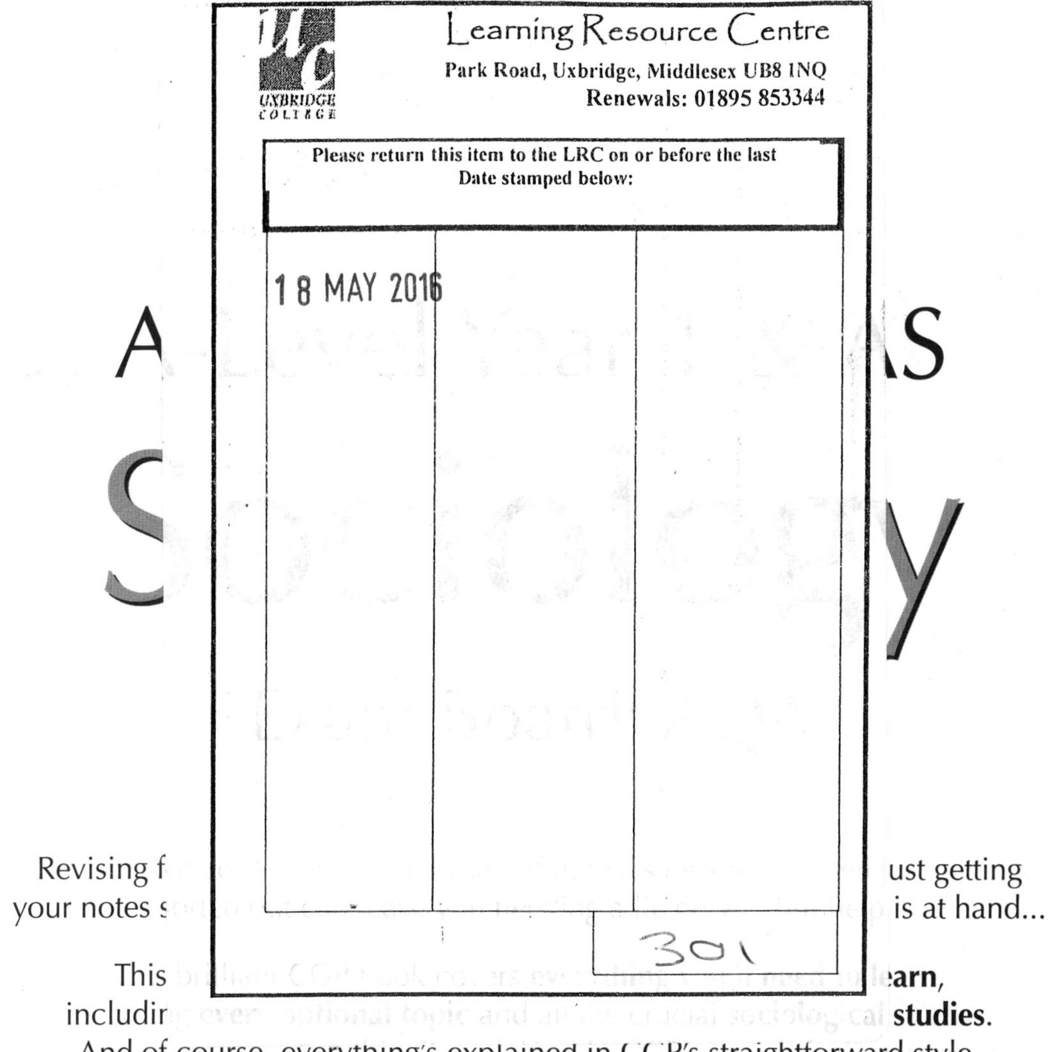

Revising f… …ust getting
your notes s… …is at hand...

This … …arn,
includir… …studies.
And of course, everything's explained in CGP's straightforward style.

We've also included **exam-style questions** throughout the book, along with a section of advice on how to pick up as many marks as possible in the final tests!

A-Level revision? It has to be CGP!

Contents

The Basics of Sociology

Section One — Sociological Methods

Section Two — Education

Section Three — Culture and Identity

Section Four — Families and Households

Section Five — Work, Poverty and Welfare

Section Six — Health

Do Well In Your Exam

We deliberately haven't included answers to the questions — that's because there are lots of valid ways to give your answers. Instead, we've put in a section on how to write answers and do well.

Published by CGP

Editors:
Emma Bonney, Emma Cleasby, Sharon Keeley-Holden, Caley Simpson and Rebecca Tate.

Contributors:
Anna Hazeldine, Sean Purcell, Kate Redmond, Neil Renton, Frances Rippin, Claire Thompson and Andrew Walker.

Acknowledgements:

Government Statistics or National Statistics. Source: Office for National Statistics licensed under the Open Government Licence v. 3.0 https://www.nationalarchives.gov.uk/doc/open-government-licence/version/3/

Page 24: The classification of one in ten children as poor. From *Poverty in Britain: what can we learn from household spending?* by Mike Brewer, Alissa Goodman and Andrew Leicester, published in 2006 by the Joseph Rowntree Foundation. Reproduced by permission of the Joseph Rowntree Foundation.

Page 27: Research on ethnic minority workers and promotion. From *In-work poverty, ethnicity and workplace cultures* by Maria Hudson and Gina Netto et al, published in 2013 by the Joseph Rowntree Foundation. Reproduced by permission of the Joseph Rowntree Foundation.

Page 27: Table of ethnicity and free school meal entitlement. Contains Parliamentary information licensed under the Open Parliament Licence v. 3.0 http://www.parliament.uk/site-information/copyright/open-parliament-licence/

Page 33: International reading and science rankings. From OECD (2014), *PISA 2012 Results in Focus, What 15-year-olds know and what they can do with what they know.*

Pages 48, 72, and 75: Employment, childbearing and death rate statistics. Crown copyright - from Social Trends 38 (2008)

Pages 54, 82 and 96: Life expectancy, wealth and working-class health statistics. Crown copyright - from Social Trends 33 (2003)

Pages 63 and 66: © NatCen. Source: Kathleen Kiernan 'Men and women at work and at home' in Roger Jowell, Lindsay Brook, Gillian Prior and Bridget Taylor, editors (1992) 'British Social Attitudes: the 9th Report' Aldershot: Dartmouth Publishing Company

Page 64: Margaret Thatcher quote. Source: Margaret Thatcher Foundation

Page 68: Information on referrals to social services. Department for Education. Contains public sector information licensed under the Open Government Licence v. 2.0 http://www.nationalarchives.gov.uk/doc/open-government-licence/version/2/

Page 68: Statistics Copyright © United Nations 2000-2008

Pages 74 and 83: Information on visa applications and relative poverty. Contains public sector information licensed under the Open Government Licence v. 3.0 http://www.nationalarchives.gov.uk/doc/open-government-licence/version/3/

Page 78: Statistics from the National Society for the Prevention of Cruelty to Children (NSPCC) © 2008 NSPCC

Pages 80 and 81: Poverty statistics published under a Creative Commons Attribution-ShareAlike 2.0 UK: England & Wales License - http://creativecommons.org/licenses/by-sa/2.0/uk/

Page 81: Poverty statistics. From *Poverty and social exclusion in Britain* by David Gordon et al, published in 2000 by the Joseph Rowntree Foundation. Reproduced by permission of the Joseph Rowntree Foundation.

Page 83: Paid work and ethnicity statistics. From *Poverty among ethnic groups how and why does it differ?* by Peter Kenway and Guy Palmer, published in 2007 by the Joseph Rowntree Foundation. Reproduced by permission of the Joseph Rowntree Foundation.

Page 99: Discrimination by health care professionals. Source: Mencap

ISBN: 978 1 78294 354 9

With thanks to Duncan Hall and Glenn Rogers for the proofreading.
With thanks to Ana Pungartnik for the copyright research.

Cover photo © iStockphoto.com/Kativ

Clipart from Corel®
Printed by Elanders Ltd, Newcastle upon Tyne.

Based on the classic CGP style created by Richard Parsons.

Themes in Sociology

OK, so before you get going with all the ins and outs of sociology, I'm going to try to answer some key questions. Starting with "what actually is sociology anyway?" Well, that's an excellent question...

Sociology is the **Study of Society**

1) Sociology is the study of **human society**, including its **development**, **functions** and **organisation**.
2) There are generally considered to be **three 'founding fathers'** of sociology — **Karl Marx**, **Emile Durkheim** and **Max Weber**. There's more information on their beliefs over the next couple of pages, but here are the **basics**:

Karl Marx (1818-1883)

Marx believed that **capitalism** oppresses the **working class**, and that there needs to be a **revolution** to make all people **equal**.

Emile Durkheim (1858-1917)

Durkheim was a **functionalist**. He believed that society is made up of different **institutions**, each with its own **function** — these institutions work in **harmony** to create a **stable society**.

Max Weber (1864-1920)

Weber believed that sociologists should study both **structures** and **actions** to understand society. He thought that an individual's behaviour is shaped by **structural factors** (such as the **law**) and **subjective factors** (such as **emotion**).

Culture, **Socialisation** and **Identity** are **Core Themes** in Sociology

There are some **key ideas** that you need to be able to **apply** to **many different topics** of your sociology course. They're covered **briefly** here, but they'll pop up **throughout** this book — you have been warned...

Culture is a Society's **Way of Life**

Norms are behaviours and views that society sees as normal. Values are beliefs and ideas about what is right and wrong.

1) The **culture** of a group of people refers to the way they **live** — their **language**, **beliefs**, **norms**, **values**, **knowledge** and **skills**. It **reinforces** the sense of **community** in a society.
2) Cultures **vary** from **place to place** — e.g. **British** culture is different to **Indian** culture. It also varies with **time** — **today's** culture is very different to the culture of **100 years ago**.

There's more detail about culture on pages 36-37, socialisation on pages 40-41 and identity on pages 44-45, but these pages contain more detail than you need to learn (unless you're studying that optional topic).

Socialisation is how **Culture** is **Passed On**

1) **Socialisation** is the way in which **culture** is passed on from **generation to generation**.
2) It begins in **childhood**, where you **learn** how to **behave** and what to **believe**, and continues into adult life. Socialisation comes from **families**, **schools**, **friends**, **religion**, the **media** and **work**.
3) A society's **values** are **internalised** by socialisation, so that they become part of your **way of thinking**.

Identity is quite a **Complex Idea** in Sociology

1) **Identity** is hard to define — there are different **levels** to it. The most **basic** level of your identity is made up of **simple facts** — your **name**, **age**, **appearance** etc.
2) On a **deeper** level (the one sociologists are more interested in), your identity is the way **you see yourself**, and the way you are viewed by **others**. This is called your **social identity**. It's influenced by things like **class**, **ethnicity**, **gender**, **age** and **sexuality**, and also by your **roles** in society — e.g. **teacher**, **friend**, **cousin**.

Chuck saw himself as a sensitive poet. Unfortunately, society just saw him as a firefighter.

Globalisation is a **Very Important Idea**

Globalisation is the idea that the **world** is becoming **more connected**. Improved **technology** and **communication**, an increase in **transnational corporations (TNCs)** and more **migration** have all meant that **national boundaries** are **breaking down**. Globalisation affects many different areas of sociology — e.g. some sociologists say that **culture** is now globalised.

Themes in Sociology

Social Differentiation, Stratification and Power are also Core Themes

There are a few more **key ideas** that you need to get to grips with. As on the previous page, they **apply** to many **different aspects** of sociology, so they appear throughout the book.

Social Differentiation is the way society is Divided Up

Any society can be **divided up** into **different groups** — this is known as **social differentiation**. The groups can be based on **biological** features (e.g. age, sex), **cultural** features (e.g. class, religion) or more personal characteristics, like abilities. You'll see **many different examples** of social differentiation throughout sociology.

There's another form of differentiation in sociology called structural differentiation. This is when different institutions in society become more and more specialised.

Stratification is the way society is Divided Into Layers

Stratification also splits society into **different groups**, but the groups are **ordered in layers**, with a definite **hierarchy**. The groups can be based on things like **status**, **income**, **religion**, **ethnicity**, **gender** and **age**, but are usually based on **social class** (especially in **Western** societies). The **top layer** is made up of the **richest** and **most powerful** people, and the **bottom layer** is the **poorest people** who have the **least power**. In between, there are many different layers, known as **strata**.

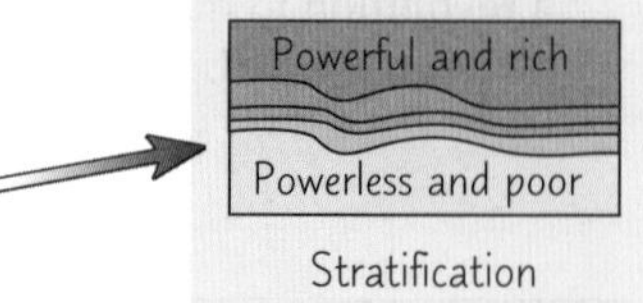

Stratification

Power is usually based on Wealth

1) **Power** can be seen as the **ability** to get someone to **do something** that they **wouldn't normally do**. A lot of sociology focuses on the **balance** (or **imbalance**) of **power** in society.
2) A person usually has power because of their **wealth**, **job** or **social class**, but could also have it because of their **gender** or **religion**, for example.
3) Some sociologists argue that people who have power use it to **control society** so that they can **remain** in power (e.g. by **oppressing** those with less power).

There are Different Sociological Methods and Theories

1) Sociologists do **research** to try to find **explanations** for how society works and why it changes. They can use different **research methods** for this, including:

- **interviews**
- **questionnaires**
- **observations**
- **documents**
- **government statistics**
- **experiments**

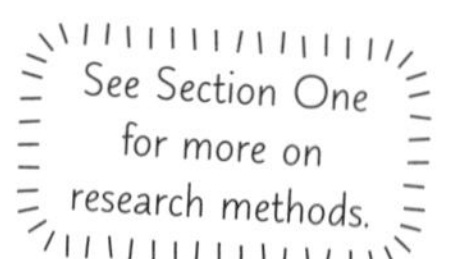

Louisa (third from right) was covertly observing the 2nd Highland Regiment.

2) Once the data has been **collected**, it needs to be **analysed** and **interpreted**. Sociologists look for **patterns** and **correlations**, and use these to draw **conclusions**.
3) Sometimes, sociologists carry out research that relates to the **main theories** of sociology. The main theories are **Marxism**, **functionalism** and **interactionism** (also called **interpretivism**), as well as **feminism** and **postmodernism**. There are also subcategories, such as **neo-Marxism** and **radical feminism**. There's a bit more **detail** about these theories over the next few pages, and they'll come up **throughout this book** as well.

Sadly, the examiners have all the power...

Remember, you need to be able to relate all these core themes to the sociology topics you're studying. You won't get an exam question just about 'power' — it'll be about power in relation to education, or health, or whatever topics you've learnt about. Unfortunately, you don't need to know about power in relation to superheroes or villains, or the power to travel through time.

Sociological Theories

There are lots of different theories about how society shapes individuals — or how individuals shape society. You need to have a decent idea of what functionalism, Marxism and interactionism are, as well as a couple of other theories.

Functionalism Says the Individual is the Product of Society

1) **Emile Durkheim** believed that society is made up of various **institutions**, each of which has a useful **function**. So Durkheim and his followers are known as **functionalists**.
2) They look at **how society is structured** — you can call functionalism a **structural theory**. Functionalists look at how institutions in society work, and how they **affect individuals**. Here are some examples:
    - **The Family** — has the function of socialising children.
    - **Education** — has the function of preparing young people for adult society.
    - **Religion** — has the function of uniting society through shared beliefs.
3) Functionalists believe that the **institutions** of society are structured to allow society to **run as smoothly as possible**.

Functionalism is a type of consensus structuralism because it states that society is structured to function harmoniously.

Not Everyone Agrees with Functionalist Thinking

1) **Interactionists** (also called **interpretivists**) think that functionalists don't focus enough on the **individual** (see p.4).
2) **Marxists** say functionalism ignores the **unequal power** of some groups. They think that society is structured to **serve the interests of the rich**, not to keep society ticking along as smoothly as possible.

Marxism Says the Individual is the Product of Economic Forces

Karl Marx

Karl Marx focused on the **effects of capitalism**. He thought that a society's **economic system** (the **infrastructure**) influenced its non-economic institutions (the **superstructure**), and that the superstructure, in turn, determined the society's **beliefs** and **values**.

Marxists believe that the most important force in society is class conflict

1) In **capitalist societies**, workers are employed to produce goods which are sold by their employers at a **profit**.
2) Only a bit of this money ends up in the workers' wages — most of it's **kept by the employer**.
3) Marx said that if workers were allowed to **notice the unfairness** of this, they'd revolt. So, to **avoid revolution**, the **capitalist system shapes the superstructure** to make sure that the workers accept their lot in life.
4) **Institutions** like the family, education and religion are part of the **superstructure**. They **lead individuals** into **accepting** the **inequalities of capitalism**.

Marxism is a type of conflict structuralism because it states that there is conflict between the two main classes of society.

Marx believed that society was divided into **two classes**:

- The **bourgeoisie** were the **ruling class** — they were the minority but had all the money and power.
- The **proletariat** were the **working class** — they formed the majority of society but had little or no power.

Neo-Marxism is a **20th century** version of Marxism, developed to be more **relevant** to the modern world. Neo-Marxists focus on **ideology** (a set of **ideas** and **beliefs** about how things should be). They study how this ideology is **communicated** and **enforced** by the **ruling class** to maintain its **power**.

Not Everyone Agrees with Marx either...

1) **Functionalists** say Marx put too much emphasis on the role of **economic structures** in shaping ideas and beliefs.
2) **Interactionists** say he placed too much emphasis on **class** and not enough on individuals.
3) **Postmodernists** say social class doesn't have such an important influence on **individual identity** any more. They say people are defined by the **choices** they make, not by whether they're a worker or a boss.

Sociological Theories

Feminists Say Women are Oppressed by Men

Feminists believe that society is **patriarchal** — that it's **run by men**, and that things are done in men's **best interests**. They believe that there are many **inequalities** in society based on gender, and want to make society more **balanced**. There are many different **strands** of feminism — the main ones are:

Feminism is also a structuralist theory.

Liberal Feminism

Liberal feminists want **equal rights** and **opportunities** for women. They believe that introducing more **opportunities** for women into the **existing structures** of society (e.g. the legal system) is the **best way** to try to bring about **equality**.

Radical Feminism

Radical feminists believe that society is **structured** to **oppress women**, and that **society itself** needs to change. They believe there's an **imbalance of power** in **all** relationships, and that all women are always expected to be **subservient** to all men.

Marxist Feminism

Marxist feminists combine the beliefs of **Marxism** and **feminism** — they believe that **women** are **exploited** by **capitalist societies** (which are run by **men**).

Feminists don't even agree with Each Other...

Radical feminists criticise **liberal** feminists for not acknowledging that it's more than just **institutions** that are patriarchal — it's **all relationships**. For example, **families** have a male-dominated structure too.

Interactionists Say Individual Actions are Most Important

1) Many sociologists say that society is actually determined by the **behaviour and interaction of individuals**. Theories like this are called **action theories** because they emphasise the **action** of individuals, as opposed to **structural theories** like functionalism and Marxism, which are all about the big structures of society.
2) **Interactionist** (or **interpretivist**) theories start with the idea that all individuals **interpret** society around them — people **try to make sense** of society. Interactionists say that culture comes from **people's own ideas** of how people **interact** with each other.
3) Interactionists don't say structures aren't important, but they do suggest that each of us **responds** to social structures in our **own way**. We aren't just products of socialisation — we all have **free will** and make **choices**. An important point here is that the **results of individual choice** can be **large-scale social change**. For example, **Jonathan Gershuny (1992)** made an interactionist analysis of gender roles in the home.

   1) Some **women decided** they wanted to **work outside the home**. That's the **individual choice** bit.
   2) Male partners then took on **more childcare** and housework. It became **acceptable** for men to adopt roles in the family that had been considered **feminine**. That's the **large-scale social change** bit.

What do you know... Not Everyone Agrees with the Interactionists

Marxists say interactionists don't pay enough attention to **conflict** or to the fact that some social groups are more **powerful** than others. **Functionalists** say they don't acknowledge the importance of the **socialisation process**.

Learn the Main Points of Each Theory

To **sum up** — here's a nice table showing the **main ideas** of functionalism, Marxism, interactionism and feminism.

Functionalism	Marxism	Feminism	Interactionism
Society is made up of different institutions that function together as a whole.	Society is split into two classes. The ruling class oppress and exploit the working class.	Society is patriarchal and women have fewer rights and opportunities than men.	The behaviour of and interaction between individuals determine how society works.

Sociological Theories

New Right *Sociologists Say* ***Traditional Values*** *are Important*

1) Like **functionalism**, the New Right is a form of **consensus structuralism**. New Right theorists are **similar** to functional theorists in that they believe society needs **values** and **institutions** to maintain **social order**. New Right theories focus on subjects such as **family**, **education** and **welfare**.
2) They argue that a **nuclear family** is one of the most important social institutions. They argue that **traditional roles** within the nuclear family (the **man** goes out to **work** and the **woman** stays at **home**) are **crucial** to maintain **social order**.
3) New Right sociologists such as **Charles Murray** say that the traditional family is **under threat**, which has led to a **decline** in **moral standards** and the **breakdown of society**.

A nuclear family is made up of parents and their dependent children, all living together.

Feminists *disagree with the* ***New Right***

As you've probably guessed by now, not everyone **agrees** with New Right theories. In fact, not many people agree with them — in particular, **feminists** criticise the New Right's ideas of **traditional roles** within the family, which they see as being **oppressive to women** and reinforcing a **patriarchal** society.

Postmodernists *Say* ***Society*** *is* ***Changing***

Postmodernism came about as a **reaction** to **modernism** — so let's start with a **brief explanation** of modernism:

> **Modernism** is the period of **industrialisation** and **urbanisation** that began with the **Industrial Revolution**, when **rational**, **scientific** thinking was valued. Modernist theories include **Marxism** and **functionalism**. Modernist theories are also known as **'metanarratives'** (**big, all-encompassing stories** that explain why things are as they are).

Postmodernists say that society has **moved on** from modernism — it's no longer **ordered** and **structured** in the same way. Society is a lot more **flexible**, and there's more **choice** of **cultures** and **lifestyles** due to increased **globalisation**. They claim that **metanarratives** are no longer appropriate — there are **many different ways of understanding** society, rather than one universal truth or theory.

Other Sociologists *disagree with* ***Postmodernists*** *(of course they do)*

1) **Functionalists** disagree with postmodernists because postmodernism ignores the role of **institutions**.
2) **Interactionists** disagree with postmodernists because postmodernism ignores how individuals **interact**.
3) **Marxists** disagree with postmodernists because postmodernism ignores **inequalities**. No one's ever satisfied.

You've probably realised by now that pretty much **all** the theories **criticise each other**. If you know what **each group** of sociologists believe, then you can probably work out what they think of a **particular theory** or **idea** (and why).

Practice Questions

Q1 What is 'socialisation'?

Q2 Name three different research methods.

Q3 What's the main difference between structural and interactionist approaches?

Q4 Give two examples of consensus structuralism.

Q5 Name three strands of feminism.

Exam Question

Q1 Give a definition of the term 'metanarrative'. [2 marks]

I'm a post-Marxist neo-functionalist feminist...

These theories come up again and again throughout sociology, so ***learn these pages****. Make sure you can jot down a few sentences about what functionalists, Marxists and interactionists think about the relationship between individuals and society, and the main arguments of feminism, the New Right and postmodernism too. Then take a deep breath before carrying on.*

Research and Methods

Sociologists do research to get evidence which helps them understand society.
Unfortunately, it's not all that straightforward to study human behaviour. If only we were ants in an ant farm.

Sociologists Have Three Aims When Collecting and Using Data

1) Sociologists try to make their research **reliable** and **valid**.

- **Reliable** research can be **repeated** to get the **same results**. Reliable data is data that **another researcher** would be able to get by using the **exact same methods**.
- **Sociological research** isn't generally as reliable as research in the **natural sciences** (physics, biology, chemistry, etc.).

- **Valid** data is a **true picture** of what the researcher is trying to measure.
- Even **reliable** data isn't always valid. For example, you could use **unemployment statistics** to measure how many people **don't work**. This wouldn't give a true picture, because these statistics don't include **students** who don't work, or people who are **unable** to work.

There are several reasons why research may **not** give a true picture:

- Respondents in an interview may **forget** things, **exaggerate** or just plain **lie**, e.g. they may say they recycle all their rubbish when really they don't.
- Asking people about their attitudes to an event a **long time afterwards** often isn't valid. People **change their views** over time, and may **alter their description** of the past in the light of their **current beliefs**.

2) You can't research the whole population, so you have to take a **sample** (see p.13). Sociologists try to make their samples **representative** — reflective of the population as a whole. To do this, it needs similar proportions of different ages, genders, classes and ethnic groups. If a sample is **representative** then sociologists can **generalise** — i.e. conclude that the results are likely to apply to the entire population.
3) Sociologists aim to be **objective** and **avoid bias**.

Primary Data is Collected First-Hand

The researcher collects primary information **first-hand** — they find it themselves. You could use methods like **interviews**, **questionnaires**, **observations** or **experiments**. You generate quantitative or qualitative data (see p.7).

1) Primary data is obtained from **first-hand research**. It doesn't rely on **another sociologist's research** and you can carefully **choose your method** to make your data as valid and reliable as possible.
2) Primary data is always **brand new** and **bang up to date**.
3) **Some methods** of getting primary data can be **expensive** and **time-consuming**.
4) **Some methods** may put the researcher in a **dangerous situation**.
5) **Some methods** may be **unethical** if you don't give **informed consent** (p.9).
6) The **researcher's own values** may mess with the research process. This creates **bias**.
7) You **can't always get access** to the group you want to study.

Secondary Data is Existing Information

Secondary data sources include **official statistics**, **diaries**, **letters**, **memoirs**, **emails**, **TV documentaries** and **newspapers**. You gather the data together and analyse it, but you don't generate the data.

1) You can **quickly** and easily collect secondary data.
2) You can **easily** use **secondary data** to **compare different societies**.
3) With secondary data you can study **past events and societies**. You can **compare past** and **present**.
4) You don't have to worry about **informed consent**.
5) The **existing data** may not be **valid** or **reliable** — you're **stuck** with the way the research was **originally done**.
6) Documents may not be **authentic**, **representative** or **credible**. Official statistics can be **biased**.
7) You **might not be able to find** the information that you need from existing data.
8) **Your values** don't influence the **collection** of the data (though they might influence your **choice of sources**), but the **researcher's values** might have ruined the validity of the **original research**. **Your values** can get in the way of **how you analyse** the data.

Research and Methods

Quantitative Data can be *Reliable* but *Not Very Valid*

Quantitative data is **numbers** and **statistics**. You can easily put quantitative data into a graph or a chart.

There are several advantages of using quantitative data in sociological research...

1) With quantitative data, you can **test your hypothesis** and look for **cause and effect** relationships.
2) You can **compare** your statistics against existing statistics, and look for **trends over time** and between societies.
3) It's **easy** to **analyse tables**, **charts** and **graphs** — especially line charts, bar graphs and pie charts.
4) You can **repeat** questionnaires and structured interviews to **test reliability**.
5) Quantitative methods allow **large samples**, so the findings can **represent** the **general population**.

However, quantitative data also has its problems...

1) **Statistics** can **hide reality**. **Categories** in **interviews** or **questionnaires** can **distort** the truth.
2) Statistics don't tell you anything about the **meanings**, **motives** and **reasons** behind behaviour — there's not much **depth** and **insight** into **social interaction**.
3) Statistics can be **politically biased**. The method may have been chosen in order to get the 'right' data.

Qualitative Data can be *Valid* but *Not Very Reliable*

Qualitative data gives a detailed picture of what people do, think and feel. It's **subjective** — it involves **opinions**, **meanings** and **interpretations**. You can't easily turn qualitative data into a list of numbers or a graph.

There are plenty of reasons why using qualitative data is a good idea...

1) **Qualitative sociological data** gives **insight** into **social interaction**. It's a **detailed description** of social behaviour.
2) Qualitative data lets you find out the **meanings** and **motives** behind behaviour.
3) You don't have to **force** people into **artificial categories** like in questionnaires.
4) Qualitative methods let you build up **trust** and research **sensitive topics**.

The motives behind some behaviour can present a difficult challenge for the sociologist.

There are also some drawbacks of using qualitative data in research...

1) Qualitative investigations are **difficult to repeat** — they **aren't very reliable**.
2) The research is often on a **small scale** — so the findings might not **represent** the whole population.
3) **Positivists** say qualitative results **lack credibility** because they're **subjective** and open to interpretation.
4) The **researcher** can get the **wrong end of the stick** and **misinterpret** the group or individual they're studying.

Practice Questions

Q1 Give one reason why research may not be valid.

Q2 What is meant by the term 'representativeness'?

Q3 Give two strengths of primary data.

Q4 What is the difference between quantitative and qualitative data?

Q5 Give two criticisms of qualitative data.

Exam Questions

Q1 What are the drawbacks of using secondary data in sociological research? Outline two examples. [4 marks]

Q2 Evaluate the disadvantages of a sociologist using quantitative data. [16 marks]

Ready, aim, research...

Data is to the sociologist what clay is to the sculptor, or what pigeon liver and celeriac are to the chef — you can't do great work without the best raw materials. Studying methodology may not have the Hollywood glamour of criminology or the rustic charm of politics, but without data sociologists have nothing to do. So you'd best learn where and how to find it.

Key Issues in Research and Methods

Sociologists use different methods to carry out their research, and lots of issues determine which method they choose. You can separate them into three groups — theoretical issues, practical issues and ethical issues.

Theoretical Issues *Affect Your* ***Choice*** *of* ***Method***

Two important **theoretical approaches** to sociology are **positivism** and **interpretivism**. You need to know how they affect someone's choice of research method.

Positivism looks at the **institutions** in society. It's called **macrosociology**.
Interpretivist sociology looks at the **individual**. It's called **microsociology**.

Jake's parents had developed a perfect method for keeping him out of trouble.

Positivists *Use* ***Reliable Methods*** *That Give* ***Quantitative Data***

1) **Positivists** say behaviour is influenced by **external social factors**.
2) They think sociology should be **scientific** and **analyse 'social facts'**. Social facts are things that **affect behaviour** and can be **easily measured**. They're **external** things like laws, **not internal** things like people's opinions.
3) So positivists measure human behaviour using **quantitative data**.
4) They use **statistics** to measure the **relationships** between different factors. They're interested in **cause and effect** relationships, e.g. the factors that cause underachievement in schools.
5) They use sources like **questionnaires** and **official statistics**. These are **objective** and **reliable**.

Interpretivists *Use* ***Valid Methods*** *That Give* ***Qualitative Data***

1) **Interpretivists** (also called **interactionists**) believe that you can only really **understand** human behaviour using **empathy** — by putting yourself in **other people's shoes**. They think that it is important to uncover and understand the **meaning** individuals give to **their actions** and to **the actions of others**.
2) **Interpretivist sociologists** use methods that let them discover the **meanings**, **motives** and **reasons** behind **human behaviour** and **social interaction**.
3) Interpretivists reckon that the **scientific** methods used in **positivist** research **don't tell you much** about how **individual people** act in society. They don't believe in the existence of 'social facts' — they think that the findings of research are always **subjective** (they depend on your opinion).
4) Interpretivists say you can't count meanings and opinions and turn them into statistical charts. They reckon **sociology isn't scientific** because **humans can't be measured** like ants in an ant farm. People don't always understand questions in questionnaires and they don't always tell the truth to researchers.
5) Interpretivists like to use methods that produce **qualitative** data — they try to understand human behaviour from the point of view of the **individual person**. They use methods like **participant observation** and **unstructured interviews** to build up a **rapport** (a feeling of mutual trust and understanding) with individuals, so they can produce a valid and detailed picture of what they think.

Participant observation means being actively involved in the research as both participant and observer.

Practical Issues *also have an Impact on* ***Method***

1) **Time** — Some methods need more time. **Covert participant observation** (see p.17) takes a **long time**. The researcher has to get into the group they're studying and win their trust before starting the actual research. A **social survey** (p.13) doesn't need the researcher to participate all the time and the **workload can be shared** in a team.
2) **Money** — This affects the **length** and **method** of the research. Money is needed to **pay the researcher**, for **transportation** to interviews, and to pay for **resources** like computers. **Large-scale social surveys** are **expensive**. The 2011 census cost £480 million. A small focus group will cost a lot less.
3) **Characteristics and skills of the researcher** — It'd be difficult for a **female** researcher to be involved in a participant observation of **monks** in a monastery. Some researchers may be OK with **dangerous situations** and others may prefer to **stay at their desk** and do **detailed analysis** of statistics.
4) **Access and opportunity** — If researchers **don't have access** to certain groups to carry out interviews or observations then they have to turn to **secondary sources**.

Key Issues in Research and Methods

Ethical Issues can be grouped into *Four Main Areas*

Studies should **try** to meet these **four ethical ideals**. Some studies **fall short**, and some **methods** deliberately avoid them.

1) **Consent** — All participants must have openly agreed to take part.
2) **Avoidance of deception** — Researchers should be open and honest about the study and its implications.
3) **Confidentiality** — The details of all participants and their actions must remain confidential and private.
4) **Avoidance of harm** — Participants should not be physically or psychologically harmed by the research process.

Covert Studies are *Criticised* for not getting *Free, Informed Consent*

1) The researcher should get participants' **consent** before they conduct their study. Sociologists should be **open** and **honest** about the work they wish to carry out. It's important that the respondent knows what they're signing up for.
2) People with **learning difficulties** may **not fully understand** what participation would entail. This is problematic. It can be argued that **uninformed consent** isn't really consent at all.
3) Consent can be **difficult to obtain**, especially from **secretive** groups (e.g. Scientologists, the Freemasons, gangs) or when the research is about a **sensitive** topic (e.g. crime, sexuality).

1) Covert methods (e.g. **covert participant observation**, see p.17) involve **not telling** the group being studied that they actually are being studied. They're often criticised for their **lack of honesty** and the absence of **true informed consent**.
2) Covert participant observers argue that to **negotiate access** into **sensitive** or **dangerous** groups such as criminals, the researcher often has to either **pretend to be part of the group**, or not inform the group of the **true purpose** of the study.

	Laud Humphreys' "Tearoom Trade" (1970) was a covert observation of secretive homosexual activity
The group:	The group Humphreys wished to study were men who engaged in homosexual activities in **public places** (especially public toilets). They were **secretive** about their activities for three main reasons — homosexuality was **taboo** in mainstream society, sexual activity in public is **against the law**, and some of the men may have been married men leading a **"secret life"**.
Covert study:	Humphreys probably wouldn't have gained access to this group if he'd openly and honestly informed them about the nature of the research and then sought their permission. Even if he did gain their permission, it's likely that they'd have **acted very differently** if they were aware that they were being observed. Humphreys therefore posed as someone who watches homosexual acts for a sexual thrill. This enabled him to gain the **trust** of the group and observe **genuine actions**.

Other sociologists argue that work like Humphreys' shouldn't be conducted, even if it gives valuable insights to sociology.

Milgram was *Criticised* for *Deceiving* his Participants

	Milgram (1974) was not honest with participants in his experiments on obedience
Background:	Milgram conducted a series of experiments in which volunteers were told to administer electric shocks to another person (who was actually an actor) on the other side of a glass screen, when that person failed to give the correct answers in a memory test. Many volunteers kept on giving punishment shocks until the actor pretended to pass out.
Deception:	• Milgram lied about the purpose of the experiment. He told the volunteers that they were doing an experiment about **memory**. • The electric shocks **weren't real**. The person who the volunteers were "shocking" was an actor, pretending.
Results:	The results of the experiment were **very useful**. The experiment showed how people are ready to **obey** authority without **question**. This helped people understand how **ordinary people** take part in war crimes and genocide.

The experiment **wouldn't have worked** if the volunteers **knew** the real purpose of the experiment. If they knew that their **obedience** was being tested, they might have deliberately been less obedient. If they knew the shocks weren't real, they wouldn't have behaved in the same way. Milgram **had to be dishonest** for the experiment to work at all.

This experiment has been **repeated** more recently, but with adjustments to try to reduce the risk of **psychological harm**. Many of Milgram's original participants showed signs of **distress** during the experiment, and some of them were disturbed by how **easily** Milgram had **manipulated** them. However, Milgram did **debrief** all of his participants afterwards so they all **understood** the study, and did **follow-up work** to check on their psychological state. He found that some participants saw the experiment as a **valuable learning experience**.

Key Issues in Research and Methods

Respondents** have a **Right** to **Confidentiality

1) All respondents taking part in a piece of research must have their **basic right to privacy** valued and **upheld**. The **data** gathered from them and their **personal details** must not be distributed to anyone **outside** the **research process**.
2) When the report is finally produced, respondents must be made **anonymous**. Any descriptions of people, geographical locations and institutions have to be written in a way that prevents readers from easily recognising the participants. **False names** may be used — in which case the researcher should **clearly state** that false names have been used, in case someone who **shares** the name is **mistakenly identified** as having taken part in the research.
3) Of course, if a researcher **breaches** trust and confidentiality, potential participants will be **put off** taking part in future studies. Research participants must feel they can **trust** the researcher, especially if the research is of a sensitive nature — e.g. a self-reported crime study, or a sexual health survey.

*Researchers must make sure that **Nobody** is **Harmed** by **Taking Part** in a study*

1) Emotional and physical harm is **never acceptable** in sociological research, and work is actively criticised and rejected if it has allowed harm to come to those involved.
2) Researchers studying topics such as **mental health** or **geriatric care** may have contact with **vulnerable groups** of people, or witness **situations** and **experiences** that cause individuals **harm** — e.g. inappropriate living conditions, or abuse by carers. There is an ethical question as to whether they should **stop** or **suspend** the research in order to **remove** the individual from the dangerous situation.
3) Some topics that are discussed may be **traumatic** for the respondents — they would need to be **informed** of the possible temporary mental and emotional harm before starting the study. Remember, it's important to make sure that all consent is **informed consent** (i.e. that the person fully understands all the implications and aspects of the research before they agree to take part).

***Some Sociologists** can justify **Bending** or **Breaking** ethical rules*

There's a lot of **good** that can come from sociological research. Many sociologists can **justify** breaking or slightly bending some of the **ethical rules** — if the data that they'll gather is likely to make a beneficial contribution to society. This justification becomes even stronger if potential ethical problems are minimised — e.g. if there's **minimal harm** and **full confidentiality**, but just a **wee bit of deception** (the basis of covert participant observation).

1) For example, **Nigel Fielding (1981)**, in a study of the **National Front** (an extreme right-wing political party with a secretive hierarchy) argues that he needed to conduct covert research otherwise he wouldn't have been able to gain access to the group and gather information.
2) **"James Patrick" (1973)** was a false name given to a researcher conducting a study on **violent gangs** in Glasgow — to ensure his **own safety** and protection.
3) **Roy Wallis (1977)** wasn't entirely **honest** when researching Scientology. He didn't say he was a sociologist when he signed up to a Scientology course. If he had been honest, the Scientologists may have told him to go away. Wallis was also forced to **name** some of his sources, during a **legal battle** between the Church of Scientology and another researcher. This broke the rule on **privacy** and **anonymity**, but in this case Wallis had **no choice**.

Practice Questions

Q1 What are the four main ethical considerations a sociologist needs to be aware of in their study?

Q2 Why are covert methods seen as unethical?

Q3 Give two reasons that sociologists might use to justify breaking ethical rules.

Exam Question

Q1 Evaluate the importance of ethics when conducting sociological research. [16 marks]

Danger, sociologists at work...

Well, obviously you wouldn't decide to do a covert observation of how people react to being hit on the head. Because that would be wrong. The key point is that sometimes there are justifications for breaking ethical guidelines, but only when the research is likely to provide such useful information that it's worth it. Most of the time, the best option is to stick to the rules.

Research Design

The first step in sociological research is figuring out what you're going to research.
The second step is condensing your topic down into a single question, or a single hypothesis.

Sociologists pick a **Topic** based on their own **Preference** and **Knowledge**

1) Sociologists often **specialise** in different fields of the subject and therefore will often choose a topic that they have experience or knowledge of — for example, **Steve Bruce** specialises in **religion**.
2) Sociologists try to pick a topic that they think they'll find **enjoyable** and **interesting** to research. It's best not to try a piece of research that you won't enjoy — it only leads to a poorly constructed report that may be either flawed or just plain boring.
3) Also, certain topics become popular in sociology at different times. For example, research in the **mid-twentieth century** often focused on **stratification** and the **class system**. **Nowadays**, the focus of sociologists has moved on to other topics such as **World Sociology**. To gain **prestige**, **funding** and public or academic **interest**, sociologists are more likely to focus their research on topics that are currently **in vogue**.
4) Sociologists and other academics who want to make a **change** in society prefer research that could help develop **solutions** to **social problems**.
5) Sociologists may feel that a particular issue is **neglected** by other researchers, so they'll research the issue to try and '**plug the gap**' — and encourage others to embrace the issue as well.

Funding and **Cooperation** for **Research** have an impact on the choice of **Topic**

1) There are a wide range of potential **sources of funding**. Some research is funded by **charities**, e.g. the Joseph Rowntree Foundation. Some is funded by **industry**. Some is funded by the **government**. A lot of quantitative studies are done **directly** by **government agencies**.
2) The organisation which funds the research is sometimes called a **gatekeeper**, because it often has the final say in the **choice of topic**, the **way** that the topic is **researched** or whether a topic gets researched at all. Government agencies often do research into areas covered by current or proposed **government policy**. **Industrial** grant providers tend to fund research that gives their industry some **practical benefit**.
3) Additionally, a researcher needs to decide whether or not they will be able to get the **cooperation** of the groups they'll be studying if they choose a particular topic. If potential subjects refuse to give their help for the research, then the topic may not be viable.

The researcher's **Career** in **Sociology** is another factor in selecting a topic

1) Sociologists have their eye on their **careers**, just like everyone else. Researchers would jump at the chance to conduct a study that improves their **employability**. Interesting, original or popular topics that are well researched, with good clear results, improve an academic's chance of having their work **published**. Getting work published, particularly in one of the **big sociological journals**, really **improves a researcher's standing** in academia.
2) A quick way for a sociologist to progress in their career is to respond to another sociologist's work. The aim can be either to **prove** the other sociologist **wrong**, or to **add something** to their research. Practically speaking, this could mean investigating the same topic, but using slightly different methods, or investigating a different group of people.
3) This can mean that particular social groups are researched a lot. For example, **routine office workers** are frequently researched in order to test out **theories of stratification** — some systems classify them as working class and some as middle class. Each sociologist who wants to **disprove** or **add to** earlier research on classification has to research **yet another** bunch of routine office workers. Beekeepers **never** get this level of interest from sociologists.

Reviewing the **Field** is crucial to a good research topic

"Lush, undulating, 4/5"

1) **Reviewing** and **critiquing** existing **data** and **literature** is an important feature in any sociological report. It requires the researcher to spend time reading **articles**, **publications** and other sources of information already produced on the subject.
2) The researcher then **analyses** this material to help clarify the issues around the subject.
3) Reviewing the field gives the researcher useful information on the types of **methodology** used in **previous studies**. They can see whether specific methods, e.g. structured interviews, worked in the past. They can see if research samples were big enough, and form ideas about how big their own sample should be.

Research Design

Research Questions give *Focus* to sociological research

1) Once the researcher has chosen a broad topic area, they need to **narrow down** the focus of their research so they don't spread their work out too thinly and end up with not enough detail. They do this by coming up with a **single research question** that their research aims to **answer**.
2) A good research question should focus on **one part** of the topic, and it should be **clear** and **easy** to **research**.
3) Questions should be as **value-free** as possible. In other words they shouldn't be **biased**, or **suggest potential social changes**. So, "Should governments provide vocational education to 14-year-olds?" isn't a good research question because it asks for a **value judgement** on social policy. "What are the attitudes of employers, parents and teachers towards vocational education for 14-year-olds?" is **better**.

Hypotheses are *Statements* that make *Predictions* that can be *Tested*

1) A hypothesis is a **statement** that makes a **prediction**. A hypothesis acts as a **starting point** for research. The research will aim to either **show that the hypothesis is true**, or **show that it's false**.
2) A hypothesis states a **relationship** between **two factors** — e.g. "Sociology teachers wear corduroy trousers" or "Material deprivation causes educational underachievement".

Terms like "democracy" need to be *Operationalised* — i.e. *Made Measurable*

1) Sociology prides itself on giving names to **concepts** and **ideas** that aren't **easily explained** or measured. For example, it's **tricky** to measure things like 'democracy', 'development' and 'culture'.
2) You end up measuring these concepts by measuring **something else** that's **linked** to the tricky concept — sociologists call this an **indicator**. This is called '**operationalising**' a concept. It means making it operational, or workable, by finding a way to measure it.
3) Researchers do this **every time** they conduct a piece of research, because you **can't research** something if you **can't measure** it. Each difficult concept needs an **indicator**, e.g. electoral participation or diversity of electoral results for democracy.
4) Researchers need to be able to **justify** how they **operationalised** their concepts in their final report. This is often a **subjective** process and the way a researcher operationalises may be **criticised** by other sociologists.

Triangulation is where you *Combine Methods* or *Data*

Triangulation is when sociologists try to combine different methods or data to **get the best out of all of them**.

1) Triangulation gives a more **detailed picture** than when you only use one method, so it's more **valid** (see p.6).
2) When you triangulate, you can **check** different sets of data against each other.
3) Triangulation combines **strengths** and **weaknesses** of different types of data.
4) It can be **expensive** and **time-consuming** to do the same research by lots of methods. Sometimes it's **not possible** to use triangulation — e.g. when there's only one viable method to get the data.

A *Pilot Study* is a *Small-Scale Practice Run*

1) A **pilot study** lets you test the **accuracy** of your questions, and check if there are any **technical problems** in your **research design**. You can use them to make studies **more valid** and **reliable**, test how **long** the research will take, and **train** your interviewers.
2) Though they can be **time-consuming**, **expensive** and create lots of **work**, they show that the project is **feasible**, and can help you secure **research funding**.

Not that sort of pilot.

Research Design

Social Surveys Give Quantitative Data

1) **Social surveys** collect information about large target populations, using **questionnaires** or **interviews**.
2) Social surveys tend to be used by **positivists** as a **primary source** of **quantitative data**. This data can be analysed to discover overall **patterns** and **trends**.
3) They're **reliable**, so they're used by **government agencies** and **research companies**.

The target population is the group that is being studied, e.g. 'women over 50'.

Before You Can Start a Social Survey You Need a Sample

1) It's **too expensive** and **time-consuming** for sociologists to survey the **whole target population**. They select a **sample**.
2) If the **characteristics** of the **sample** reflect the **characteristics** of the **target population** — with similar proportions of people in terms of age, class, ethnicity and gender — then the sample can be said to be **representative** of that target population. The extent to which a sample represents the target population is known as its **representativeness** (p.6).
3) If the sample is sufficiently **large** and **representative**, then it should be possible to make **generalisations** from it about the **wider target population**. The extent to which you can accurately do this is the sample's **generalisability**.

Representative Sampling

Representative sampling involves picking names out of a 'sampling frame'. A sampling frame is a **complete list** of the population being sampled, which needs to be **accurate**, **complete** and without any **duplicate** entries.

1) In simple **random sampling**, names are taken completely at random, e.g. randomly selected from a list by a person or a computer, so each member of the population has an **equal chance** of being selected.
2) **Systematic** sampling involves choosing a random **starting point** in the sampling frame and selecting every *n*th value, e.g. every fifth name. There may be bias if there's an underlying pattern in the sampling frame.
3) **Multi-stage sampling** means selecting a sample from **within another sample**. It's often used to select samples for opinion polls to measure voting intention. First, a selection of constituencies is chosen to represent the whole country, then postcodes within that constituency are selected, then houses from those postcodes.
4) In **stratified random sampling** the population is put into **segments** called '**strata**' based on things like age, gender or income — e.g. age 18-24, 25-34, 35-44, 45-54, 55-64, 65+. Names are selected at random from within each segment.
5) **Quota sampling** is a bit like stratified random sampling, but it's not random. The selection is made by the **interviewer**, who'll have a quota to meet — e.g. "interview 20 women between 25 and 34". Interviewers tend to pick people who look 'nice', which introduces bias. It's quick and useful, though.

Non-Representative Sampling

Some target populations may be **difficult** to **access** — e.g. criminals, the very young or very old — or the characteristics of the population may be **unknown**. In these cases you can use **non-representative sampling** methods.

1) **Snowball sampling** means finding **initial contacts** and getting them to **give you more names** for your research.
2) **Purposive sampling** is when researchers select non-representative samples, often in order to **falsify** a hypothesis. E.g. **feminist** sociologists trying to disprove the idea that gender roles are determined by biological difference deliberately looked for samples where women's roles **weren't different from men's roles**, or weren't traditionally 'feminine'.
3) **Opportunity sampling** is used when researchers need to select a non-representative sample **quickly** and **easily**. Researchers can use **captive audiences** — these are **groups** of people who are gathered together for another reason, like a group of **school-children** or **office workers**. Researchers also go to **public areas** and select people who are nearby.

Practice Questions

Q1 Why is reviewing the field useful?

Q2 Name and explain one representative and one non-representative sampling method.

Exam Question

Q1 What factors should be considered when choosing a research topic? Outline two examples. [4 marks]

The scarecrow award — for being outstanding in your field...

Now you know how sociologists plan research — pick a topic, check out previous studies, formulate a question, make some hypotheses, operationalise the concepts, do a pilot and choose samples. Oh, and find funding. I definitely would've been a researcher if I'd known it was that easy. Revise these pages and maybe you can become the sociologist I can only dream of being.

Questionnaires

Are questionnaires A) the main way to conduct a social survey, or B) flashy people who enjoy asking questions? (Hint: It's A.)

Questionnaires Mainly Give Quantitative Data

Reginald was lamenting the lack of an 'all of the above' option.

1) **Questionnaires** mainly use **closed questions** and **multiple-choice answers**.
   e.g. *"What's your favourite fish? a. Haddock b. Cod c. Salmon d. Hake e. Other"*
2) Some questionnaires use **open-ended** questions. e.g. *"What's your favourite fish?"*
3) The **reliability** and **validity** of a questionnaire depends on **how it's designed**.
   - **Closed** questions give you **quantitative** data, which **positivists** like.
   - **Open-ended questions** can give you some insight into **meanings** and **motives**. They give you **qualitative** data, which **interpretivists** prefer.

Questionnaires should...

1) Use **clear, simple questions** which are **easy to understand**.
2) Give **clear instructions** and make it **easy** for the respondent.
3) Have a nice **clear layout** that doesn't **intimidate** people.
4) Give a **range of options** on **multiple-choice** questions.
5) **Measure** what **you want to measure**.

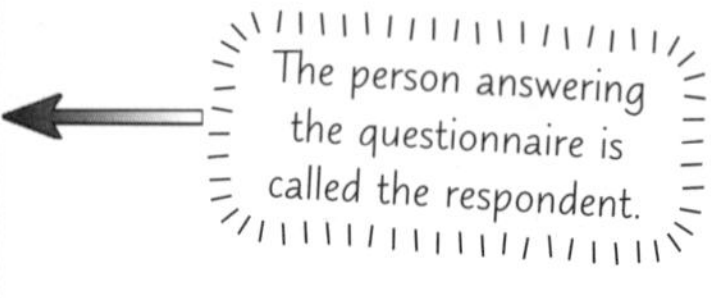

Pilot studies (see p.12) are useful for questionnaires. Researchers can test whether the questions make sense to the respondents.

Questionnaires shouldn't...

1) Ask **embarrassing, threatening** or **complex** questions.
2) Ask **two questions instead of one**.
3) Be **too long**.
4) Use **sociological** terms that **few people understand**.
5) **Lead** the respondent to **answer a question** in a **particular way**.

1) Questionnaires can be used to investigate topics such as **TV viewing habits**, **purchasing habits**, **voting behaviour** and **experiences of crime**.
2) The **Crime Survey for England and Wales (CSEW)** is a questionnaire that is carried out **continually** by the British government. They survey about **38 000** people a year and publish new results **annually**.
3) The **British Social Attitudes Survey** is carried out annually by the **National Centre for Social Research**. Each year they select around **3000** British adults at random and send them a questionnaire.

Questionnaires have several **Advantages**

1) Questionnaires are **easy to administer**, and they can collect a **lot of data** in a **short time**. Closed questions provide quantitative data which can be **quickly** analysed too.
2) Questionnaires are **reliable**.
3) Questionnaires are **anonymous** and don't require the respondent to sit **face-to-face with an interviewer**. This makes them suitable for **sensitive topics**. For example, the National Survey of Sexual Attitudes and Lifestyles was a **postal questionnaire** rather than a face-to-face structured interview.
4) A **large sample** can be given a questionnaire, so if the sample is representative (see p.6), the questionnaires should produce **representative data** that can be used to make generalisations.

Questionnaires have **Limitations** *— they aren't very* **Valid**

1) Respondents **may not tell the truth**. They may lie, or they may be mistaken.
2) Questions may be **misleading** or **mean different things** to **different people**. This means they may not accurately measure what you **want to measure**.
3) Respondents can't give any **extra information**, even if it would be really helpful to the researcher.
4) Because the respondent fills in the questionnaire on their own, there's no one there to **explain** the questions if the respondent doesn't understand them.
5) Postal questionnaires have a **low response rate**. If it's **too low** it won't be a **representative** sample.

Interviews

There are two kinds of interview — structured and unstructured. Sociologists use interviews when they want to be able to have a chat with their respondents. Well... okay, it's a little bit more complicated than that.

An Interview is a Conversation Between a Researcher and a Respondent

1) An **interview** is a **conversation** between a **researcher** and an **interviewee** where the researcher asks a set of questions.
2) You have to pick the **sample**, organise the **interview**, select / train your **interviewers**, **ask the questions** and **record the answers**. **Bias** can get in the way at each stage. An interviewer should create a **friendly relaxed atmosphere**.

Structured Interviews are Questionnaires given Face to Face

1) **Structured interviews** are like **questionnaires** given to **individuals** or **groups**, except an interviewer is present to ask the questions.
2) **Structured interviews** ask the **same questions** each time. The questions are closed questions, with set **multiple-choice answers**.
3) They give **quantitative data** and they're very **reliable**.
4) They're used in **large-scale social surveys**.
5) The main plus point over a postal questionnaire is that the interviewer can **explain** and **clarify** the questions.
6) Also, most structured interviews get a much **higher response rate** than questionnaires. People tend to agree to be interviewed (unless the research topic is sensitive or taboo).
7) However, they're **more expensive** than questionnaires — you need to **pay for the interviewer**.
8) The interviewer has to **follow the list of questions** so they **can't ask for more detail** if the respondent says something **particularly interesting**.

Unstructured Interviews give Qualitative Data

Pilot studies allow the researcher to find out what kind of question gets a substantial response. They also tell the researcher whether they need to warm up with a gentle chat to gain rapport with the respondent before asking more meaty questions.

1) **Unstructured interviews** are **informal**, with **no rigid structure**.
2) They are also **flexible** — they can be used to find out facts or attitudes.
3) They're good for researching **sensitive issues** where the interviewer has to gain the respondent's **trust** — for example, sexuality, domestic violence or crime.
4) They use **open-ended questions** and give **qualitative** data. They're quite **valid**.
5) The interviewer needs to have **skill** so they can **probe** to **find out more detail** about the interviewee's **opinions**.
6) They're used with **smaller samples**, which means they're **not very representative**.
7) It takes a **long time** to write up an **unstructured interview** — you have to write down a **whole conversation**, not just the **answers** to particular **multiple-choice questions**.

In constrast, Becker (1970) suggested that an aggressive interview style could actually uncover more honest responses that a participant might otherwise have kept to themselves.

Interviewers can have an effect on people's answers

1) Respondents in interviews may give the sort of answer they **think** the **interviewer wants to hear** — or the **exact opposite**, if they're feeling uncooperative.
2) Interviewers can give **subtle direction** towards certain responses — often **without realising** they're doing it.
3) These are known as **'interviewer effects'** (or 'researcher effects'). They make the data **less valid**.

Practice Questions

Q1 Give two advantages and two disadvantages of questionnaires.

Q2 Give two differences between structured and unstructured interviews.

Q3 What are 'interviewer effects'?

Exam Question

Q1 Evaluate the disadvantages of a sociologist using interviews. [16 marks]

Sociologists could be everywhere, watching us... shhhh...

Don't just learn what questionnaires and interviews are — you have to be aware of their pros and cons. You might also be asked whether one of these methods would be appropriate for educational research (there's more about that on p.34-35).

Experiments

You can use experiments to give you quantitative primary data.
Observation will give mostly qualitative primary data, and there are lots of different types.

Experiments Let You Find Cause and Effect

1) Experiments are used by **natural scientists** — biologists, chemists etc.
2) The researcher starts with a **hypothesis** and they use the experiment to **test** it out.
3) All the variables are kept constant, apart from the one you're interested in — the **independent variable**. Scientists **change the independent variable** and observe the effects on the **dependent variable**. If you were testing the effects of temperature on electrical resistance, **temperature** would be the **independent variable** which **you control** and **electrical resistance** would be the **dependent variable** which you **measure**.
4) The results are **turned into numbers** — the scientist looks for **patterns** and **cause-and-effect** relationships.
5) This method has been developed and used by **social scientists** to look for **social** causes and effects.

There are Two Kinds of Experiment

1) **Lab experiments** are done in a **controlled environment**. The researcher **changes** the **independent variable**, and observes the effect on the **dependent variable**. The researcher usually uses a **control group**, which is **left alone** to see what happens if you **don't do anything** to the **independent variable**. This method is often used by psychologists.
2) **Field experiments** are a response to the criticisms of lab experiments. They take place outside of the lab in **real social settings**, and those involved are often **unaware**. This method is used by **interpretivist** sociologists.

Strengths of lab experiments

1) The **researcher** has **control** over the experiment.
2) You get **quantitative** data.
3) You can **replicate** the research.

Limitations of lab experiments

1) It's **hard** to **reproduce real social situations** in a lab — lab experiments are **artificial**.
2) It is **difficult** to **isolate single variables**. **Social behaviour** is influenced by **many factors**.
3) There are often **moral** and **ethical** issues in lab experiments.
4) People may feel **intimidated** or **act differently** in the lab.

Strengths of field experiments

1) They're done in **natural social settings** and are more like **real life**.
2) They can show the **hidden meanings** of **everyday social interaction**.

Limitations of field experiments

1) You **can't control the variables** like you can in lab experiments.
2) If people **know they're being studied** they may **change** their **behaviour**.
3) There's an **ethical problem** in carrying out experiments when the subjects **aren't aware** that they are taking part in an experiment.

In any kind of experiment, researchers can measure things in a biased way if they have expectations about the results.

When People Know They're Being Studied, They Sometimes Act Differently

1) When people are more **interested** in something, they **try harder**. They may try harder at what they're doing because they know they're being observed and want to appear in a good light. This is called the **Hawthorne effect**.
2) People usually have an idea of what kind of **response** the **researchers want**. People often either give the researchers the **response they think they want** or the **exact opposite** — depending on whether they want to please the researchers or whether they want to be stubborn.
3) These effects mean data from experiments may not be **valid**.

Observations

Observation is Watching Behaviour in Real-Life Settings

1) In **covert observation**, the researcher **doesn't tell the group** they're being observed. The British Sociological Association (BSA) advise that you should only use covert participant observation when there's **no other way** of obtaining the data. For example, **Nigel Fielding (1981)** used covert observation when researching the National Front (a far right-wing political party) because he believed he would encounter hostility if they knew he was a sociologist.
2) **Overt observation** (direct observation) is when the group is aware of the research and they know who the researcher is. For example, **Beverley Skeggs (1991)** used overt observation when studying female sexuality among students at a college.
3) **Participant observation** is when the researcher **actively involves themselves in the group**.
4) **Non-participant observation** is when the researcher **observes** the group but isn't actively part of the group.

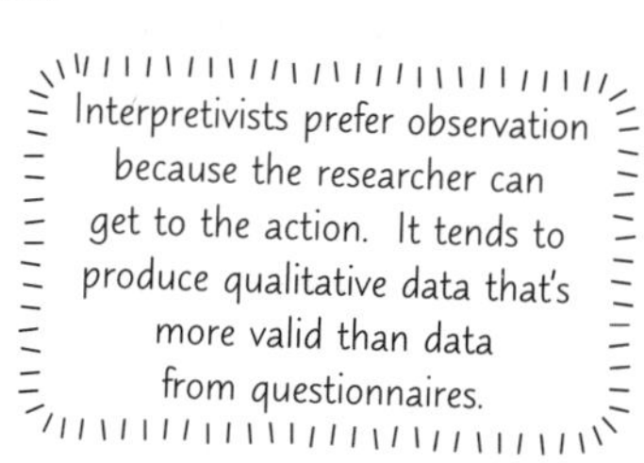

Participant and Non-Participant Observation Have Pros and Cons

1) Participant observation gets the researcher **right to where the action** is — so they can **check out the dynamics of a group** from **close up**.
2) **Participant observation** allows you to research the workings of deviant groups.
3) The researcher gets **first-hand insight** of people in **natural real-life settings**.
4) If it's **covert**, people **can't mislead** the researcher.

But...

1) The researcher may get too involved and find it **hard to stand back** and **objectively observe** the group.
2) **Overt research** may **influence** the behaviour of the group.
3) The researcher in a **covert observation** may join in with illegal acts if they're in a deviant group.
4) You **can't repeat the research**. It **lacks reliability**. A covert observer may find it difficult to remember all the events and accurately record them.
5) There are **ethical** and **practical** problems in **getting in**, **staying in** and **getting out** of the group.
6) The research usually includes a **small group** so it's not **representative** of the population.
7) It is **hard work**, **time-consuming** and **expensive**.

1) In **non-participant** observation, the researcher **isn't drawn into the group** so they can be more **objective** about the group's behaviour.
2) If you want to observe **deviant** groups, you have to be very **inconspicuous**.

But...

1) **Observing from the outside** stops you from getting to where the **action** is.
2) **Overt research** may **influence** the **behaviour** of the group.

By day three of her covert participant observation of landscape painters, Jules was blending in seamlessly.

Practice Questions

Q1 Name two advantages of field experiments over laboratory experiments.

Q2 What is the 'Hawthorne effect'?

Q3 What is the difference between overt and covert observation?

Exam Question

Q1 What are the drawbacks of using non-participant observation in sociological research? Outline two examples. [4 marks]

Anyone up for an experiment on how people cope with being millionaires...

If you're not really into science, this business about dependent and independent variables might seem a tad confusing. Don't be too confused — just remember that the dependent variable is the one you measure to see how it's changed. When it comes to the stuff on observations, remember to think about the reliability and validity of the different types.

In-depth Research Methods

This page covers some specific types of research methods that study particular groups in a very detailed way.

Case Studies focus on just One Thing

1) Case studies are **detailed investigations** of **a specific thing** — e.g. one person, one group, one institution or one event.
2) One particular kind of case study is the **life history**, which studies one person's whole life.
3) Examples of case studies include **Willis's (1977)** study of one group of boys in a school (p.23) and **Venkatesh's (2008)** study on the organisation and impact of one criminal gang.
4) **Interpretivists** like case studies because they can provide very **detailed data**, and they can give the researcher great **insight** into the subject under investigation.
5) **Positivists** dislike case studies as they **aren't representative** of wider populations, and so they can't be used to make accurate generalisations because of the **small sample size**.

Focus Groups are a Type of Semi-Structured Observation

1) A **focus group** is a **small sample**, perhaps fewer than ten people. The sample are **put in a room together**, and asked to talk about a particular issue or to try to answer a specific set of questions. The discussion is **observed by a researcher**.
2) Because this is more like a **natural conversation**, the subjects may feel **more able to express themselves** than if they were speaking **directly to an interviewer**. Sometimes the focus group is **left alone** and a **video camera** or **audio recorder** is used to **record the discussion for later analysis**. Sometimes researchers **stay with the group** and **take part in the discussion** — they use the focus group to conduct a **group interview**.

Longitudinal Studies are Social Surveys over a Period of Time

Longitudinal studies are done at **regular intervals** over a **long period of time**. They're often **large-scale quantitative** surveys, and they tend to be used by **positivists**. However, some studies like the TV programme *Seven Up* are more **qualitative**.

Seven Up was a TV documentary that asked 14 kids aged 7 what they thought about life, and what they wanted to be when they grew up. The programme makers came back to interview the children every seven years. The latest instalment was Fifty-Six Up.

Strengths of longitudinal studies

1) You can **analyse changes** and **make comparisons** over time.
2) You can study how the **attitudes** of the sample **change** with time.

Limitations of longitudinal studies

1) It's **hard** to recruit a **committed sample** who'll want to **stay** with the study.
2) It's **hard to keep contact** with the sample, which may make the study less valid.
3) You need **long-term funding** and you need to **keep the research team together**.
4) Longitudinal studies rely on **interviews** and **questionnaires** which might not be **valid** or **reliable**.

Ethnography Studies the Way of Life of a Group

1) **Ethnography** is the scientific description of a specific culture by someone with first-hand experience of observing that culture. It was first used by **anthropologists** to study **traditional societies**. They joined the community, learnt the language, and noted their observations.

Anthropology is the study of humans.

2) It is based on small-scale fieldwork that tends to produce **qualitative** data. It's **valid** because you can study behaviour in **natural settings**.
3) You can use ethnography to see what a whole **community** get up to, or to find out just one **individual's life history**.
4) You can use all sorts of methods to get **primary data**, including **case studies**, **focus groups** and **longitudinal surveys** and **observations** (p.17).
5) Researchers may also analyse **documents** such as **diaries** and **letters**, which are **secondary data** (p.19).

- Ethnography is **in-depth research** which gives **inside knowledge** about a community.
- You get a **valid** picture from ethnography, but it relies on the **researcher's interpretations** of what people do and say.
- It's **difficult** to **make generalisations** from small-scale research, and it may not be **reliable** (it's difficult to reproduce).

Secondary Data

You can get quantitative secondary data from statistics, and qualitative secondary data from documents.

Statistics *are a Source of* ***Secondary Data***

Official statistics are a source of secondary data. They're produced by local governments, central government and government agencies.

1) **Hard statistics** are **objective**. Politicians can't fiddle with them. Statistics on births and marriages are hard statistics.
2) **Soft statistics** are more **subjective**. Politicians can fiddle with them. Statistics on **crime**, **poverty** and **unemployment** are soft statistics. In the 1980s and 1990s, the government **changed the method** used to **measure unemployment** over 20 times.
3) **Social Trends** was a collection of **government surveys** published annually until 2012 — a **great source** of **secondary data**.
4) The **UK census** is a survey of every household every 10 years. Every household has to fill in the form **by law**.
5) The **Crime Survey for England and Wales (CSEW)** looks at victims of crime. The data is collected by a questionnaire.

Non-official statistics are statistics collected by organisations other than the government. For example:

1) **TV ratings** collected by the **British Audience Research Bureau**.
2) **Surveys** carried out by **special interest groups**, such as charities, or by other **sociologists**.

I ♥ statistics

Documents *and* ***Mass Media*** *are a Source of* ***Secondary Data***

1) A document is **written text**. It can be either on paper or in a digital format, e.g. an online text.
2) Documents can be **personal** — like **letters**, **diaries**, **autobiographies** and **memoirs**. Documents can also be **official**, like **school** records, **health** records, **church** records and **social work** records. **Public** documents are produced by charities, businesses and local government.
3) Documents can be **expressive** — more to do with **meanings**, like a **diary**. Documents can be **formal** — like **official documents**. **Interpretivists** prefer **expressive** documents because they're a big source of **qualitative data**.
4) **Content analysis** is a method of **systematically** analysing a communication (e.g. a speech, film or letter) to understand its **meanings**. It is often used to study the mass media, e.g. research by the Glasgow University Media Group.
5) There are **problems** with documents. They can be **difficult to understand** if they're old. They might be **fakes**. They might contain **lies** — especially personal documents.

Sociologists ***Compare*** *Different Secondary Documents*

1) Sociologists look for **similarities** and **differences** between secondary documents. They can compare different **times**, different **cultures** and different **groups** within society by looking at secondary data.
2) Researchers can analyse real social behaviour and make comparisons without having to set up artificial experiments.
3) Durkheim used this **comparative method** in his famous 1897 study of suicide. He looked at the rates of suicide in different European societies. He found that the suicide rate was **consistent over time**, **but varied between societies** and varied for **different groups** within society.

Practice Questions

Q1 What is ethnography?

Q2 Give three examples of official statistics.

Q3 What is the difference between hard and soft statistics?

Exam Questions

Q1 What are the drawbacks of using longitudinal studies in sociological research? Outline two examples. [4 marks]

Q2 Evaluate the disadvantages of a sociologist using official statistics. [16 marks]

Studying research methods? Infiltrate a gang of sociologists...

I once infiltrated a chocolate factory in the name of ethnography. I got caught sampling a box of triple-layered chocolate bars and had to leave pretty quickly. Make sure you know the kinds of secondary data and in-depth research methods sociologists use.

The Role of the Education System

Different theories try to explain the role or function of education in society. Some of them look at the positive functions, some look at how education maintains inequality, some look at education as a business. Time to learn about learning.

Functionalism Says Education Has Three Functions that Help Society

1) Education plays a part in **secondary socialisation**, passing on **core values.**
2) Education **sifts and sorts people** for the **appropriate jobs**. This is called the **allocation** function.
3) Education teaches the **skills** needed in **work** and by the **economy**.

1) **Durkheim** said that education passes on **norms** and **values** in order to **integrate** individuals into society. Education helps to **create social order** based on cohesion and value **consensus**, and to strengthen **social solidarity**.
2) **Parsons** describes school as a bridge between the family and adult roles of society. Schools pass on a **universal value** of **achievement**. Parsons says that education **selects** children into **appropriate roles** because it's **meritocratic** (meaning that the best students rise to the top). He agrees with Durkheim that education helps to make people agree about norms and values.
3) **Davis and Moore (1945)** say that every society sorts its members into different positions. They think that there are **rules** for how education does this — called "**principles of stratification**". They believe that there has to be a system of **unequal rewards** (more money or status) to **motivate** people to train for the top positions.

The **functionalist** perspective says that education is **meritocratic**. A **meritocracy** is when social **rewards** are allocated by **talent** and **effort** rather than because of a position someone was **born** into.

Talent + motivation + equal opportunity = qualifications and a high position in society

Marxism Says Education Legitimises Inequality through Ideology

1) Education **prepares children** for the **world of work** by giving them **skills** and **values** employers need.
2) Education passes on **ruling class ideology** that **supports capitalism**.
3) Education **legitimises inequality**.

1) **Bowles and Gintis (1976)** say that there's a **correspondence** between **pupil experiences of school** and **adult work**. Pupils are **prepared** for the world of work by the school system:
   - Pupils are taught to accept the **hierarchy** at school. Work also has a hierarchy.
   - Pupils are **motivated by grades** to do **boring work**. Workers are **rewarded with pay** to do **boring work**.
   - The **school day** is broken into **small units**. So is the **work day**.
   - At school and work **subservience** (following the rules) is **rewarded**.
2) Bowles and Gintis say that the '**hidden curriculum**' (see p.22) also **prepares people for work**.
3) Marxists claim that, as well as these skills and values, education also passes on **capitalist ideology**. **Althusser**, a neo-Marxist, sees education as part of the "ideological state apparatus". In other words, it's a **tool** of capitalism which is used to pass on the belief that society is fair, even though it isn't — it **legitimises inequality**. Althusser thinks education produces a **docile and obedient workforce** who will not challenge authority.
4) **Willis (1977)** says that education **doesn't turn out** an **obedient workforce**. Some kids form an **anti-school subculture** and cope with school and then adult work by mucking about (see p.23).
5) **Bourdieu** used the concept of **cultural capital** (language, skills, knowledge and attitudes) to explain how middle-class children generally go on to fill the top jobs in society (there's **plenty** on this on p.25).
6) Marxists say that education **legitimises** this inequality through **meritocracy**. They claim that meritocracy is a **myth**, so **working-class pupils** are blamed for their poor results, when in fact they're a result of their **social class**.

There are Similarities and Differences Between Functionalist and Marxist Views

1) Both functionalism and Marxism look at the **big picture** — institutions and the whole structure of society. They tend to **ignore social interaction** — with the exception of Willis. Both say education has a **huge impact** on the individual and that it's **closely linked** to the **economy** and **work**.
2) The biggest **difference** is how they see **inequality**. Marxists say education helps to **reproduce and legitimise inequality**. Functionalists say education passes on the value of **meritocracy** and lets people **better themselves**.

The Role of the Education System

There are **Problems** with **Functionalist** and **Marxist Views**

Criticisms of Functionalism

1) Evidence of **differential achievement** in terms of class, gender and ethnicity suggests that education is **not meritocratic**.
2) **'Who you know'** is still more important than 'what you know' in some parts of society. So the allocation function isn't working properly.
3) It can be argued that the education system **doesn't prepare people** adequately for **work**. For example, the lack of engineering graduates indicates education is failing to produce what **employers** and the **economy** needs.
4) Functionalism doesn't look at how education may serve the interests of particular groups in terms of **ideology** and **values**. It **doesn't explain conflict**.

Criticisms of Marxism

1) Marxism assumes people are **passive victims**. It **exaggerates** how much working-class students are **socialised** into **obedience**. Willis showed how students actually resist authority.
2) Most people are **aware of the inequality** in education, and **don't think** that this inequality is **legitimate**.

The problem with both approaches is that they don't look at interaction and social processes within the school (see p.24-25).

Feminists say that the Education System is **Patriarchal**

1) Some feminists argue that the hidden curriculum (p.22) unofficially **reinforces gender differences**.
2) There are still **gender differences** in **subject choice** in schools. Gender stereotyping may still exist.
3) Girls are now outperforming boys at school — but **boys** still **demand more attention** from the teacher.
4) **Men** seem to dominate the top positions in schools (**head teacher**, **deputy head**) and even more so in universities.

Liberal feminists want **equal access to education for both sexes**.
Radical feminists believe men are a bad influence, and want **female-centred education** for girls.
Marxist feminists want to consider gender inequalities **combined with inequalities** of **class** and **ethnicity**.

The **New Right** believes that **Education** should provide **Individual Choice**

1) **New Right** theorists believe in the power of **individual choice**, and prefer this to the **state intervening** in people's lives.
2) They claim that the role of a school should be more like the role of a **business**. Businesses have to **compete** with one another to **attract consumers** and provide those consumers with the products they **want** and **need**. New Right theorists claim that this forces all businesses to **continually improve their standards**.
3) State schools are run by the **state**, so they **don't** have to **compete** for their consumers (pupils, parents and employers). New Right theorists say that this has caused **poor standards**. They want to **accelerate** the creation of an '**education market**' (see p.31), where a school's role is to provide what its community **wants** and **needs**.

Practice Questions

Q1 Name three functions that the education system performs, according to functionalists.
Q2 What is meant by meritocracy?
Q3 Give two problems with the Marxist theory of education.
Q4 What are the differences between Marxist and functionalist approaches to education?
Q5 Why do New Right theorists believe that schools should be run more like businesses?

Exam Questions

Q1 Give a definition of the term 'meritocracy'. [2 marks]

Q2 How do schools prepare students for the workplace? Outline three ways. [6 marks]

I like this idea of consumer power — all breaks and no lessons, please...

*Mmm, there are lots of theories here. But if you know what functionalism, Marxism, feminism and the New Right are, then their views of school **aren't that surprising**. What's that, Marxists think education reproduces class inequality? Shocker.*

Relationships and Processes within Schools

These pages are all about what actually happens inside schools, day in, day out. Most people experience a school at some point in their lives, so you should be able to relate to quite a bit of this stuff. Which should make it easier to learn. Dandy.

School also Teaches you a **Hidden Curriculum**

1) As well as the **formal curriculum** of subject content (English, science, geography and so on), schools pass on a set of **social norms** and **values** to their students. This is called the **hidden curriculum**.
2) Turning up to lessons **on time**, dressing **smartly** in the correct uniform and **working hard** to **achieve rewards** are all part of the hidden curriculum. They all teach students things they will need in **adult life**.
3) The hidden curriculum is part of many areas of school life. For example, a **hierarchy** of management staff, teaching staff and students teaches **respect for authority**. Punishments for failing to do homework teach students about the importance of **following instructions**.

The chaps had searched all night for the hidden curriculum, but without success.

Labelling Theory says that **Teachers** can create **Self-Fulfilling Prophecies**

1) **Labelling theory** was a very popular idea in sociology in the 1970s and 1980s. It states that people **decide** on the **characters** of others and **treat** them accordingly, whether the label is 'fair' or not.
2) According to this theory, **labels** are an important part of **teacher-pupil relationships**. If a student is labelled by their **teacher** as a 'troublemaker', they're **disciplined more harshly** than their classmates. Meanwhile, a student labelled as a 'bright spark' is given encouragement to help them to **succeed even further**.
3) Labelling can create a **self-fulfilling prophecy**. This is where the student **internalises** the label they've been given as part of their **identity** (see p.23), and 'acts up' to the label. For example, 'troublemakers' might behave poorly because that is how they think their teacher **expects** them to behave anyway.

> Some studies have shown that teachers label students based on **ethnic**, **gender** and **class stereotypes**. E.g. **Gillborn and Youdell (2000)** found that **black pupils** were more likely to be **disciplined** than their white classmates for the **same behaviour**, and black students felt that their teachers had **low expectations** of them.

There are **Different Ways** to **Organise Teaching** in a School

The ways in which schools decide to **sort** their pupils into **classes** can have a **big impact** on pupil achievement.

Streaming	Setting	Mixed Ability
Students are sorted into classes according to **ability**, and they **stay** in these groups for all or most of their subjects.	Students are sorted into classes according to **ability**, but on a **subject-by-subject** basis. E.g. a student could be in the top class for maths and the lowest class for music.	Students are sorted into classes that **aren't** based on **ability**, so that the highest and lowest achieving students are **taught together**.

1) There are possible **advantages** and **disadvantages** to each of these systems.
2) The main argument in favour of **setting** and **streaming** is that students can work at their own **level** and **pace**.
3) One problem with **streaming** is that students are likely to be **better** at **some subjects** than **others**, so some 'bottom stream' students **aren't challenged enough** in certain subjects, whilst some 'top stream' students **struggle** in some subjects.
4) Both **setting** and **streaming** can lead to **low self-esteem** for those in the lowest ability classes. **Ball (1981)** also found that teachers had **high expectations** for the highest ability classes. These students received even more attention and encouragement, while those in the lower classes suffered from **negative labelling** and performed poorly — setting and streaming can actually **increase** the differences in student achievement.
5) **Mixed-ability** classes can avoid worsening **gaps** in pupil achievement, but studies have shown that teachers still hold **low expectations** for lower ability students, and often **lower the level** of their teaching to suit them. This can mean that there isn't enough challenging work for the higher ability students.

Relationships and Processes within Schools

Pupils *can Form* ***Subcultures*** *within Schools*

A **subculture** is a group who share ideas and behaviour patterns which are different from the mainstream culture.

1) Two of the most commonly discussed subcultures are **pro-school** and **anti-school**, but there are **many** different subcultures within a school, e.g. sporty students, academic achievers or "lads".
2) Subcultures can have a **positive** or a **negative** effect on student **achievement**.
3) There is much debate about **how** and **why** students form subcultures within schools:

Streaming

Lacey (1970) claimed that it was a result of **streaming**. He conducted his study in a **grammar school** (p.30). Even though all pupils had been selected as "bright" at age 11, **bottom stream** pupils still formed an **anti-school subculture**, because they were **labelled** as failures.

Ethnicity

Fuller (1984) looked at a group of **black girls** in Year 11 at a comprehensive school. They were **high ability**, but felt that their teachers were **racist**, so they didn't work for their teachers' approval. Instead, they formed a **subculture**, worked alone and succeeded.

Social class

Willis (1997) studied a group of **boys** who had formed an anti-school subculture. He found that the 'lads' deliberately disrupted lessons as a way of **gaining respect** from others within the subculture. He also observed that these boys were **working-class** and likely to get **manual** jobs after school — they seemed to believe that school was of **no use** to them in the future.

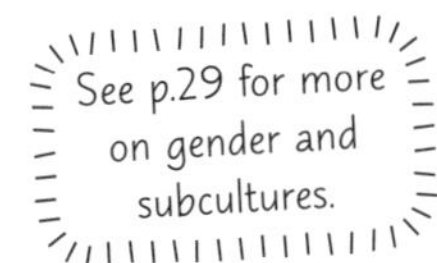

Identity *is a* ***More General Way*** *of Studying School Pupils*

1) Factors such as labelling, self-fulfilling prophecies, the organisation of teaching, and subcultures all have an **impact** on the achievement of school pupils, and it can be hard to work out the **specific** effects of each factor.
2) Instead, considering a pupil's **identity** (the way they view themselves, and the way others view them — see p.1) can be a way of **bringing together** all of these factors, and thinking about them alongside factors outside of school, such as parental attitude and whether they're suffering from poverty.

For example, if a **male pupil** identifies himself as '**non-academic**', this may have **begun** with a **teacher label**, but the biggest factor may **now** be a **subculture** of other, like-minded pupils, who are also 'non-academic'. He may choose to take a physical education GCSE, because he thinks of it as a **traditionally male** subject and he's already in a **top-ability set**, while adopting an **anti-school attitude** in English and history lessons. At home, he may not have access to **books** that would help his English or history performance. Overall, the difference in his **achievement** in various subjects gets **larger**.

3) One **disadvantage** of studying pupils' identities is that they're very **complex**. If a sociologist wants to study the effect of a **specific process** within school (such as setting) on achievement, then identity can make this difficult. Using the example above, if this student's achievement fell in history, it would be tricky to work out whether this was due to the set he was in, or one of the various factors that form his 'non-academic' identity.

Practice Questions

Q1 What is the hidden curriculum?

Q2 How can teacher labels lead to the formation of self-fulfilling prophecies?

Q3 Define the term 'subculture' and give two examples of subcultures which could appear in a school.

Exam Question

Q1 Outline two ways in which students may be organised into teaching groups in schools. Explain each one. [10 marks]

"Yes, I did stick loo roll to the ceiling, but I was fulfilling a negative label, sir..."

Even if sociology can't get you out of detention, it can tell you a lot about how schools work. All of these processes and relationships affect pupil achievement, so make sure you're clear on key terms like streaming, labelling and pupil subcultures.

Class and Differential Achievement in Education

Sociologists have investigated how social class affects how well people do at school. Financial and cultural factors are studied, as well as in-school factors like streaming.

Social Class tends to Affect Educational Achievement

I wonder if class affects how well you do in a school of fish.

1) Pupils from **professional** backgrounds are significantly **more likely** to enter **higher education** than those from unskilled backgrounds.
2) Pupils from **middle-class** backgrounds are more likely to study for **A-levels**, whereas **working-class** pupils are more likely to take **vocational** qualifications.
3) Pupils from disadvantaged backgrounds are **less likely** to start school being able to **read**.
4) Pupils from **unskilled backgrounds** on average achieve **lower scores** on SATs and in GCSEs and are more likely to be placed in **lower streams** or **sets**.

Some sociologists have suggested that different socio-economic groups have **different relative IQs**, and this accounts for discrepancies in educational attainment (**Eysenck (1971)** and others), but this is **very controversial**. It's also difficult to work out whether or not any **potential** IQ differences would be more **important** to achievement than social factors.

Processes Inside School — Labelling, Streaming and Subcultures are Factors

1) **Negative labelling** of students can lead to a **self-fulfilling prophecy of failure** (p.22). **Becker (1971)** and **Keddie (1971)** say that teachers tend to evaluate pupils in comparison to an imaginary **ideal student**, by looking at their **social class** (as well as appearance, personality and speech).
2) **Ball (1981)** found that the pupils in top **streams** (p.22) tended to be from **higher social classes**.
3) As a response to negative labelling and frustration with low status, pupils may form **anti-school subcultures** (p.23). **Woods (1983)** argued that there are lots of different reactions to school, but **non-conformist** reactions were more likely to come from **working-class** students.

These explanations are useful when looking at **day-to-day experiences** in schools. The problem is that they don't explain how **factors outside of school** (e.g. poverty, cultural deprivation) can influence achievement.

Material Deprivation Outside School Can Affect Achievement

The theory of **material deprivation** says that **economic poverty** is a big factor in low achievement at school.

1) In 1997, the **Joseph Rowntree Foundation** classified **one in ten** children as **poor** — which was defined as being in a family that couldn't afford at least three things other families took for granted.
2) **Halsey (1980)** found that the **most important factor** preventing working-class students staying on at school was a **lack of financial support**.
3) **Douglas (1964)** found that children in **unsatisfactory living conditions** (poor housing, lack of nutritious food, overcrowding) didn't do very well in ability tests compared to kids from comfortable backgrounds.
4) **Unemployment** or **low income** means less money for books, internet access and school trips. Low income families can't afford **nurseries** and **private schools** and they can't afford to support their kids through **uni**.
5) Poverty and unsatisfactory living standards may cause **health problems** and **absence from school**.

Cultural Deprivation Outside School Can Affect Achievement

The theory of **cultural deprivation** says that **working-class culture** and **parenting** aren't aimed at educational success.

1) **Douglas (1964)** thought the **level of parental interest** was the most important factor in affecting achievement. For example, middle-class parents are more likely to attend open evenings. Bear in mind though that **working-class parents** may not go to open evenings because they work **inconvenient shifts** — not because they aren't interested.
2) Some sociologists say that working-class kids don't have the **knowledge** and **values** that help achievement. **Books**, **museum visits**, **home internet access** and **parental knowledge of education** may help middle-class pupils to succeed.
3) Some **styles of parenting** emphasise the importance of education more than others.

Class and Differential Achievement in Education

Some Sociologists say **Class Affects Attitudes** to **Education**

1) **Sugarman (1970)** said that pupils from non-manual backgrounds and manual backgrounds have **different outlooks**. The pupils from **manual** backgrounds lived for **immediate gratification**. The pupils from **non-manual backgrounds** were **ambitious** and **deferred their gratification** — they invested time in studying and planned for the future.
2) **Leon Feinstein (2003)** found that social class continued to have a **significant impact** on educational achievement. He argued that **redistributive policies** (like Sure Start — see p.32) should carry on throughout a **student's entire education**, rather than being restricted to their pre-school years.
3) **Hyman (1967)** said that the **values** of the working class are a **self-imposed barrier** to improving their position. He said that the working class tend to place a **low value** on education.

ethnocentric = prioritising the values and culture of a particular group.

But...

Material and cultural deprivation theories **don't** explain how **factors inside school** affect achievement.

Cultural deprivation theory **generalises a lot** about differences between middle-class and working-class life. It **ignores** working-class families who **do** place a high value on education, and tends to **assume** that working-class families have **no culture** at all, or that working-class culture can't be **relevant** to school. This is **ethnocentric**.

The **method** may be **unsound**, e.g. attending parents' evenings might not be a good measure of parental interest.

The two Bs (**Bernstein** and **Bourdieu**) Investigated **Differences** in **Achievement**

1) **Bernstein (1970)** found that working-class pupils in the East End of London weren't comfortable with the style of language required by school. They used a **restricted code** — short forms of speech.
2) **Middle-class students** knew how to use the same **elaborated code** as the **teachers** — a much more wordy style of speech with everything made very explicit.
3) In terms of **language**, the working-class kids were at a disadvantage.

1) **Bourdieu (1971, 1974)** reckons middle-class students are at an advantage because they have the right kind of "**cultural capital**" — the right **language**, **skills**, **knowledge** and **attitudes**.
2) He thought that the **more cultural capital** you have, the **more successful** you'll be in education — and he believed that working-class pupils don't have **access** to cultural capital.
3) **Middle-class** families **pass on cultural capital** and **expectations** from parents to children. This is called **cultural reproduction**.

Problems with Bernstein's theory	Problems with Bourdieu's theory
There are **variations within** the middle class and working class. Different sections of these groups **vary** in how they use the **elaborate code** — the 'posh language' of teachers.	**Halsey et al (1980)** found that **material factors** are important. **Lack of money** may **stop kids staying on at school** or **getting to university**.
Some sociologists have developed his ideas to say working-class speech patterns are inferior or somehow 'wrong' — controversial... **Labov (1973)** thinks the elaborated speech code is just **different**.	**Not all working-class students fail**, even if they don't have cultural capital.

Practice Questions

Q1 Explain how processes outside school can cause underachievement by children from working-class backgrounds.

Q2 In what way might cultural deprivation theory be considered ethnocentric?

Q3 What is cultural capital and who does it help in education?

Exam Question

Q1 Evaluate the idea that differences in educational achievement by social class result from factors outside school. [20 marks]

Immediate gratification sounds good to me...

A warning — the exam might ask you something like "Assess how factors inside and outside school affect achievement". To answer that, you'd need to look at home and school factors for ethnicity, gender AND class. So revise p.26-29 as well.

Ethnicity and Differential Achievement in Education

Ethnicity is another factor that can influence how well people do at school.
Quick reminder — ethnicity means the shared cultural traditions and history which are distinct from other groups in society. Modern Britain is said to be a multicultural society made up of many different ethnic groups.

Some Ethnic Groups *Do* Better *Than* Others

There are big **variations** between the **average achievement level** of different ethnic minority groups.

Higher levels of achievement

1) **Chinese** pupils are the highest achievers at GCSE. **Indian** pupils also perform above the national average.
2) Students who are from **mixed ethnicity** backgrounds tend to perform above the national average at GCSE.
3) **Female black** and **male Asian** groups have some of the highest rates of students entering **higher education**.

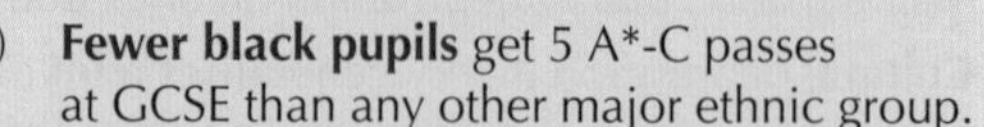

Lower levels of achievement

1) **Fewer black pupils** get 5 A*-C passes at GCSE than any other major ethnic group.
2) **Roma**, **white** and **Bangladeshi** students are the least likely to continue into **higher education**. (However, it's worth noting that Bangladeshi pupils achieve **above** the national average at **GCSE**.)

There must be reasons behind these statistics — probably more than one factor, and probably some **social** and **economic** factors.

Some people say that **intelligence is inherited** — i.e. people underachieve because they've inherited low IQ.

However, **IQ tests** can be **biased**. Sometimes they ask things that aren't really a test of brains, but really a test of **cultural knowledge**. The **Swann Report (1985)** found that if you took into account social and economic factors there were **no significant differences in IQ** whatsoever between different **ethnic groups**.

Processes Inside School — Labelling, Curriculum *and* Prejudice *are Factors*

Labelling theory

Labelling theory says that teachers have **different expectations** of **different ethnic minority groups**. **Gillborn (1990)** found that teachers sometimes **negatively label black students**. African-Caribbean students were seen as a **challenge** to school **authority** — and were more likely to be excluded from school. Gillborn calls this the 'myth of the black challenge'. Teachers had high expectations of Asian students, which could lead to a self-fulfilling prophecy of **success**. In contrast, negative labelling could result in a **self-fulfilling prophecy of failure**.

School Curriculum

The school curriculum could also be seen as **ethnocentric** — i.e. that it might fit the mainstream, white, middle-class culture better than other ethnicities. It could be **Europe-centred** too. Languages in the National Curriculum are mainly **European** — even though Mandarin Chinese is being taught more, kids usually learn French and German. **Assemblies, school holidays** and even **history lessons** may not fit with the culture and history of particular groups.

Institutional Racism

Some sociologists see British education as **'institutionally racist'**. This is where **policies** and **attitudes** unintentionally discriminate against ethnic minority groups. **Wright (1992)** found that even though members of staff said they were **committed to equal opportunities, Asian girls** got **less attention** from teachers and felt their cultural traditions were disapproved of (e.g. they might get told off for wearing a headscarf if it isn't part of the school uniform). **African-Caribbean boys** were more likely to be punished and **sent out of class**.

1) Some sociologists say that these factors may lead to **low self-esteem** for ethnic minorities. **Coard (1971)** said that black students are made to feel inferior in British schools.
2) On the other hand, **Mirza (1992)** found that black girls had **positive self-esteem** and **high aspirations**. The girls experienced discrimination but had **strategies** to minimise the effects of racism. It **wasn't low self-esteem** that affected their achievement — it was being **unwilling to ask for help**, or unwilling to **choose certain subjects**.

Ethnicity and Differential Achievement in Education

Factors Outside School — **Cultural Deprivation** Can Affect Achievement

1) **Language** can be a barrier for children from **immigrant families** when they **first arrive** in the UK.
2) However, the **Swann Report** found that **language didn't affect progress** for **later generations**.
3) **Driver and Ballard (1981)** also found that Asian children whose **first language** was **not English** were **as good at English** as their **classmates** by the age of 16.
4) **Labelling theorists** would say that language might not be a barrier, but **dialects** or having an **accent** might **influence teacher expectations** and lead to **negative labelling**. For example, a teacher might **assume** that a child isn't good at English because they have a foreign accent and put them in a lower set.

1) Some studies say that **family life varies** for different groups and this can influence achievement.
2) **Driver and Ballard (1981)** say that the **close-knit extended families** and **high parental expectations** increase levels of achievement in **Asian communities**.
3) **Archer and Francis (2006)** found that **Chinese parents** saw education as hugely important and this seemed to create a **desire for achievement** in Chinese families.
4) Some sociologists say the relatively high levels of **divorce** and **single-parenthood** in African-Caribbean households could result in **material deprivation**. On the other hand, the **independence** of **African-Caribbean women** can mean that girls get **positive role models**.

Ethnicity Combines with **Material Deprivation** to Affect Achievement

On their own, cultural factors and factors inside school may not seem all that convincing. If you bring **material factors** and **social class** into the equation you get a more complex picture.

1) The **Swann Report** found that **socio-economic** status was a factor in the lower levels of achievement of **African Caribbean** pupils.
2) **Pakistani**, **Bangladeshi** and **African Caribbean** groups are more likely to be in **lower class positions** such as routine occupations (assembly line workers, factory workers) and elementary occupations (cleaners, labourers). This may result in poor housing, periods of unemployment, poverty and **material deprivation**.
3) **Chinese**, **African Asian** and **Indian** groups are more likely to be in **higher class** positions and **less likely** to experience material deprivation.

African Asians means people of Indian origin who lived in Kenya and Uganda and then moved to Britain in the 1970s.

Some recent studies have claimed that **prejudice** in society may contribute to these lower class positions. Research by the **Joseph Rowntree Foundation** found that **ethnic minority** workers in **low-paid jobs** often face **barriers** to **promotion**.

Free school meals are given to children from families on certain financial **benefits**, so they can be a good **indicator** of material deprivation:

Ethnic group	% of pupils at end of KS4 entitled to free school meals
Bangladeshi	38.5%
Pakistani	28.0%
Indian	9.7%
Chinese	7.4%

Data from the year 2012-2013.

Practice Questions

Q1 Why do sociologists dislike genetic explanations of intelligence and educational success?

Q2 Name one factor inside school that explains the underachievement of some ethnic minority groups.

Q3 Give an example of how social class combines with ethnicity to affect achievement.

Exam Question

Q1 How might schools themselves affect the educational achievement of students from ethnic minorities? Use one example to briefly explain your answer. [2 marks]

It's more complicated than you might have thought...

Remember that not all ethnic minorities underachieve — so don't go storming into your exam answer with a pre-prepared rant that it's all about white / black racism. There are always several different factors that affect each ethnic group.

Gender and Differential Achievement in Education

Gender is another factor that can influence how well people do at school.
Since the 1980s, things have changed. Sociologists used to talk about female underachievement.
Now there are worries that boys are falling behind. Geez Louise, make your minds up...

Four Facts about Gender and Differential Educational Achievement

Boys used to outperform girls at school in the UK — this had a lot to do with the fact that female education was seen as **less important** for much of history. However, there's been a shift, and it's now **boys** who are **falling behind**:

1) Girls get **better results** in primary school National Curriculum tests.
2) Girls get **better results** in **nearly every subject** at **GCSE**.
3) Girls are **more likely** to **pass** their **A-levels**.
4) **More women** than men go on to **university** in the UK.

Factors Inside School Explain Why Females Now Do Better

1) **Mitsos and Browne (1998)** say teaching has been **feminised**. Women are **more likely to be classroom teachers**, especially in primary schools. This gives girls **positive role models**.
2) **Textbooks** and **teaching resources** have changed and are less likely to **stereotype girls** into passive roles.
3) The National Curriculum **forced** girls to do **traditionally 'male'** subjects. For example, more girls started to do **science**. Other Local Education Authority and government initiatives tried to encourage girls to do these subjects, e.g. WISE (Women In Science and Engineering) and GIST (Girls Into Science and Technology).
4) **Swann and Graddol (1993)** think that high female achievement is a result of the **quality of interaction** they have with their **teachers**. Most of the time teachers spend with girls is used to **help with their work** but most teacher time spent with boys is focused on **behaviour management**.
5) **Jackson (1998)** says that schools label boys **negatively**. Boys are associated with poor behaviour, which gives the school a bad name, and with **low achievement**, which lowers the school's **league table position**. This negative label becomes a **self-fulfilling prophecy**.

Archer (2006) says that Females Still Face Problems at School

1) **Archer (2006)** argues that the current **underachievement** by boys in education masks the **continuing problems** that girls still face.
2) She claims that **high-achieving Asian** and **Chinese** girls get negatively labelled by teachers as **robots** who are **incapable of independent thought**.
3) She also argues that **black working-class girls** are negatively labelled as **loud and aggressive**.
4) She concludes that the ongoing achievement of girls is '**fragile and problematic**'.

Factors Outside School Explain Why Females Now Do Better

1) Some sociologists argue that girls are **socialised** into ways of behaving that are **well-suited** to classroom environments — to be quieter, to listen to authority figures and to read a lot.
2) Policies such as the **Equal Pay Act** and **Sex Discrimination Act** have helped to create **more equal opportunities** in the wider society. This has **changed the values** of society and attitudes in school.
3) **Sue Sharpe (1994)** found that girls' priorities have changed. They now want **careers** and qualifications. More women go out to work, so girls see **positive role models** in work. Girls nowadays often want to be **financially independent**.

> The Equal Pay Act (1971) makes it illegal to pay men and women different wages for the same work. The Sex Discrimination Act (1975) means employers can't discriminate on the basis of gender.

4) The **feminist** movement caused a **change in female expectations**, and made more people **aware of inequality**. People are now more careful about negative stereotyping, sex discrimination and patriarchy.
5) Changes in the **labour market** have created opportunities for women. Since the 1970s, there has been a **continual increase** in the size of the **service sector** (jobs like healthcare and retail), which is traditionally female-dominated, and a **shrinking** of the **primary sector** (e.g. farming and mining), which is traditionally male-dominated.
6) Changes in **family structure** have changed female aspirations. On average, women now marry and have children **later in life**, so they can pursue a career first. There's also been a move towards **more equal roles within households** (p.49), partly as a result of the feminist movement, so that women are more able to seek work **outside** of the home.

Gender and Differential Achievement in Education

There are Several Reasons Why Some Boys Underachieve

Burly men in Santa hats can read books, too.

1) Boys may be having an **identity crisis**. The rise of **female independence**, the decline of the **breadwinner** role for men and the rise in **male unemployment** might mean that boys don't see the point of education. This may lead to anti-school subcultures.
2) **Interpretivists** say that teachers have **lower expectations of boys**. Teacher expectations may lead to a **self-fulfilling prophecy** of poor behaviour. **Negative labelling** may explain why they're more disruptive. Boys are more likely to be **excluded** from school.
3) The **feminisation** of **teaching** means that boys don't have as many **role models** in the classroom.
4) **Reading** can be seen as 'girly'. Boys who **avoid books** may not develop vital **communication skills**.

Subcultures help to Explain Gender and Achievement

Negative labelling and putting students into different **streams** or **sets** can cause some pupils to rebel against the school's values. They form **subcultures**. These can be either **pro-school** or **anti-school** subcultures.

1) In the 1970s **Willis** looked at why working-class kids get working-class jobs. He studied a group of boys later called "Willis's lads". The lads **rejected school** and formed an **anti-school subculture**. They **coped** with their own underachievement by having a **subculture where education didn't matter**, and where having a laugh was more important.
2) **Mac an Ghaill (1994)** says that **subcultures are complicated**. There are **lots of different types**. Boys may join a **macho lad subculture** because of a crisis of masculinity. But boys could also join **pro-school subcultures** and be proud of academic achievement.
3) **Fuller (1980)** studied a group of **African-Caribbean girls** in **London** who formed a **subculture** that worked hard to prove negative labelling wrong.

There are Different Ways to Explain Gender and Subject Choice

Girls tend to choose **essay-based** A-levels like English and religious studies.
Boys tend to go for **technical** ones like maths and physics.

1) **Subject choice** may still be influenced by **gender socialisation**. The ideas of **femininity** and **masculinity** can create different **expectations** and **stereotypes** of what pupils should study.
2) **Kelly (1987)** found that **science** is seen as a **masculine subject**. Boys dominate the science classroom.
3) **Parental expectations** may encourage students to follow what they see as the traditional '**normal**' choice for their gender. There's a pressure to **conform** to a social norm.
4) **Teachers** may also have an effect on subject choice. Most physics teachers are male, for example, meaning that there are more male than female **role models** within this subject.

In 2015, 28 500 boys and 7787 girls entered the A-level physics exams.

Practice Questions

Q1 Give two stages of education where girls tend to outperform boys.

Q2 Give two reasons why subcultures are formed by some pupils.

Q3 Give one reason why boys and girls might choose different subjects.

Exam Question

Q1 Apply your own knowledge and material from Item A to evaluate the idea that socialisation is the most important factor in female educational success. [20 marks]

Item A

Girls are now achieving better results at school than boys. More girls also move on to university than boys. Some sociologists argue that this is because girls are socialised into behaviour that suits the classroom environment.

Girls are DOOMED... no wait, boys are DOOMED... no wait... ah, forget it...

*Remember that there's a **lot of generalisation** with all of the sociological theories in this book. You can't just assume that Josephine beat Joseph in the sociology exam because she's a girl. She might have done more revision. (No hints here.)*

State Policy and Education

All governments are interested in education. The 1870 Forster Education Act introduced elementary schooling for 5–10 year olds in England and Wales. Since then there have been some major changes. Place your votes, please.

The **1944 Education Act** Introduced the **Tripartite System** and the **11+**

Before the **Second World War**, many poor people couldn't afford **secondary education** because it wasn't **free**. The **1944** Act (often called the **Butler Act**) made secondary schools free for all and raised the **leaving age** to 15. You took the **11+ exam** (like an IQ test) at the end of primary school and then went to one of **three types** of school:

1) **Grammar schools** were for the able kids who passed the 11+. Pupils were taught traditional subjects ready for **university**. About **20% of kids** got in to grammar school.
2) **Secondary modern schools** were for the **75-80%** of pupils **who failed** the 11+. Secondary moderns offered **basic education**.
3) **Technical schools** were meant to provide a more **vocational** education for those pupils with aptitude for **practical subjects**.

This system took a largely functionalist approach (since it was based on the idea of role allocation — see p.20).

This **tripartite system** aimed to improve the education of all children, but several problems remained:

1) The **11+ didn't necessarily measure your intelligence**. It was **culturally biased**, and suited the middle class more than the working class. It actually **legitimised** social class inequality, by incorporating it into a **system**.
2) **Few technical schools were built**, so the vocational part of the plan didn't work that well. Most children ended up either at grammar or secondary modern schools. These schools were supposed to have '**parity of esteem**' — they were supposed to be considered as having **equal value** — but grammar schools were seen as the best.
3) Kids who failed the 11+ were **labelled as failures**, which sometimes turned them off education.
4) If well-off middle-class pupils failed, their parents could still afford to send them to **private schools**.

In **1965** the Labour Government made Schools **Comprehensive**

The Labour government insisted that Local Education Authorities (LEAs) **reorganised most schools** so that everyone had **equality of opportunity**. 'Comprehensive school' means it's universal — everyone's meant to get the same deal.

Positive aspects of the comprehensive system	Criticisms of the comprehensive system
There's no 11+, so 80% of the school population don't get labelled as failures.	Most comprehensive schools still sort pupils into streams or sets (p.22) depending on test scores, so it's still possible to feel like a failure without the 11+.
High-ability pupils generally still do well with this system. Lower-ability pupils do better in comprehensive schools than in the old secondary moderns.	Comprehensives in working-class areas have worse GCSE results than those in middle-class areas.

Comprehensive schooling **hasn't achieved equality of opportunity**. Schools tend to be 'single-class', depending on the **local area**. Where people can afford to live (and how good the local schools are) is important in educational attainment.

In **1976** the Push for **Vocational Education** Started

In 1976, Labour Prime Minister James Callaghan made a speech saying that British education and industry was in decline because schools didn't teach people the **skills they needed in work**. All governments since then have had policies designed to create a closer link between school and work. This is called **vocationalism**.

These vocational reforms include:

1) **Youth Training Schemes (YTS)** started in 1983. These were job training schemes for school leavers aged 16-17.
2) **NVQs** (1986) and **GNVQs** (1992) were introduced — these were **practical qualifications**.
3) The **New Deal**, introduced in 1998, meant people on benefits had to attend courses if they didn't accept work.

There are some **problems** with vocational education:

1) Some sociologists argue that vocational education aims to teach **good work discipline**, not skills.
2) Some Marxist sociologists say that vocational training provides **cheap labour** and that governments encourage people into training schemes to **lower unemployment statistics**.
3) Vocational qualifications often aren't regarded as **highly** as **academic qualifications** by universities and employers.
4) Some feminist sociologists argue that vocational qualifications **force** girls into traditionally 'female' jobs, such as beautician and childminder.

State Policy and Education

*The **1988 Education Reform Act** — Choice, Inspections and More Tests*

In the late 1980s, the **Conservative** government introduced some **major reforms** in education.
These reforms were based on **New Right** ideas (see p.21), so they were focused on:

- widening **choice** within the education system.
- encouraging **more competition** to create a '**market**' in schools (this is called **marketisation**).

Education should link to the economy

The government introduced **more vocational courses** and more **work placement schemes**.

There should be better standards in education

1) The government introduced a **National Curriculum** of **compulsory subjects** for all **5- to 16-year-olds**. English, maths and science ('**core subjects**') had to be given more space in the timetable.
2) **OFSTED** (Office for Standards in Education) was set up to **inspect** schools and make sure they were doing a **decent job**. You might have seen **teachers** getting somewhat **frantic** before an inspection.
3) Schools could **opt out** of their local education authority and become **grant-maintained schools**. This means that they got money **straight from the government** and could **spend it how they liked**. The government believed this would **improve standards**.

There should be a system of choice and competition

1) Parents could **choose** which school to send their child to — if the school had **space**.
2) Parents could use **league tables** to help them choose. **League tables** show **how many** kids at each school **pass their exams**, and how many get **good grades**.
3) Schools worked like **businesses** and **advertised** for students.

David (1993) describes this situation as a 'parentocracy', because the power in education is held by parents, rather than by teachers and schools.

There should be more testing and more exams

1) Pupils had to sit **SATs** at **7, 11 and 14**, and **GCSEs** at **16**.
2) The results could be used to form **league tables**, and to monitor school **standards**.

There are several criticisms of these policies:

1) Sociologists like **Whitty (1998)** argue that middle-class parents have an **advantage** in an educational **market**. Since they are more likely to have succeeded in education themselves, they have the **knowledge** and **attitudes** (what Bourdieu called **cultural capital** — see p.25) to choose a good school for their child. They may also have the **financial** capital to **move** to an area with better schools. Increasing parental choice can actually **reinforce social class inequality**.
2) Constant **testing** can be **stressful** for students, and can encourage **labelling** and **self-fulfilling prophecies** (p.22).
3) **Ball (1995)** claimed that the new **National Curriculum** was the 'curriculum of the dead', because its emphasis on the core subjects was **outdated**.

Practice Questions

Q1 What was the aim of the 1944 Education Act?

Q2 Name the three types of school in the tripartite system.

Q3 Briefly explain two problems with comprehensive schools.

Q4 Briefly describe two changes brought about by the 1988 Education Reform Act.

Q5 Explain one way in which middle-class parents may benefit from an education 'market'.

Exam Question

Q1 How did the Butler Act remove inequalities in education? Use one example to briefly explain your answer. [2 marks]

They'll never make their minds up...

Governments have been trying to "Sort Out Education Once And For All" and "Shake Up Britain's Failing Schools" for ages. But whatever happens, kids go to school, teachers teach them things, and there are exams at the end of it all...

State Policy and Education

These pages examine and evaluate the motivation behind recent state policies in education.

New Labour (1997-2010) Followed Third Way ideas

When Labour took power, they wanted to intervene to do something about **educational inequality**, but they also wanted **choice** and **diversity**. This approach is called '**third way politics**' — it's a bit like the old Labour policies of **state intervention** and the New Right policies of marketisation **combined**. Party leaders called themselves 'New Labour'.

1) New Labour continued the process of **marketisation** begun by the previous Conservative government. For example, they allowed schools to **specialise** in certain subjects — e.g. by becoming Music Colleges or Mathematics Colleges — to try to **create diversity** and **increase choice for parents**. They also allowed **faith schools** to be set up.
2) New Right thinking made education more **privatised**. Agencies were given **contracts** for things like improving reading and writing in primary schools. New Labour claimed that this would improve efficiency and standards, because the contracts were **competitive**, but some people argue that the **privatisation** of education takes too much control away from schools.
3) The government also pursued some **interventionist** policies, such as:
    - **reducing infant class sizes** to a maximum of **30**.
    - introducing **numeracy hour** and **literacy hour** in **primary schools**.
    - trying to **increase** the **number of people going to university**.
4) A big change in education for 16- to 18-year-olds came with **Curriculum 2000**. Policy changed to make A-level education broader. A **vocational A-level** was introduced (intended to be of equal worth to an academic A-level). **Key skills** qualifications were also launched, and were supposed to be useful for all jobs.

Some Policies Aimed to Promote Gender Equality

Girls

The **1988 National Curriculum** gave all pupils equal entitlement to all subjects for the first time. This has been credited with the increased achievement of girls in the last 20 years.

Initiatives such as the **Computer Club for Girls** (CC4G), **Women Into Science and Engineering** (WISE) and **Girls In Science and Technology** (GIST) encourage girls to get involved with subjects they have **traditionally avoided**.

Boys

In 1999 the government gave **grants** to primary schools to hold **extra writing classes** for boys to help push up their **SATs scores**. In 2005 the **Breakthrough Programme** introduced **mentoring**, **after-school classes** and **e-tutorials** for teenage boys in an attempt to improve their exam performance.

Some New Labour Policies Aimed to Reduce Class Inequality

Compensatory education tries to make up for **material** and **cultural deprivation**, by giving **extra help** to those who need it. This is an **interventionist** approach. New Labour introduced several compensatory policies during their time in power:

1) **Sure Start** began in 1999. It was a government programme to improve early education and childcare in England, and offered up to two years of **free childcare** and **early education** to all three- and four-year-olds.
2) The **Education Maintenance Allowance (EMA)** gave up to £30 per week to students who stayed on in education post-16. A series of **bonuses** were available for good attendance and progress. EMA was **means-tested** so only children from poorer families could benefit from it.
3) **Education Action Zones** were introduced in 1998 as a way of tackling educational inequality by **area**. Local public, private and voluntary organisations worked together and combined their **resources** to try to raise standards.
4) **Free school meals** (which were means-tested) and **breakfast clubs** also aimed to reduce class inequality.
5) The **Academies Programme** opened new schools in **disadvantaged areas** where existing schools were judged to be '**failing**'. They were run in partnership with local business **sponsors** to try to improve performance.

The EMA was ended in England by the new government in 2010.

1) However, sociologists such as **Benn (2012)** have **criticised** New Labour because their policies aimed at **reducing** educational inequality seemed to be **inconsistent** with policies that threatened to **increase** it. For example, they introduced **university tuition fees** of £1000 per year in 1998, and increased them to £3000 in 2004. These fees are a **barrier** to higher education for many working-class students.
2) For Benn, therefore, **third-way politics** was **too contradictory**. She calls this the 'New Labour paradox'.

State Policy and Education

Privatisation and *Marketisation Progressed* under the *Coalition* Government

In the 2010 General Election, no one party won a majority of MPs in the House of Commons, so the Conservative and Liberal Democrat parties formed the **Coalition** government, led by Conservative Prime Minister David Cameron.

1) The Coalition government **changed** the **academies** programme. Any school classed as 'Outstanding' by Ofsted could apply to become an academy without a **sponsor**. Failing schools were made into **sponsored academies**. The increasing numbers of schools run by **private organisations** means that the **privatisation** of the education system has **advanced**.
2) They also introduced **free schools**, which are set up by groups of parents, teachers or religious groups and don't have to teach the National Curriculum. The government hoped that this would provide **more choice** in **disadvantaged areas**.
3) Under Education Secretary Michael Gove, there were also changes to the **National Curriculum**:
   - A-levels were changed to a **linear** structure — all exams must be taken at the **end** of the course.
   - In a similar way, **coursework** and **modular exams** were **removed** at **GCSE**.
   - Far more **formal grammar** was included in the primary English curriculum.
4) The government also introduced the **pupil premium**, which provided **extra funding** for schools with students on **free school meals**. The funding was supposed to be spent on improving the educational experience of **these pupils**.
5) There are some **criticisms** of Coalition education policies:

- Critics say that, in some disadvantaged areas, the **academies** and **free schools** attract all the best teachers, which **undermines** other local schools.
- It is difficult to track whether **pupil premium** funding is actually being spent on **disadvantaged** pupils, or whether it is being **absorbed** into the whole school budget.
- The maximum **tuition fees** in higher education **increased** to £9000 per year. This can be seen as **socially exclusive**, because it's also increased the **loans** that most students need. This debt can be off-putting for working-class students.

Max was disappointed to find that his new 'free' school was not the lawless utopia he had imagined.

Education has been Affected by *Globalisation*

Globalisation is the idea that traditional national boundaries are **breaking down** across the world, as people become **more connected** by improved technology, multinational companies and increased migration.

It's tricky to study exactly how globalisation has **affected education**, but here are a few key ideas:

1) The British economy needs to be competitive in global industries like **technology**, so British workers need to be highly trained. This has an impact on education policy — e.g. **computer programming** has been introduced to the **primary school** curriculum.
2) Increased **immigration** to the UK has meant that there's a heavier focus on learning about **other cultures**. Schools also need to provide **specialised support** for pupils whose first **language** is not English. (In some areas of London, this applies to over 70% of students.)
3) Educational **ideas** are **shared** between nations. UK politicians have been **influenced** by countries such as Finland, whose education system is ranked very highly. However, **Kelly (2009)** has warned that as education systems become increasingly **similar**, they'll become **less relevant** to the needs of individual nations.

In 2012, Finland ranked 5th in the world for science and 6th for reading. The UK ranked 20th and 23rd respectively.

Practice Questions

Q1 What is 'third way politics'?

Q2 Give two examples of New Labour educational policies influenced by New Right thinking.

Q3 Give three educational policies of the Coalition government.

Q4 Explain one way in which globalisation has affected the UK education system.

Exam Question

Q1 Outline two ways in which the Coalition government advanced the privatisation and marketisation of education. Explain each one. [10 marks]

My education policy is to revise everything...

The New Right want policies that widen choice and give the market a chance to drive up standards. The left want the state to intervene in and have control over the education system. And New Labour wanted both. Make sure you learn about education policies for the exam (Sure Start, WISE, academies, tuition fees) — you might be asked to describe some of them.

Application of Research Methods to Education

In Paper 1, you'll be given a question that asks you to think about the advantages and disadvantages of using a particular research method to study a particular educational issue. Here are some tasty examples for you to digest.

The advantages and disadvantages of all the various research methods can be found in Section One of this book (p.6-19).

Using Unstructured Interviews *to Study* Anti-School Subcultures

1) A **subculture** is a group who share **ideas** and **behaviour patterns** which are **different** from the mainstream culture (see p.23). So an **anti-school** subculture are a group who have a **negative idea** of education, and behave accordingly.
2) **Willis'** study of **pupil subcultures** (p.23) and **Labov's linguistic deprivation** study (p.25) both used unstructured interviews.
3) Here are some ideas about **unstructured interviews** that you could mention:

Advantages	Disadvantages
Students who are part of an anti-school subculture may **not want to talk** about their school lives. Using unstructured interviews would allow the researcher to build up a **rapport** with the students, potentially giving **greater insight** into their thoughts and feelings.	Unstructured interviews are quite **time-consuming**. This means that they tend to be used with **smaller samples** — the researcher may only be able to interview a **few** students from the subculture. This means the data wouldn't be very **representative**.
School may be a **sensitive topic** for students within an anti-school subculture. Unstructured interviews are good for investigating sensitive issues, because the researcher doesn't have to stick to a fixed **questionnaire**. They can change their approach to gain the **trust** of the students and make them feel more **comfortable**.	The interviewer could have an **effect** on the interviewee, making the data **less valid**. Students may give an answer they think the interviewer **wants to hear**, or an answer that **presents** their behaviour in a more **positive** light. These are examples of '**interviewer effects**' (see p.15).
Unstructured interviews are likely to offer **greater validity** than questionnaires because they give the interviewer a chance to **adapt their questioning to the subject**. For example, if a student struggles to understand a question, the researcher can explain it.	The data collected from unstructured interviews is **qualitative**, so it would be harder to make **comparisons** between various students' ideas. It would also be harder to reproduce the data, making it **less reliable**.
Anti-school subcultures can cause **disruptive** behaviour in the classroom, as students **encourage** each other to misbehave. Using unstructured interviews would mean that students could be interviewed **away** from this **peer pressure**. This gives them more time to reflect on the issues and give a more **valid** response.	Students with a **negative attitude** towards school may also take a negative attitude towards the **interviewer**, seeing them as just another adult connected with school. This means they may not express their **true feelings**, or even deliberately **lie**, making the data **less valid**.

Using Covert Participant Observation *to Investigate* Labelling

Labelling is covered on p.22.

1) In **participant** observations, the researcher **gets involved** with the people they're studying.
2) In **covert participant** observations, the people being studied **don't know** why the researcher is **really there**.
3) Here are some things you could talk about:

Advantages

1) Teachers often label students **without realising** they're doing it, so they may not mention it in an interview or questionnaire. Being a **participant** would allow the researcher to **observe** labelling in a **natural**, **real-life** setting.
2) Teachers probably wouldn't want to **be seen** to label their students, so they might **deliberately avoid** doing it if they knew this was the issue being studied. By observing **covertly**, the researcher could get more valid data.

Disadvantages

1) **Misleading** teachers counts as **deception**, which is arguably **ethically incorrect**. It may also be difficult to find a good enough cover explanation to gain **access** to a school, and **using a cover** would also be ethically questionable.
2) The researcher may become **too familiar** with the teachers and find it hard to analyse them **objectively**. The researcher may even start to label the students themselves, so they **stop recognising** that teachers are doing it.
3) The research couldn't be **exactly** repeated, so it isn't as **reliable** as questionnaires, for example. Covert participant observation also has to be conducted with a **smaller sample**, which makes the data **less representative**.

Application of Research Methods to Education

Using **Closed Questionnaires** to find out about **Parental Attitudes**

1) Parental attitudes to education can be **positive** or **negative**. (Have a look back at pages 24 and 27 in particular.)
2) Here are some things you could include in an answer:

1) Questionnaires can be used to collect a **large amount** of data very **quickly**. This means that lots of parents could be surveyed, which would make the results more **representative**.
2) Parents may be more **honest** about their attitudes towards education if they can complete a **private questionnaire**, rather than talking to an interviewer. For example, if their attitude towards education is negative they may be unwilling to speak about this **in person**.
3) The study could be easily **repeated**, making the data more **reliable**. This could be useful for investigating the **changes** in parental attitudes over time.

But...

1) Respondents can **easily lie** about their true attitudes. This makes the data **less valid**.
2) Using closed questions doesn't allow the respondent to **explain** their answer. It might not be a suitable method for researching **attitudes** to education, which are often **complex**.
3) If parents associate the questionnaire with the **school**, then the researcher may find that the questionnaire is mostly completed by those with a **positive** attitude towards education. This would **skew** the **sample**, making it **less representative**, so the data would be **less valid**.

7 out of 10 parents lie when asked if they've ever taken a silly photo of their child.

Using **Official Statistics** to Study **Mixed-Ability Teaching**

1) **Mixed-ability classes** are one of the three main ways to **organise teaching** in a school (alongside setting and streaming).
2) There are two **types** of statistics — **hard** and **soft** (see p.19). You should try to mention both of them in an answer.

Advantages

1) Using **hard** statistics would be a **reliable** source of secondary data, because they're **objective**. Schools can't adjust them to portray mixed-ability teaching in either a positive or negative way.
2) Statistics can be easily **compared** because they're a form of **quantitative** data. For example, the outcomes of mixed-ability classes could be compared for different genders, age groups and schools. They could also be compared **over time**.

Disadvantages

1) If **soft** statistics are used, the researcher would have to be careful that the data was **valid**. It could have been **adjusted** by schools, e.g. to **exaggerate** the successes of mixed-ability teaching.
2) Official statistics don't offer as much insight into the **reasons** behind achievement as other methods like unstructured interviews.
3) At **selective** schools, the variation in abilities in mixed classes would be less great than at non-selective schools, so this could **skew** the data.

Practice Questions

Q1 Why might covert participant observation be more useful than questionnaires for studying teacher labelling?

Q2 Give one disadvantage of using closed questionnaires to investigate negative parental attitudes to schooling.

Exam Question

Q1 Apply your own knowledge and material from Item A to evaluate the advantages and disadvantages of using overt non-participant observation to investigate institutional racism in schools. [20 marks]

Item A

Some sociologists claim that schools are institutionally racist. They suggest that some groups receive less teacher attention than their peers, and are punished more harshly. Sociologists have used overt non-participant observation to investigate this claim.

So many combinations, so little time...

There's no way you can prepare for every method-and-issue pair that might pop up in the exam (though for more examples, see Section One). The best thing to do is to make sure you know the methods inside out (they're all in Section One) — that way, you can apply them to any issue the examiner throws at you (Section One might help). Maybe you should revise Section One.

Different Types of Culture

In the UK, there's more than one type of culture and there are lots of ways to look at culture — folk vs urban, high vs low, popular culture, global culture...

Culture is a Way of Life

Culture means the **language**, **beliefs**, **customs**, **values**, **knowledge**, **skills**, **roles** and **norms** in a society. It's the way of life of a **society**. Culture is **socially transmitted**. That means it's **passed on** through **socialisation** (see p.40).

> **Norms** are ways of **behaving** and / or **thinking** that are seen as **normal** in society.
> **Values** are **beliefs** about what things are **important** and what things are **right** and **wrong**. Ideas like 'freedom of speech', 'respect for human life' and 'equality' are all **values**.

A **subculture** is an identifiable **group** within a culture whose members share **values** and **behaviour patterns** which are **different** from **mainstream norms**, e.g. youth subcultures like punks and goths. Subcultures can be a form of **resistance** to mainstream culture (see p.23).

Mass Culture replaces Folk Culture

Folk culture is the culture of **pre-industrial society**. It includes things like folk dances, folk songs, fairy tales, old wives' tales, traditional folk medicine and agricultural rituals. It's mainly passed on through word of mouth.

Sociologists have looked at the ways **culture changes** as people move from **villages** into **towns** and **cities**.

1) **Robert Redfield (1947)** said that '**folk societies**' were based on strong extended families, **supportive communities** and a **local culture**. In **urban** societies these were **not present**.
2) **Georg Simmel (1950)** argued that **urban societies** showed a **reduced sense of community**, and that urban people were more **individualistic** and **selfish**.
3) Theorists from the **Frankfurt School** (see p.38) said that this reduced sense of community was linked to the development of a **mass culture**. They said that the **media** had become a **strong agent of socialisation**, and it was wiping out the differences between local cultures. Instead, it looked more and more like there was just **one big culture**, shared by **everyone**.
4) These days, the term **mass culture** is used not just to describe the effects of the **media**, but also to refer to **fashion** and other types of **consumption**, e.g. if you eat lunch in a famous burger chain, you're taking part in mass culture.

Just try and tell me folk culture is dead... I dare ya, punk...

You can also Divide culture up into 'High Culture' and 'Low Culture'

The **elite** (better educated, with more money and power) tend to have a **distinct culture** from the **masses**.

1) Shakespeare, opera, sophisticated restaurants and arty French films are the type of things that are associated with '**high culture**'.
2) Meanwhile, the masses enjoy '**low culture**' — e.g. soap operas, reality TV, musicals, fast food and Hollywood films.

This is all linked to the ideas of 'class taste', cultural deprivation and cultural capital — see p.47.

3) 'High culture' is generally considered more **difficult to appreciate** and the audience is seen as **educated** and having '**good taste**'. Aspects of 'high culture' are seen as **good for society**, though they don't make much money compared to a lot of 'low culture', so the government often **subsidises** them.
4) In recent years a lot of **funding for high culture** has come from a '**low culture**' **source** — the National Lottery®. Some customers have been hostile to the idea that the lottery is used to pay for 'arty' dance and theatre companies. They suggest it's **elitist culture** — most lottery punters **wouldn't get to see it** and probably **wouldn't like it** if they did.

Many sociologists say there's No Such Thing as 'Low Culture'

1) The ideas of '**high culture**' and '**low culture**' are very **negative**. For example, **Bourdieu (1984)** says the **whole idea** of 'high culture' is to give **status** to **elite groups** — he says that status is maintained by passing on **cultural knowledge**.
2) Marxists argue that 'high culture' is just ruling-class culture, and that the ruling class have imposed their idea of culture on the rest of society, and defined it as 'better' than working-class culture. Some Marxists argue that so-called 'low culture' is just as **complex** and **sophisticated** as 'high culture'. For that reason, they prefer to use the term '**popular culture**', which is more of a positive idea.

Different Types of Culture

Popular Culture theorists emphasise that the **Audience** is **Active**

1) '**Mass**' and '**low**' culture are both concepts that are based on the idea of a **passive audience**. They assume that the audience is being **manipulated** by the media and doesn't have much control.
2) '**Popular**' culture is a concept that is based on the idea of an **active audience**. This audience shapes and changes culture. The **Centre for Contemporary Cultural Studies (CCCS)** did a lot of research into the way this happens in youth fashions and subcultures. They analysed popular culture products like TV shows and magazines, finding **meanings** within them.

There's also a **Global Culture**

Giddens (1990) says that **technological change** has led to **globalisation**. Goods can be **transported** to anywhere in the world, and **information** can be quickly transmitted across the globe. This has meant that cultures that were once local have become global. For example, British and American pop music is everywhere. American and Indian films are popular internationally.

1) **Klein (2000)** and **Sklair (1995)** point out that a few large **transnational corporations** (TNCs), e.g. Coca-Cola®, NIKE and TimeWarner, are involved in the majority of cultural production, making cultural goods that are consumed all over the world. **Sklair** argues that TNCs and the global media have **more power** than individual **nation states**.

2) Critics of globalisation worry that these TNCs will replace the world's current **cultural diversity** (the differences in people's lifestyles because of the society they live in) with Western culture. They refer to cultural globalisation as **cultural imperialism**. **Klein (2000)** says there's already a trend towards **cultural homogeneity** (everyone having the same culture — wearing the same trainers, eating the same burgers, drinking the same fizzy drinks).

3) Supporters of cultural globalisation argue that it's a **two-way process**. Western culture is transmitted to new societies, and other identities and cultures get passed back to Western societies — e.g. through **Bollywood films** shown in Western mainstream cinemas. With the movement of people from different countries and cultures to other parts of the world, many countries are now **multicultural societies**. Postmodernists argue that this allows people to consume a **plurality** of cultures — this is called **multiculturalism**. They think that globalisation leads to **hybridity** (a **pick and mix**) of cultures rather than one culture being imposed on another.

Practice Questions

Q1 What is 'low culture'?

Q2 What do Marxists say about 'high culture'?

Q3 What is globalisation?

Q4 What is mass culture?

Exam Question

Q1 Apply your own knowledge and material from Item A to evaluate the idea that high culture is elitist. [20 marks]

> **Item A**
> Culture can be divided into 'low culture' and 'high culture'. High culture is often seen as being reserved for the elite, while low culture is consumed by the lower classes. Some sociologists argue that the upper classes use their knowledge of high culture to give themselves status and separate themselves from the lower classes.

If I watch X factor on top of Ben Nevis, does that make it high culture?

Culture is everywhere, apparently. Sociologists divide culture into different categories — unfortunately, they don't always agree on exactly how to do it. Some argue that using terms like 'low' and 'high' to describe culture isn't very helpful. You need to be familiar with the terms on these pages, because you'll need them to analyse different views of culture in the exam.

Theories of Culture

Marxism, functionalism, postmodernism — it looks brain-bursting at first, but once you get the key ideas it'll all fall into place.

Marxists Say Capitalism Creates **False Needs** and **Commodity Fetishism**

Marxists are pretty **pessimistic** about **low/mass** culture because they believe it is used to **control** the working class.

1) The Frankfurt School began as a group of **neo-Marxist** thinkers in 1930s Germany who combined Marxism and psychology. Frankfurt School sociologists **Adorno and Horkheimer (1944)** argued that mass culture encourages you to think you '**need**' to **buy things** which you don't really need, such as twenty pairs of shoes, or a TV. You don't need these things in the same way you need **food** and **oxygen**, but it's **good for capitalism** if you **think** you do. They're **false needs**.
2) **Commodity fetishism** is where false needs create **obsessions** and **desires** about consumer goods — '**must-have**' objects. An example of this is when a new mobile phone comes out and everyone wants it.
3) The Frankfurt School said that commodity fetishism was like a **religion** because **capitalism creates desires** that **only capitalism can satisfy**. This means we all end up thinking **capitalism** is **good**, because it gives us **what we want**.

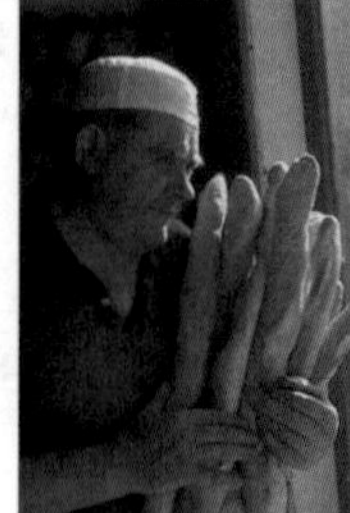
Arnold misunderstood when they asked him to knead the bread.

Some **Neo-Marxists** Say the Working Class are **Oppressed** by **Capitalism** via **Culture**

1) The **Frankfurt School** decided that the main way of transmitting **capitalist ideology** was through the **media**.
2) They argued that mass culture **helped capitalism** to oppress the working class by **destroying community** and **individuality**. It also encouraged **acceptance of authority** and **discouraged** people from **thinking for themselves**.
3) The Frankfurt School argued that things like **newspaper horoscopes** were used to suggest that a person's life experiences were down to **luck** or **fate**, rather than social structures or personal actions. **TV and radio advertising** reinforced the values of **capitalism**, while **Hollywood films** distracted ordinary people from social issues.
4) In this way, capitalism used **mass culture** to **prevent revolution** from ever happening.

So to sum up, the **Frankfurt School** took a **pessimistic** approach to mass culture:

- Mass culture is used to **dull the minds** of the **working class**.
- Mass culture promotes **capitalist ideology**.
- The population are **passive victims** of mass culture.

Other Neo-Marxists Disagree with the **Frankfurt School**

1) The Italian thinker **Antonio Gramsci (1971)** said that the idea of a **single mass culture** was too **simplistic**.
2) **Gramsci** thought that capitalism creates a big **dominant culture**. He called this dominance **hegemony**.
3) Gramsci believed that **capitalism** had to **tolerate** some oppositional cultures, rather than stamp them out. By **allowing some opposition** to exist, he said, capitalism could create the **illusion** that it was a **fair** system.
4) He had a big influence on the work of Marxists like **Stuart Hall** of the **Centre for Contemporary Cultural Studies**. Hall says that **youth subcultures** help working class youths to **resist capitalist values**.
5) Hall, and other neo-Marxists who take a more positive, optimistic view of modern culture, prefer the term **popular culture** to mass culture.

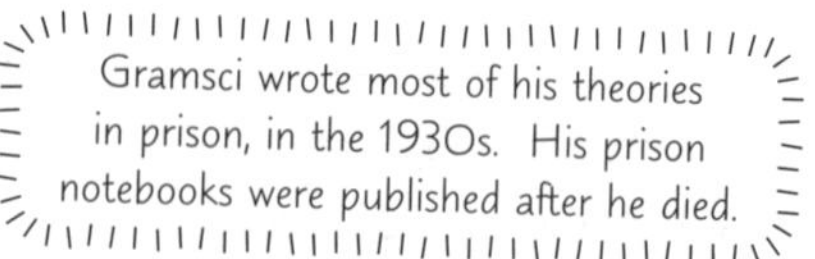

Functionalists See Culture as a Kind of **Bond**

Functionalists believe that **structures** of society are set up to allow society to **run as smoothly as possible**. **Durkheim's** functionalist theory of culture is also based on the idea of **social control**, but is more positive than that of the Marxists.

1) Durkheim's **functionalist** perspective describes culture as a kind of **social glue**. It bonds people together by creating shared interests and purposes.
2) Individuals **internalise** the **norms** and **values** (the rules and ideas) of society. This means those norms and values **become a part of who you are** — your personality and your **identity**.
3) The result is **consensus**, which means everyone sharing the **same norms and values** — Durkheim called the **shared norms and values** that **hold society together** the '**collective consciousness of society**'.
4) It also helps to **socialise** people into appropriate behaviour. This prevents society from breaking down into chaos.

Theories of Culture

Postmodernism Argues That Culture is Diverse

1) **Postmodernists** say **functionalism is outdated** because it's based on the idea that there's only one dominant or shared culture. Instead they argue that **culture** is **increasingly diverse**.
2) Postmodernists **reject** the idea that culture helps to **unify** people in society.

Stuart Hall (1992) says that diversity results in **fragmented identities**. People can **construct their identity** from a range of different cultures. Layers of identity can include nationality, gender, ethnicity, religion and political beliefs. Hall links this with the rise of **social movements** such as feminism and black power. He also says people have constructed new identities such as 'Black British' and 'British Muslim' as a response to cultural **globalisation**.

Dominic Strinati (1995) agrees with some postmodern ideas, but he says that culture is also affected by **structural** factors like class — culture traditionally consumed by **elites** is seen as **more valuable** than that enjoyed by the working class.

Interactionists Think That Culture is Determined by Individuals

Many sociologists say that culture is actually determined by the **behaviour and interaction of individuals**. Theories like this are called **action theories** because they emphasise the **action** of individuals, as opposed to **structural theories** like functionalism and Marxism, which are all about the big structures of society.

1) **Interactionists** think that individuals can choose how to behave, and aren't simply responding to social forces — culture comes from **people's own ideas** of how people **interact** with each other.
2) They see culture as being partly developed from the **bottom of society** at the **individual** level — if people **change** the way they act in relation to each other, then **culture will change too**.

Goffman (1972) studied **pedestrian interaction** on busy Western city streets — he discovered that cultural **norms** associated with the **action** of walking through the streets prevented people from **colliding** with one another. **Unspoken rules** like not looking at people for a long time and avoiding conversation enabled people to walk freely.

Feminism Links Popular Culture to Socialisation and Patriarchy

During the 1970s and 1980s, many feminists researched the relationship between **popular culture** and **gender socialisation**. Most of these studies suggested that popular culture **stereotypes** women into roles — such as housewife or sex object. These roles are then **reinforced** in society.

1) **Ferguson (1983)** and **McRobbie (1978)** studied magazines, and found that they promoted traditional female roles.
2) **Radical feminists**, such as **Andrea Dworkin (1981)** in her study of pornography, suggest that many images of women in popular culture encourage and justify **violence** against women.
3) More recently, some feminists have argued that popular cultural representations of women can also be **empowering**. For example, **Camille Paglia** has written a lot about Madonna's public image as a strong female role model.

Practice Questions

Q1 How do the Frankfurt School view popular culture?

Q2 Define 'false need' and 'commodity fetishism'.

Q3 What did Stuart Hall mean by 'fragmented identities'?

Exam Question

Q1 Evaluate the idea that culture can be determined by individuals. [20 marks]

Capitalism didn't tell me to want a new phone — the TV advert did...

According to the Frankfurt School, I didn't really need that designer dress after all. If only Theodor Adorno could have texted me to tell me. Sigh. Anyway, make sure you know the nuts and bolts of these theoretical approaches, because you'll need them if you want to get top level marks. Without mentioning relevant theorists, you aren't going to win the examiner over.

Socialisation and Social Roles

Most sociologists believe you have to learn how to fit into society, e.g. learn how to behave. This process is called socialisation. It begins in childhood and continues throughout life. As usual in sociology, there are different views about how it all works…

Socialisation** is the passing on of **Culture

1) Culture is **passed on** through **socialisation** from generation to generation. Sociologists say that through socialisation the **norms and values** of society are **internalised** — they become part of everyone's way of thinking (see p.36 for more on norms and values).
2) **Laws** often reflect norms, but sometimes **law-breaking** is the norm. Making illegal CD copies is a good example of this.
3) **Culture, values and norms** are **not fixed**. They **vary** according to the time and place. For example, British culture is different from American culture, and today's culture is different from the culture of 30 years ago.
4) There are two kinds of socialisation — **primary socialisation** and **secondary socialisation**.

*The Main **Agent of Primary Socialisation** is **The Family***

Primary socialisation comes first. In **early childhood**, individuals learn the **skills**, **knowledge**, **norms** and **values** of society. This all happens in three ways:

1) Children **internalise** norms and values by **imitating their parents / guardians.**
2) Children are **rewarded** for **socially acceptable behaviour.**
3) Children are **punished** for **socially 'deviant' behaviour.**

Children who are deprived of social contact during development often can't function as social adults. In 1970, an American girl known as 'Genie' was discovered. She'd been locked up by her father for her first 13 years and never managed to recognise even basic social norms.

*There are many **Agents** of **Secondary Socialisation***

Secondary socialisation comes after primary socialisation and **builds on it**. It's carried out by **institutions** like these:

Education

The education system aims to pass on **knowledge and skills**. Learning these skills is a part of socialisation:

1) **Functionalists**, like Durkheim, believe that school **promotes consensus** by **teaching norms and values**. They also say children learn to value belonging to a **larger group** through things like school uniform and assembly. All this is important for **fitting into society**.
2) **Marxists**, such as **Bowles and Gintis (1976)**, reckon there are two sorts of curriculum at school — the acknowledged curriculum (maths, English, geography etc.) and the hidden curriculum (doing as you're told and not questioning authority). They believe that the **hidden curriculum** (p.22) socialises pupils into **ruling-class cultures** and encourages them to **accept exploitation**.

Peer Groups

Peer groups are made up of people of **similar social status**. The peer group can **influence norms and values**. This can be towards **conformity** or **deviance**. **Youth subcultures** sometimes encourage **deviant** behaviour, like joyriding.

Conformity means doing what society likes and deviance means doing what society doesn't like.

Religion

Religion often provides **social norms and values**. Most religions promote charitable giving and teach respect for elders.

The Media

The **media** are **powerful** in shaping norms and values in the audience. Some sociologists (e.g. Althusser) argue that the media have now **replaced religion** in secondary socialisation.

The Workplace

Workplace socialisation involves learning the norms and values that enable people to fit into the world of work, such as being on time and obeying the boss.

Socialisation and Social Roles

Individuals have *Social Roles* and *Status*

According to some sociological perspectives, an important result of socialisation is that each individual ends up with a number of **roles**. These are associated with different sorts of **status**.

1) Your **status** is your **position** in a **hierarchy**. You can have low status or high status. It's the respect and recognition others give to your position. Being the **monarch of the United Kingdom** is a **status**.
2) Your **roles** are the **behaviours and actions** you take on **because of your status**. In sociological terms, a role is a set of norms that go with a status. The UK monarch has to meet the public and show an interest, they have to speak to the nation on TV on Christmas Day, and they have to travel and meet leaders of other countries. These are all **roles**.

Status can be ascribed or achieved

Ascribed status is fixed at **birth**. For example, the King or Queen of the UK **inherits their status** from the previous monarch (normally their mother or father) when they die. Head teachers, on the other hand, have **achieved** status. This means they've **earned** it through **education** and **work**. This is a **very important difference** for sociological arguments about gender, class and ethnic identities.

Individuals can be Socialised *into* Socially Constructed *Identities*

Social constructs are ideas and behaviours that are **invented** by society rather than being dictated by the **laws of nature**. Everyone adopts social constructs and sees them as normal parts of the way society works. A person's **identity** (see p.44) is made up of several **socially constructed elements**:

Social Class	**Perceived differences** between members of the lower, middle and upper classes are related to things like money, family connections and the kind of jobs people have. These categories are **social** rather than **biological**.
Sexuality	**Sexual identities** are influenced by socially constructed ideas about what kind of sexual behaviour is **normal**.
Gender	**Gender identities** are based on **social expectations** about masculine or feminine traits and behaviours, rather than on **biological differences** between men and women.
Disability	Society often underestimates people with disabilities. **Socially constructed expectations** of **disability** can be a **bigger limiting force** than the actual impairment (the physical feature or characteristic).
Nationality	**National identities** involve the relationship between people and the nation they **belong to**. They are constructed around **social expectations** like being loyal to your country.
Ethnicity	**Ethnic identities** can either **complement or compete with** national identities and are constructed around things like **shared** languages and cultures.
Age	Different societies **construct childhood** and **old age** differently — for example, some cultures have more **age-based restrictions** than others.

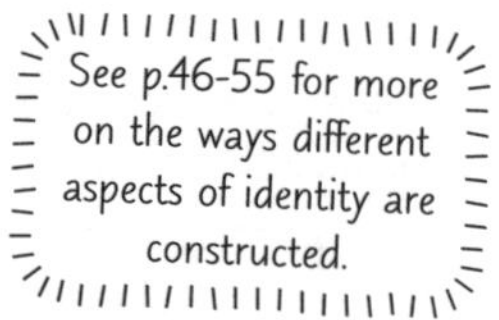

Practice Questions

Q1 What is a 'social construct'?

Q2 Name five agents of secondary socialisation.

Q3 What is a role?

Exam Question

Q1 Give a definition of the term 'ascribed status'. [2 marks]

And I thought socialisation was just something to do down the pub...

Socialisation is the process by which people learn to be members of society. The main things I remember learning when I was young are to only speak when spoken to, to always eat my greens, not to play football in the house, not to take sweets from strangers, not to pogo stick next to the cliff and not to offer myself as food to stray lions. I learnt that last one the hard way.

Theories of Socialisation

Sociologists have lots of theories about socialisation. Marxists, feminists and functionalists argue that socialisation leads to conformity. Interactionists and postmodernists think people have more choice when deciding which values to believe in.

Functionalists Say That Social Behaviour is Regulated by Social Control

1) Socialisation puts **limits** on people's behaviour. The functionalist Durkheim called this **constraint** (it's also known as **social control**). If it weren't for internalised norms and values, people would **do what they liked**.
2) Functionalists say that socialisation creates a **consensus**, where everyone has the **same values and norms**.
3) It's important for people to **conform** to the norms and values of society. When people conform to the expectations, they're **rewarded**. When people **don't conform** to social expectations, they're **punished**. Sociologists call these punishments **sanctions**. Sociologists call behaviour which doesn't conform to society's expectations **deviant**.

Parsons (1951) argues that the **nuclear family** is key to primary socialisation of children. Parents shape a child's personality — Parsons calls the family a '**personality factory**'. As a result, children feel like they **belong** in society and subscribe to its **cultural consensus**. Children want to be like their **parent of the same sex**, which influences their behaviour.

Functionalists believe that **education** and **religion** function as key agents of **secondary socialisation**.

- **Durkheim** thought that institutionalised **education** is a **link** between the family and society as a whole. **Parsons (1961)** argues that **education** teaches children about **values** such as fair **competition**, striving for **success**, and **honest** conduct. Functionalists see this socialisation as important preparation for going to **work in adult life**.
- **Religion** produces codes of behaviour by giving **sacred status** to chosen **values** — adults socialise children to follow these codes, which promotes **social conformity**.

Marxists Think Socialisation is Designed to Benefit the Ruling Class

Marxists believe that the institutions of the **family**, **education** and **religion** are used to socialise the **working class** into **acceptance** of their own **exploitation** in capitalist society. They see the process of socialisation as a form of **indoctrination** (teaching people to accept a set of beliefs without **question** or **criticism**).

1) **Marxists** agree with functionalists that education promotes **conformity**. However, they think that the values transmitted by education, like **obedience** to authority figures and **acceptance of failure**, are designed to oppress the working class.

2) This kind of socialisation is good for the **ruling class** because it prevents aspiration and teaches the **working class** that obedience to authority is **normal**.

Neo-Marxists question the effectiveness of this indoctrination and accept that people are able to rebel against this kind of socialisation.

3) **Religion** is used to socialise the working class into accepting **poverty** and their own **exploitation**. Religion **distracts** people from their **social inferiority** by promoting the idea that suffering will be worth the **reward** of the **afterlife**.

Feminists Also See Socialisation as a Form of Indoctrination

Feminists believe that the socialisation of children is designed to pass on the ideals of the **patriarchy**. Socialisation in the **family** and in **wider society** promotes **conformity** to social expectations about **gender roles** and **acceptable behaviour**.

- **Oakley (1982)** argued that parents socialise their children to **conform** to **patriarchal ideals** by praising them for behaving in supposedly **gender-appropriate ways**. For example, they might direct children towards toys traditionally associated with their gender.
- **Liberal feminists** argue that to **create gender equality** society needs to change the way children are socialised. They believe that **confronting gender stereotypes** will change **attitudes** to gender equality and create more equal **opportunities** for men and women.
- **Radical feminists** think that patriarchal ideals are **more deep-seated** in society. They argue that **revolutionary changes** to society's structure are needed to combat **patriarchal indoctrination**.

See p.48 for more on Oakley's theory of family socialisation.

Theories of Socialisation

Interactionists *see Socialisation as an* ***Active, Two-Way*** *Process*

Interactionists believe that socialisation involves **two-way social interaction**. **Handel (2006)** argued that there are three key stages in **childhood development** that are important in the socialisation process:

1) In early life, children learn to **communicate** with others around them, but they have little understanding of **how others see them** and the **impact** of their own behaviour.
2) Later, a sense of **empathy** develops — children are able to understand the **feelings** of others around them.
3) Finally, children develop a **sense of self** — this means they are able to see themselves from the **perspective of another person** and **change their behaviour** so that others view them differently.

Mead (1925) believed that play was important for developing a **sense of self**. Children learn to understand the **viewpoint** of other children and adults, and that they can **influence what happens** with their own **actions**.

Mead accepted the functionalist view that **institutions** socialise people into **shared norms**. However, he said that **social control** depends on **how far** people take on the attitudes of others. Individuals can **rebel** against socialisation.

Interactionists believe that **indoctrination** is not the **only** way to socialise people:

- Interactionists point out that **peer group socialisation** influences the behaviour of children in society. Children put **peer pressure** on one another to **rebel** against existing rules or **conform** to alternative rules they have created themselves. **Adults** can also experience peer pressure while **socialising** and at **work**.
- Your **background** can influence the way you are socialised. Interactionists argue that parents are **free** to socialise their children however they like — they don't have to socialise their children into conforming to a **fixed set** of social norms.

Some sociologists argue that interactionist theories of socialisation are too focused on the **minor details** of people's lives. They're also **criticised** for not paying enough attention to the impact of **social factors** (class, gender, ethnicity) and **institutions** (religion, education, the media) in the process of socialisation.

Postmodernists *Argue That People Can* ***Resist*** *Socialisation*

Postmodernists are big on the idea of **personal choice**. They say that in today's society people have a large amount of choice in their actions and behaviour — and in the values that they believe in.

1) **Lyotard (1979)** argues that there are lots of **competing versions** of knowledge and **truth** in postmodern society — people can **choose** who to listen to and what values to believe in.
2) **Lyotard** believes that even the most powerless person in society has **some control** over the kind of knowledge they are exposed to. No single institution has a **monopoly** on knowledge, so it's **harder** to convince people that they should stick to one way of living.
3) This **weakens** the effects of **secondary** socialisation in educational and religious institutions. There is no single, accepted version of the truth and **various cultural values** and norms exist — this helps people to **resist** socialisation.

The pro-leotard faction of the ballet were getting harder to resist.

Practice Questions

Q1 How do functionalists link religion to the process of socialisation?

Q2 Summarise the three stages of childhood development that interactionists believe are important for socialisation.

Q3 Why do postmodernists think socialisation is becoming less effective?

Exam Question

Q1 Outline two ways that people can be socialised, according to interactionists. Explain each one. [10 marks]

Chocolate cake for breakfast — now that's a norm I can get on board with...

While sociologists disagree on the motives behind socialisation (shocker), most agree that successful socialisation helps society to agree on what is socially unacceptable. Socialisation is the reason you don't see people in business suits hopping to work on a pogo stick or galloping down the street like a horse (which, let's face it, would be a lot more fun...).

The Self, Identity and Difference

There are two main sociological approaches to identity — structuralist views (see p.3-4) look at how identities are caused by social structures. Social action views (see p.4) focus on the role of social interaction in constructing identities.

'Identity' is a Tricky Concept in *Sociology*

1) At a basic level, your **personal identity** is the sort of stuff that would appear on an identity card — name, age, physical appearance, distinguishing marks, place of birth. These are **easily checked**, hard to change **facts** about who you are.
2) In **sociology**, identity has a **deeper meaning**. It refers to the **way we see ourselves**, and the **way others see us**. This sort of identity comes from things that are more **complicated**, and sometimes **less fixed**, than the basic identity card stuff. Social class, ethnicity, friendships, work, gender, age and sexuality are all factors that contribute to your **social identity**.
3) Your social identity is often linked to **roles you perform** in society (e.g. daughter, student, volunteer, best friend) as well as the **social groups** you are a part of (e.g. female, middle class, Asian, teenager).

Structuralists Believe that Identity is *Caused* by *Social Constructs*

Structuralists agree that **institutions** socialise people into **shared identities** and **values**.
They disagree on which **values** are being upheld and **who benefits** the most.

Marxists

- Marxists think people's **identity** depends on their **class position** in the capitalist system. They argue that the cultural **values** and **norms** that influence identity are **created** and **maintained** by the **upper classes** with the aim of protecting capitalism.
- Socially constructed ideas about **cultural consumption** can cause people to develop different class identities — knowledge of **high culture** is considered to be a key part of **upper-class identity**, while consuming **mass culture** is part of **working-class identity** (p.36).

Functionalists

- Functionalism argues that **social institutions** allocate people different roles in society, based on the **best fit** for their talents and efforts. However, some functionalists argue that this isn't always **successful**.
- **Merton (1957)** said that all institutions have **manifest functions** (**intended** outcomes) and **latent functions** (**hidden** or **unintended** outcomes). For example, the **manifest** functions of the **education system** are providing **skills**, **knowledge** and **equal opportunities** to increase **social mobility**. However, the **latent** function is to maintain **socially constructed ideas** about the kind of future people can expect to have, based on their **social class identity**.
- **Trumpbour (1989)** found that **wealthier** university students expect education to prepare them for **professional** roles and leadership, while **poorer** pupils expect to be prepared for **lower status jobs**.

Feminists

- **Feminists** argue that the **patriarchal structure** of society has influenced **gender identity** by causing people to believe in gender **stereotypes** and socialising people to hold **sexist** views about male and female identity.
- **Marxist feminists** say that **capitalist** and **patriarchal** social structures have influenced female identity on a **subconscious** level. Some argue that patriarchal views have been a key part of female identity for a long time, which makes it difficult for women to **change the way they think about themselves** and their role in society.
- **Difference feminists** criticise these arguments — they think that women should be treated as a **diverse** group with **many identities**. The social forces that shape the identity of one woman **might not apply** to another.

Postmodernists say that We can *Construct* Our *Own Identities*

Postmodernists say **structures** like social class are no longer the most important part of the **construction of identity**.

1) Postmodernists argue that it's possible to **construct** a **unique** identity by drawing on **different cultural sources** — postmodern society allows you to **consume** food, clothes and other products from various cultures.
2) They argue that identity is becoming increasingly **unstable** because individuals can **choose** their own lifestyle and identity — this leads to **diversity**.
3) Critics of this argument point out that being able to buy and consume **whatever we like** depends on how much **money** we have and whether we have a steady **job** or **income** — these things are linked to our **social class**.

The Self, Identity and Difference

Goffman's Dramaturgical Model says Identity is Deliberately Constructed

Goffman (1956) says that you can **control** the way you present your identity during **social interaction**. You can **construct an identity** by controlling the **impressions** you give of yourself to other people — he calls this '**impression management**'.

1) Goffman saw **society** as a **big stage**. You behave differently when interacting with people depending on **where** social interaction is happening.
2) When you are in '**front stage**' environments (e.g. work, school, public places) you **carefully control** the **impression** you give to other people and **act out a specific role** (e.g. student, teacher, manager).
3) Once you are '**backstage**' (e.g. at home or with people you know very well) you **stop performing that role** and reveal the parts of yourself that you **hide** while playing a front stage role.
4) There is a **gap** between the **role** you play on the front stage and on the back stage — he called this '**role distance**'.

Cooley Wrote about Self-Image and Difference

Cooley (1902) argued that the way you **think** other people see you affects your **behaviour** and **self-image** — he called this the '**looking-glass self**'.

1) Cooley argued that you are always **unconsciously constructing** your identity. When you **imagine** yourself through the eyes of **other people**, you change your behaviour. You **become** the person that **you think they think you are**.
2) Cooley based his theory on the idea that **people are aware** of the ways that their personal behaviour and views are **different** from **social norms**. This helps you to define who you are in **opposition** to other people.

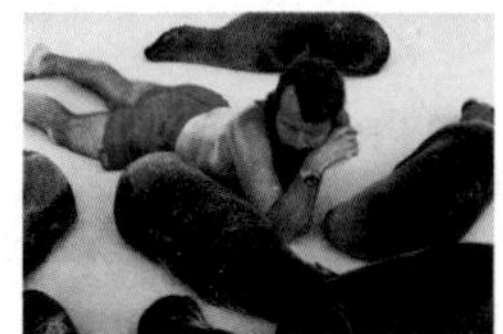

Nigel had taken the whole 'identifying with others' thing a bit too far.

Labelling Theory says We're Given Labels which Affect Our Behaviour

Labelling theory argues that the way **other people see and judge you** automatically **influences** who you are.

1) The **classic example** of labelling theory is the **self-fulfilling prophecy** of **educational failure** (see p.24). This is where a child is **labelled** as a bad student and actually **becomes** a bad student as a result.
2) Very **strong labels**, e.g. '**criminal**' or '**pervert**', can take on what's called **master status**, which means they replace an individual's other labels. As a result, people **change** their behaviour to fit the label that they've been given.
3) **Becker (1963)** said that people who are labelled as '**deviant**' become **outsiders** and their deviant label becomes their **main source of identity**. For example, once someone is labelled as a **thief**, this will always be their **master status**.
4) **Wilkins (1964)** discovered that people who have been labelled as '**deviant**' or **outsiders** often join a **subculture**. This makes them feel like they **belong**, but it also **creates more differences** between them and the rest of society.

Schooling can contribute to the **creation of differences** between **students** from different social classes. Some sociologists have found that teachers are more likely to label **working-class** pupils as **deviant**. Working-class pupils are often placed in **lower sets** as a result — this can lead to these students developing **lower self-esteem** and **aspirations** than their middle-class peers.

Labelling theory is a kind of interactionism — you can choose to accept or reject labels. Being called a failure will only turn you into a failure if you accept the label.

Practice Questions

Q1 Briefly explain two feminist theories on the construction of identity.

Q2 Describe Goffman's dramaturgical model.

Q3 Give two examples of labelling theories.

Exam Question

Q1 How might a 'deviant' label contribute towards the creation of difference? Use one example to briefly explain your answer. [2 marks]

I was a pirate for Halloween once and now people keep asking me to parlay...

Structuralists think we've got hardly any say in who we are. Interactionists say what other people see is pretty important, and we can control how we're seen. Postmodernists reckon we can be whatever we want (like a fire-breathing unicorn... probably).

Class Identities

The following pages explore different aspects of social identity, starting with class.

Societies are Stratified — Divided into Layers

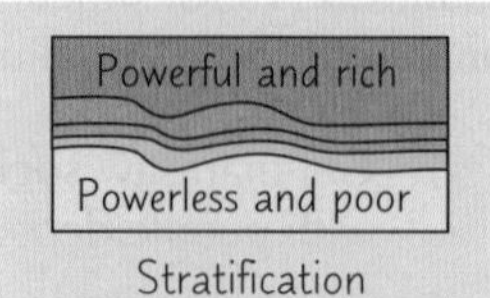

Stratification

1) **Social class** is an important part of **identity**. Most societies are **stratified** by social class.
2) **Stratification** is the division of societies into **layers**. The **richest** and **most powerful** are at the **top**. The **poorest** and **most powerless** are at the **bottom**. In between are lots of **strata** (which means layers, like the layers in rock) organised in a **hierarchy**.
3) **Social class** is the main stratification system in **modern, Western capitalist societies**, such as the **contemporary UK**.

There are Different Ways to Define Social Class

- Marx divided society into just two classes — the **proletariat** (the workers) and the **bourgeoisie** (the bosses).
- For the **UK census**, the **government** used to use a scale based on the **jobs** people do.
- Sociologists usually talk about just **four basic social classes**:

1) The **upper class** are **wealthy** and **powerful**. The original upper class were the **landowning aristocracy**. Their wealth is **passed on from generation to generation**. People who have made a lot of money from business or from the entertainment industry are also sometimes considered to be upper class.
2) The **middle class** earn their money from **non-manual work**. Teachers, doctors, managers and pretty much anyone who **earns their living sitting in an office** are middle class. The middle class is **getting bigger** because there are **more non-manual jobs** these days, and fewer manual jobs.
3) The **working class** make their money from **manual work**. Farm labourers and factory workers are working class. The working class have **poorer life chances** than the middle class.
4) The **underclass** get their money from **state benefits**. They include the long-term unemployed and the homeless. The underclass have **the poorest life chances**.

Class Culture Affects Identity

Sociologists often link **identity** to **social class**. **Who you are** is connected to your **class culture** and **class identity**.

1) **Barry Sugarman (1970)** argued that middle-class and working-class children are socialised into **different norms and values**. **Middle-class** children are encouraged to plan for the future (**deferred gratification**) whereas **working-class children** are encouraged to live for the moment (**immediate gratification**). Deferred gratification is a big part of studying and training for a **professional career**.
2) **Charles Murray (1994)**, a New Right thinker, suggested that **certain values keep people poor**, for example believing in the **acceptability** of living on **state benefits**. He argued these values are **passed on** from one generation to the next.
3) **John Scott (1991)** looked at the ways the **upper class** use the **public school system** (this means the **top private schools** like Eton and Rugby) to create **social networks** which then follow through into **high-status universities** (such as Oxford).
4) In the state education system, **middle-class children** tend to form **pro-school subcultures** (such as homework clubs) and are more likely to be placed in top sets. **Working-class children** are more likely to be **anti-school** and to find themselves in lower sets. (For more detail on this, see p.24-25.)

Negative Stereotypes About Social Class Can Influence Identity

Skeggs and **Loveday (2012)** studied the effects of **negative stereotyping** on **working-class identity** and sense of **self**.

- The study's participants felt like they were being held **responsible** for being born into a system with **structural inequalities**. They were being characterised as **selfish** or **greedy** individuals while other classes were allowed to **profit** from greedy behaviour.
- They identified strongly with values like **loyalty** and **caring for others**. They argued that people in the middle and upper classes don't value these things in the same way.
- The study found that **struggle** is a key part of the **performance** of working-class identity — the lower classes bitterly accept **class oppression** and **endure** poverty because they do not have the **power** to change their position.
- Skeggs and Loveday argued that members of the middle class often **negatively stereotype** people from lower classes, and use this form of **class oppression** to maintain their position by claiming **moral authority** over the lower classes.

Skeggs and Loveday argued that you need some kind of social, cultural or economic capital (see p.47) before you can present yourself as someone with social value.

Class Identities

Bourdieu said the *Upper Class* use *Cultural Capital*

Bourdieu (1984) argued that there are **different** kinds of **capital** in society:

1) **Economic capital** — your income or wealth
2) **Social capital** — being a member of a group or network of people
3) **Cultural capital** — the knowledge and skills you need to fit into the top level of society.

The competition to be Greece's Next Top Statue was getting a bit heated.

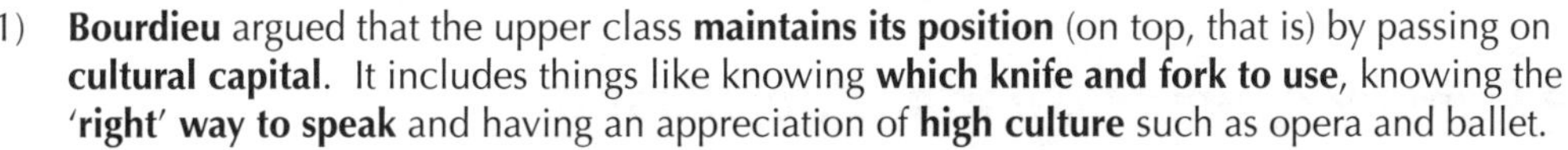

1) **Bourdieu** argued that the upper class **maintains its position** (on top, that is) by passing on **cultural capital**. It includes things like knowing **which knife and fork to use**, knowing the '**right**' **way to speak** and having an appreciation of **high culture** such as opera and ballet.
2) He also said that **middle-class** families try to **develop cultural capital** in their own children in order to **improve** their class position. These parents **encourage** their children to read 'good' books, experience theatres, go to art galleries and so on.
3) By contrast, he said that **working-class** families **don't develop** this form of **cultural capital**.
4) Bourdieu also argued that you need **social capital** to back up your **cultural capital**. **Middle-class children may be limited** by a lack of social capital, even if they've gained a lot of cultural capital.

Many Sociologists say Class Isn't *the* Most Important Influence *any more*

1) Most sociologists agree that identity used to be based on how and where people **earned their money** (social class). Many **postmodernists** say that these days identity is based on how and where people **spend** their money (consumption).
2) They also claim that people's **leisure activities** are **no longer class-based**.
3) Traditional **working-class** activities included things like **bingo**, **darts** and the **pub**. The **middle classes** were associated with **DIY**, **dinner parties**, **golf** and **bridge**.
4) Nowadays, lifestyles are based more on **individual choice** than class background. Middle-class people do traditional working-class leisure activities and vice versa.

Postmodernists also argue that there isn't any difference between high and low culture any more — globalisation means people have access to a range of media images in an instant, resulting in a mass culture (see p.36).

New Right theorist **Peter Saunders (1990)** argues that today an individual's identity **isn't** based on social class. He claims that the old **divisions** between social classes have **disappeared** in our modern, **equal-opportunities** society.

Marshall (1988) suggests that the working class still see themselves as working class, but they are more **fragmented** than in the past due to the **loss of traditional industries**. This has meant that traditional working-class identities have weakened.

Bradley (1996) thinks class identity has become **less important** — **social class** used to determine a person's identity, but now it is **more common** for identity to be made up of **several fragments** based on ethnicity, gender and age, as well as class.

Practice Questions

Q1 What are the four social classes usually discussed in sociology?

Q2 What does the term 'immediate gratification' mean?

Q3 How does negative stereotyping influence the identity of the lower classes?

Q4 According to Marshall, why have working-class identities become fragmented?

Exam Question

Q1 Give a definition of the term 'deferred gratification'. [2 marks]

Some very classy pages to revise...

Most sociologists are keen on figuring out what makes the working class different from the middle class. Agents of socialisation like the family and social class (see p.1) are a common explanation. Postmodernists, on the other hand, argue that social class doesn't really exist in this twenty-first century world. I hope the Marxists don't hear them say that — things could get ugly.

Gender Identities

Gender is about masculinity and femininity (as opposed to straightforward biological boy/girl differences).

Sex is Not the Same as Gender

In sociology, **sex** means the **biological differences** between men and women. **Gender** means the aspects of **masculinity** and **femininity** that are **not biological** but **cultural**. They are **learned through socialisation**.

Sociologists focus on **gender**. One reason for this is that there are **gender inequalities** in education and employment that **can't be explained** by the **biological** differences between men and women.

The Family is the Primary Agent of Gender Socialisation

Ann Oakley's (1974) research led her to identify **four** ways in which **family life** usually teaches children the **norms** and **values** associated with **masculinity** and **femininity**:

1) **Manipulation** — parents **often encourage** 'normal' behaviour and interests for the child's sex and **discourage** what's seen as **deviant**. This **manipulates** the child's self-image — the child becomes interested in 'normal' behaviours. For example, girls are often dressed up in pretty dresses so that being pretty becomes important to them. Girls are sometimes told off for being 'unladylike' — shouting, playing loudly, getting mucky.
2) **Canalisation** — parents often **channel** their **children's interest** in particular directions. **Boys** may be given **construction toys** like LEGO® and **aggressive toys** like toy guns. **Girls** may be given **beauty toys** like toy jewellery and make-up, **mothering toys** like dolls and prams, or **housewife toys** like toy kitchens.
3) **Verbal appellation** — parents may **use language and names** to **define what's appropriate**. For example, 'you're an angel' (girl) versus 'you're a cheeky monkey' (boy), or 'what a beautiful little girl' versus 'what a big strong boy'.
4) **Different activities** — parents may involve children in **different aspects** of the **household**. For example, girls help wash the dishes, boys help wash the car.

School is a Secondary Agent of Gender Socialisation...

1) Girls and boys are treated **differently** in **education**. Sociologists say that education passes on **gender stereotyped assumptions** about how males and females should behave. Remember that gender stereotyped assumptions can **disadvantage boys** as well as girls.
2) There are still **gender differences** in **subject choice**. Boys are more likely to study physics and I.T. at A-level. Girls tend to dominate in art and English.
3) **Skelton (2002)** argues that schools both **create** gender stereotypes and **maintain** those learnt at home.

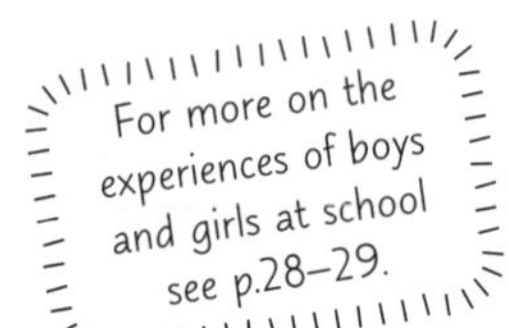
For more on the experiences of boys and girls at school see p.28–29.

...and so are the Media

1) The **mass media** help to build gender roles. For example, **females** in Hollywood films are often presented as **weak**, in need of rescuing by a strong male hero.
2) **Angela McRobbie (1978)** has argued that teenage female magazines **reinforce conventional notions of femininity**, emphasising the importance of getting and keeping a man, being 'beautiful' and so on.

3) **Wolf (1990)** suggests that **advertising** tends to present an unobtainable '**ideal image**' for women, reinforcing the notion that women should **look good** for **men**.
4) **Joan Smith**, in her 1997 book *Different for Girls*, also argued that **culture creates** and **perpetuates** gender differences.

Gender Stereotypes can Affect Employment Opportunities

1) **Traditional gender roles** can have an **impact** upon the **opportunities** and **experiences** of men and women in the workplace and at home. According to Social Trends 38 (2008), **19% of men** are employed as **managers or senior officials**, compared to **11% of women**.
2) It is still difficult for women to reach the **top levels** of **traditionally 'male' professions**. For example, the majority of **judges** are male.

Gender Identities

Gender Roles *are Changing — for* ***Females…***

1) In the **1970s**, when Sue Sharpe first researched **teenage girls' attitudes**, she found they valued **marriage** and **motherhood**. When she repeated the research in the **1990s**, she found that this generation of teenage girls stressed their **career ambitions**.
2) **Diana Gittins (1993)** looked at the **rising divorce rate** and said this was evidence that women's **attitudes to marriage** had changed a great deal. They were much **less willing** to **accept** relationships they weren't happy with. This was a sign that the old **passive female gender roles** were a **thing of the past**.
3) One important factor is the fact that more women **go out to work**, and earn good money. It is now more common for women to be the **biggest earners** or only earners in their household than it was in the past. The increase in office-based work is referred to as the **feminisation of the workforce**.
4) There has also been an **increase** in **female deviant behaviour** — for example girl gangs, as studied by **Ann Campbell (1984)**.

…And for ***Males***

1) Research by **Jonathan Gershuny (1992)** shows that **childcare** and **housework** are **shared** between men and women much more than in the past. The so-called '**new man**' does the dishes and changes the baby's nappies. Statistics show an increase in the number of **househusbands** — men who stay at home, cook, clean and care while their female partners go out to work.
2) One cause of men staying at home might be the **loss of traditional jobs** and **roles** for men. **Heavy industry has declined** and the majority of jobs now require **traditionally feminine skills** such as communication. Boys aren't socialised to have these skills as much as girls are, and girls are now socialised to be ambitious and dominant — traditionally masculine traits.
3) **Máirtín Mac an Ghaill (1994)** says these changes have led to a **crisis of masculinity** where **men no longer know** what their **role** should be. This idea says that men are **shut out** from their **traditional** roles, and **not adequately socialised** to be able to **fit into new roles**.

Masculinity *in the* ***Media*** *has Become* ***Feminised***

1) **Rutherford (1996)** points out that images of men in the media are now being used in traditionally female ways — e.g. to be ogled at. Male stripper groups like the Chippendales are a good example. He also looks at the marketing of **men's cosmetics and toiletries**. There are far **more** of these products now than in the past, and the images used to advertise them are often of **half-naked male models**. These are signs that men's roles have moved closer to women's. Rutherford calls this the **feminisation of masculinity**.
2) **Wilkinson (1997)** suggested that increasingly male and female **values** are **coming together**, with both men and women **creating** their **own identities**.

Findings like this have led some sociologists to believe that **traditional ideas** of **masculinity** and **femininity** are now in **decline**. **Postmodernists** say that **both men and women** now see **consumption** and **leisure** as the **key factors** in shaping their **identity**, rather than masculinity and femininity.

Practice Questions

Q1 What is the difference between sex and gender?

Q2 Name two secondary agents of gender socialisation.

Q3 What did Rutherford mean by the 'feminisation of masculinity'?

Exam Questions

Q1 How might socialisation influence femininity? Use one example to briefly explain your answer. [2 marks]

Q2 Evaluate the idea that the family is the most important agent of gender socialisation. [20 marks]

I never liked pink much anyway...

With these pages, you need to learn about traditional masculinity and femininity AND how these gender roles are changing as society changes. As usual, those postmodernists claim nothing matters any more except shopping and leisure. Troublemakers.

Ethnic Identities

British society includes many different ethnic groups. Ethnicity can be an important part of identity. Not to forget gender, religion, class, nationality and occupation. One thing you can say for identity — it ain't simple...

Sociologists Use the Term Ethnicity, not Race

Race is a way of classifying people by **visible biological features**, like skin colour or bone structure. The idea of race is linked to **racism**, the idea that some races are inferior to others.

That's one reason most sociologists agree **ethnicity** is a better term to use when you're talking about society. People from the same **ethnic group share** the **same culture** and **socialisation**.

Ethnic Minorities have Different Cultural Features

Ethnic minorities in the UK are often people whose families came here from former colonies (like **Jamaica** and **India**) from the **1950s onwards**. The **2011 census** says that **14% of the population** of England and Wales are from ethnic minorities.

Ethnic minorities have distinctive **cultural features** from their countries and **cultures** of origin. This means stuff like **values, customs, religion, diet, language** and **clothing**. These **cultural features** give each ethnic minority its **ethnic identity**.

It's a long time since the 1950s, so Britain's ethnic minorities have been through a lot of **changes**. The way **ethnic identity changes over time**, from one generation to the next, is something a lot of sociologists study (see below).

Culture based on **shared origin** is still an **important influence** on **ethnic identity** though. Some ethnic groups work hard to keep distinctive cultural features going. For example, **Modood et al (1997)** suggested that cultural origins still play a key role in influencing the behaviour of Asians, particularly the older generation.

Children are Socialised into an Ethnic Identity

Quite a few studies have looked at the way **parents pass on ethnic identity** to their children. This is **primary socialisation** — the socialisation that takes place as part of **family life**.

Rosemary Hill (1987) found **the family** was very **important** in the Leicester Asian community. She also said that some children learned 'Western' ideas about marriage, education, work and so on from white peers. Hill thought this led to **generational conflict** between parents and children from ethnic minorities.

John's latest attempt to be more Western had failed to impress.

Roger Ballard (1994) disagreed. He found that young Asians **negotiated** the two aspects of their lives (home and outside the home). That meant that at **home** they'd behave in **traditional** ways to fit in with their parents, but **outside** the home they'd **'act Western'**.

Shaun Hides (1995) studied the use of **artefacts** in ethnic minority homes. He was interested in the way things like **furniture**, **pictures**, **ornaments** and **religious items** helped **reinforce** ethnic identity. Hides found that the wearing of **traditional dress** was a really important part of this. **Women** wore traditional dress **more often** than men, and Hides concluded that **women** had the most **important role** in keeping ethnic identity going.

Ethnic Identity is Also Created by Secondary Socialisation

1) **Racism** in British society can affect secondary socialisation. For example, studies by **David Gillborn (1990)** and **Cecile Wright (1992)** suggest that African-Caribbean pupils are often **labelled** as a **problem** by teachers. This can lead to a **self-fulfilling prophecy** where pupils form an **anti-school subculture** because that's what the school seems to **expect** them to do.
2) The **peer group** is important too. Academic **Tony Sewell** said in an interview in **2000** that he thinks young African-Caribbean males are too influenced by popular culture. He believes that they encourage each other to be interested in **expensive consumer goods** (e.g. cars, the latest mobile phones, clothes) instead of **education**.

Ethnic Identities

Some Sociologists Say that **Ethnic Identities** are a **Response to Racism**

1) When **African-Caribbean** and **Asian** families first arrived in Britain, they faced lots of **prejudice** from the white population.
2) Some people from ethnic minorities felt there **wasn't any point** trying to **integrate** into the mainstream.
3) One way minorities responded to **discrimination** in work, housing and education was to **hold on** to their **ethnic identity** and **resist** full assimilation into the mainstream.
4) **Cashmore and Troyna (1990)** show how people in ethnic minorities turned to **each other** for **support**, for example in religious groups like the (mostly black) **Pentecostal Church**.

New Ethnic Identities are Emerging

1) **Stuart Hall (1996)** talks about **new ethnicities** which are very **varied**. He says that the **old ideas** of condensing ethnicity to **white / black** are being **challenged**. There are lots of **different kinds** of Asian ethnicity and black ethnicity. Hall also points out that for ethnic minority people, **gender** identity, **class** identity and **sexuality** can actually be **as important** or **more important** than ethnic identity.

2) Many sociologists argue that **young people** from **ethnic minority** backgrounds are developing **hybrid identities** — based on a mixture of influences. **Paul Gilroy (1987)** examined how black and white culture has become mixed together. **Maria Gillespie (1995)** looked at how young Sikhs brought bits of **mainstream popular culture** together with **Punjabi traditions**.

3) **Tariq Modood (1997)** found that **ethnic identities** were **changing**. Things like wearing **ethnic clothes** were **less important** for young people than for their parents. **Younger** people were more likely to be **political** and **upfront** about their **ethnic identity**. On the other hand, second generation immigrants were **more likely** to **see themselves** as **British** or partly British than first generation immigrants.

4) **Basit's (1997)** study suggested that ethnic identities are **dynamic** and **changeable**. Basit's interviews with British Asian schoolgirls suggested that they **combine elements** of both British and Asian cultures. They created their identity based on their Asian culture's **ethnicity, language** and **religion**, but in the **context** of a **British society**. This made their identity particularly **unique**, as the girls' parents thought that their daughters would not feel as **comfortable** if they were to go to Pakistan or Bangladesh to live, because of the **impact of British culture** upon them.

Practice Questions

Q1 What's the difference between 'race' and 'ethnicity'?

Q2 What makes ethnic minorities distinctive from the mainstream population?

Q3 How can secondary socialisation affect ethnic identity?

Q4 Briefly outline the view that ethnic identities are a response to racism.

Q5 What are Stuart Hall's views about the emergence of new ethnicities?

Q6 What are hybrid identities?

Exam Questions

Q1 Outline two ways that the family influences ethnic identity. Explain each one. [10 marks]

Q2 Evaluate the idea that ethnic identities are becoming more diverse in modern UK society. [20 marks]

So many identities, so little time...

Sociology is full of these 'hot button' topics. Debates about racism, identity and multiculturalism come up in the newspapers and on the radio quite a lot. For you as a sociology student, the important thing is to know the main theories about how ethnic identity is learnt by socialisation. Make sure you can explain how modern life is changing the way identity is formed.

National Identities

Yup. Yet more aspects of identity.

National Identity *is about Feeling you* ***Belong*** *to a* ***Country*** *and its* ***People***

Durkheim said that national identity (nationalism) has an important function. It makes **individuals** feel that they **belong** to a **larger group**. **Benedict Anderson (1983)** reckons that **nationalism has replaced religion** in giving people's lives meaning.

National identity can have **negative** effects. It can be used to **exclude** certain groups. For example, if someone defines being British as being **white**, then they are **excluding black and Asian British people**. When an organisation excludes ethnic minorities like this, it's called **institutional racism**.

1) **Symbols** and **rituals** are important to national identity. The symbols of a nation's identity include things like its **currency**, its **flag**, and its **national anthem**.
2) Every nation has its own **national rituals**. These are events when people are **expected** to **think** about what it **means** to be English or Scottish or French, etc. A good example from Britain is **Remembrance Sunday** when there are processions and ceremonies to remember British soldiers who died fighting in wars.

National Identity *is a* ***Product of Socialisation***

Schudson (1994) says that individuals are **socialised** into a **national culture** and identity by agents of socialisation such as **education** and the **mass media**. For example, the National Curriculum says all children must learn about Shakespeare.

The **hidden curriculum** also contributes by having school celebrations for national events such as the **Queen's Jubilee**, or letting pupils watch 'important' national football matches at school.

The **media** are also very important in building up national identity. They do this by **broadcasting national rituals** — things like Royal funerals or the state opening of Parliament.

Stuart Hall (1992) writes about the way each country has its own collection of **stories** about itself. National identity is about **learning** and **sharing** these tales of **wars won**, **great sporting victories** and so on. These are **passed on** from one generation to the next.

Traditional National Identity *is on the* ***Decline***

Some sociologists suggest that during the last 20 years, people have found it **harder** to **identify** with Britishness. British national identity isn't as strong as it was, and some would say it **doesn't exist** any more. There are a few reasons for this:

1) **Big business** is now **international**, and companies like the McDonald's fast food chain appear all around the world. People in Britain are often **working for companies** based in **Japan**, or **Germany** or the **USA**. Some **British companies** have been **bought by corporations** from **overseas**. Sociologists call this breaking down of national boundaries **globalisation**.
2) Mainstream **TV**, **fashion**, **music** and **film** are often dominated by **American products**. Many people think that the result of this is that Britain and other countries are **losing their own cultures**.
3) Britain today is **multi-ethnic**. It contains many **different** groups, religions and languages.
4) Britain has strong **regional differences**. Scotland, Wales and Northern Ireland have strong national identities of their own. Under the New Labour government, regional identities were given a boost by **devolution** — regions being given **more political power** by central government, e.g. the creation of the National Assembly for Wales in 1998.

New National Identities *are Being Formed*

The old 'Britishness' is partly being replaced by a **new multicultural national identity**. Things like food, fashion and music bring together **British traditions** with **multicultural influences** from **inside Britain** and **international influences** from the **rest of the world**. Our new 'national dish', chicken tikka masala, is an example of this.

There are some **obstacles** to the creation of this new British identity, one of which is **racism**. A lot of the traditional British identity was based on the idea that the British were **different from** (and **better than**) the rest of the world. Some people may prefer this traditional view of 'Britishness' and be **resistant** to the idea that British society and identity are changing.

Sexuality and Identity

Sexuality is another part of **Identity**

1) **Sexuality** means a person's **sexual orientation** — whether they are heterosexual, homosexual, asexual or bisexual. It can also imply **sexual desire**. It is something which **society** can seek to **control**.
2) **Attitudes** towards sexuality **vary** between different cultures and over time. **Jeffrey Weeks (1986)** argued that sexuality is a **social** and **historical construct** — taking on **different meanings** depending on the society and time period.
3) In the past in the UK, **monogamous heterosexual relationships** were the **norm** in **mainstream culture** — and people who tried to live differently were often treated **very negatively**. People with different sexual orientations sometimes formed **subcultures** — **alternatives** to the mainstream (see p.36).
4) **Agents of socialisation** such as religion, the media and the law can **pass on attitudes** about sexuality.

Religion passes on ideologies that control sexuality

1) Religion tends to **promote** a **norm** of **heterosexuality** and **marriage**. Many religions forbid homosexuality and sex outside of marriage, e.g. Catholicism.
2) **Feminists** argue that religion **oppresses female sexuality** by imposing a **strict norm** of staying a **virgin until marriage**, only having sex to have babies and being **sexually passive**.
3) **Functionalists** think that the **control** and channelling of **sexuality** is crucial to the continuation of society. They think it's important to have a **stable family** for kids to be born into, and a monogamous sexual relationship between husband and wife to keep society stable.
4) The **New Right** claim that a **moral decline** caused by **secularisation** has encouraged homosexuality, abortion and pornography. They say these are **threats to social order**.
5) **Postmodernists** think this is all old-hat and that religion doesn't have that big an influence on sexuality any more. They say individuals have choice in the **construction** of their **identity** — including **sexual identity**.

Representations of sexuality in the media can be stereotyped

1) **Homosexual** relationships and **heterosexual** relationships are often treated differently in the media. For example, very **few** main characters on TV and in film are gay.
2) **Early media reporting** of **HIV/AIDS** had a prejudiced aspect. It was initially openly characterised as a 'gay disease'. Some tabloid newspapers in the 1980s referred to AIDS as a 'gay plague'.
3) Increasingly though, the way that the **media** has **represented gay people** has been **more positive**, for example the television series *Queer as Folk*, and the films *Beautiful Thing* and *Brokeback Mountain*.

Social attitudes towards sexuality are reflected in the law

1) Homosexuality used to be **illegal** in the UK. It was **decriminalised** in England and Wales in **1967** — but the **age of consent was 21**, higher than for heterosexual people.
2) In 1988, **Section 28** came into force. It **prevented** local authorities from **'promoting' homosexuality**, i.e. presenting gay relationships as acceptable. The scope of this law was ambiguous — but many **teachers** thought it meant they **weren't allowed** to **talk about homosexuality** with pupils.
3) Over the last few decades, there have been moves towards **equality**. For example, the **age of consent** for gay men was **lowered to 16** in 2000, Section 28 was scrapped in 2003, **civil partnerships** for gay couples were introduced in 2005, the **Equality Act (Sexual Orientation) 2007** made it illegal to discriminate against gay men and women in the provision of goods and services, and the **Marriage (Same-Sex Couples) Act 2013** legalised **gay marriage**. These all reflect **changing attitudes** in **society**.

Practice Questions

Q1 Give one example of a national symbol and one example of a national ritual.

Q2 Give three agents of socialisation that can pass on attitudes about sexuality.

Exam Question

Q1 How have attitudes to homosexuality changed in the UK since the 1960s? Outline three ways. [6 marks]

I'm having an identity crisis...

People don't just have one identity — they have blimmin' loads. Class, gender, ethnicity, nationality, sexuality... and there's more over the page. So square your shoulders and chin up — another four pages and you'll have polished off this section.

Age and Identity

The identity topic rolls on... Two more aspects of identity are age and disability.

*Attitudes about Age **Vary** between **Cultures** and **Change Over Time***

1) Views about age **aren't universal** — they **change over time**, and vary between **different societies** and cultures. **Age** can be seen as a **social construct**.
2) **Age** is part of social **identity**. People are **socialised** to accept the **norms** and **values** of the **society** they live in. So the way a society **views** certain **age groups** affects **people's behaviour** and **treatment of each other**.
3) People who are **similar ages** and have lived through the same **cultural and political events** are often referred to as being from the same **generation**. It can be part of an individual's **identity** that they **feel part of a generation** — e.g. the 60s generation.
4) Assumptions about at **what age** someone becomes an '**adult**', or at what age someone is '**old**' can vary between different societies and cultures.

Her cooking wasn't up to much, but if you're going to insist on hiring a two-year-old chef...

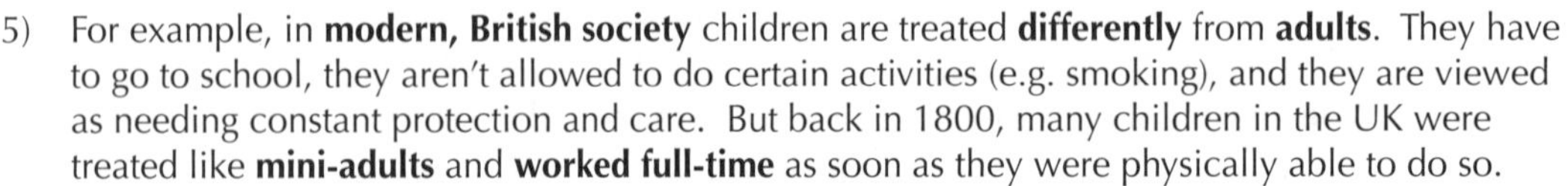

5) For example, in **modern, British society** children are treated **differently** from **adults**. They have to go to school, they aren't allowed to do certain activities (e.g. smoking), and they are viewed as needing constant protection and care. But back in 1800, many children in the UK were treated like **mini-adults** and **worked full-time** as soon as they were physically able to do so.

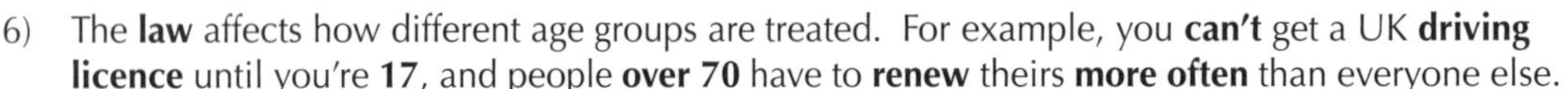

6) The **law** affects how different age groups are treated. For example, you **can't** get a UK **driving licence** until you're **17**, and people **over 70** have to **renew** theirs **more often** than everyone else.
7) **Bradley (1997)**, however, argues that age is **less important** to identity than other facts like class, gender and ethnicity. This is because people know that their age identity is **temporary** — they're not going to be a child, teenager or middle aged forever.

*The **Media** sometimes present **Stereotyped** views of different **Age Groups***

1) The way the media represent different age groups can **influence** social attitudes — and **reflect** them.
2) Some sociologists have found evidence of **ageist** attitudes in media products. **Simon Biggs (1993)** studied the way older people are presented on television entertainment programmes. He found they were often in stereotyped roles, e.g. 'forceful', 'vague' or 'difficult' — especially in sitcoms.
3) **Lambert (1984)** found that **older men** were often portrayed in **positions of power**, e.g. newsreaders. But this was not the case for older women.
4) There are also media stereotypes of **young people**. Children are often represented as **innocent**. Teenage characters in TV soaps are often **a bit wild** — prone to drug-taking, petty crime, binge drinking and unplanned pregnancy.

*Marxists think **Attitudes** to **Age** are influenced by **Capitalism***

1) Marxists suggest that age groups are defined by the **capitalist system**. For example, **adults** are people of **working age**, and the **elderly** are people who are **too old to work**.
2) **Phillipson (1982)** argues that capitalism views the **elderly** as a **burden on society**. This is because their **working life** has **ended**, and they usually have **less spending power**. Old age becomes a **stigmatised** identity.

Increasing Life Expectancy** has changed attitudes to **Old Age

1) The UK has an **ageing population**. **Social Trends 41 (2011)** said that between 1971 and 2009, the **percentage** of people in the population **over 75** rose from **4.7%** to **7.8%**.
2) This is partly because people are **living longer**. According to **Social Trends 33 (2003)**, between 1971 and 2001, **life expectancy** in the UK **increased** from 69 years to 75 years for men, and from 75 years to 80 years for women.
3) **Giddens (1986)** argues that **longer life expectancy** has an **effect on family life**. For example, people are more likely to know their grandparents or great-grandparents. Families continue for much longer after the children have left home.
4) **Postmodernists** argue that **attitudes** to old age are **changing**. **Featherstone and Hepworth (1993)** found that magazines aimed at older people portray an image of 'youthful' old age — enjoying holidays and sports, wearing fashionable clothes etc. They also argue that people can **mask their age** more than ever before, e.g. through cosmetic surgery.

Disability and Identity

Society puts Disabled People into a **Separate Category**

1) **Tom Shakespeare (1994)** argued that 'disability' is a label that society uses to **categorise people**. Being in the category of 'disabled' is often **more of a problem** than the disability itself. In this way, 'disability' can be seen as a **social construct**.
2) He argues that it's more useful to talk about **impairments** (the actual physical characteristics or symptoms). These don't make it **impossible** for people to do some tasks — they just make it **harder**. Since everyone's abilities are different, **everyone has some sort of impairment** — not just people traditionally defined as 'disabled'.
3) He also says that society should adapt so that **everyone** has access to the same services, regardless of how severe their impairments are.

There is sometimes **Prejudice** against **Disabled People**

There are **negative stereotypes** of disabled people as **weak** and **dependent on others**.

Scott (1969) studied the way that **blind people** were treated by **medical professionals**. He concluded that the blind people sometimes **learned helplessness** — they relied on sighted people for support because this was what the medical professionals **expected** them to do. Because they were **labelled** as dependent, it became a **self-fulfilling prophecy**.

Some people have challenged the idea that disabled people are unusual in being reliant on others. **Marsh and Keating (2006)** argue that everyone is dependent on other people to some extent.

Disabled People are Under-represented in the Media

1) There's very **little representation** of **disabled people** in the **media**. **Roles** for disabled people are **limited**. Research by **Cumberbatch and Negrine (1992)** looking at British television over six weeks found the roles for disabled people were based on **pity** or **comedy**. They found that **disabled actors** never appeared **just as actors** playing a person who **just happened to have a disability**, only in roles **particularly about disability**. However, there are some positive portrayals of disabled people in films and TV — e.g. in *X-Men* and *Glee*.
2) They also found that how people **interpreted** media messages about disability depended on their **personal experiences**. Those with real-life experience of disability were more likely to **reject unrealistic portrayals**, or to **reinterpret** them according to their own knowledge. This suggests that the media can only create **negative perceptions** amongst people who haven't already **formed their own ideas**.

Practice Questions

Q1 What characteristics have TV soap operas often given to teenage characters?

Q2 Give two examples of stereotypes about age groups that are sometimes presented by the media.

Q3 How do Marxists think that capitalism defines who society views as elderly?

Q4 What is Tom Shakespeare's view about how society should view disability?

Q5 How are disabled people usually portrayed in the media, according to Cumberbatch and Negrine?

Exam Questions

Q1 How have attitudes to old people changed in recent decades? Use one example to briefly explain your answer. [2 marks]

Q2 Outline two ways that disabled people are negatively stereotyped. Explain each one. [10 marks]

You want to retire with a pension at 17? Oh, act your age...

Age is a flexible part of identity (my dad's been 21 for decades). Everyone gets older and society's views of age change, often due to changes in population within a single person's lifetime. On the other hand, disability is much more rigid — a person is unlikely to stop being disabled, and society often unfairly views a disability as the most important attribute of an individual.

Production, Consumption and Globalisation

In a postmodern world, identity is all about shopping...

*Some Argue That **Identity** is Linked to **Work** and **Leisure***

In industrial society, **traditional patterns of employment** helped people to create a strong sense of shared identity through **work**, **family** and **location**. People often lived and socialised in **communities** close to their place of work. These communities were **self-sufficient** — they **produced** what they needed to survive. People were expected to stay in the same skilled or semi-skilled job for a lifetime, and work was closely linked to family and community traditions. This made it easier to build your sense of **identity** around your **job**.

In modern society, people have become more **geographically** and **socially mobile**, jobs are **less secure**, and families (traditional, extended and nuclear) are **less stable**:

1) Instead of **producing** everything themselves, people are increasingly **relying** on the work and services of **other people** to survive. More people are **defining** themselves based on what they **consume** (buy), **not** on what they **produce** — this means the identities people can build are more **varied**.
2) **Willis (1990)** suggests that work is now **less satisfying** because it often requires little **skill**. This leads to people using their **leisure time** to gain **satisfaction** and build their **identity**.
3) **Rojek (1995)** argues that work and leisure are often **combined** in **postmodern society** — lots of jobs exist in the **leisure industry** and more people are **turning their hobbies or passions** into **paid work**.

*Social Class Affects the Link Between **Work** and **Leisure***

Parker (1976) looked at the link between **work** and **leisure**.
He discovered **three** different patterns of **integration**:

Bourdieu (1984) argued that there is a link between cultural consumption, class and identity (see p.47).

1) The **extension pattern** — leisure and work are **actively linked**.
2) The **neutrality pattern** — work and leisure may not be linked — their relationship is **not planned**.
3) The **opposition pattern** — leisure and work are **deliberately separated**.

1) Parker found that **upper-class** people with **high-status jobs** often follow the **extension pattern** — they spend leisure time **networking** (making social contacts) or doing other things that will help them advance in their working life.
2) **Middle-class** and **working-class** people in **jobs** that are **not stressful or rewarding** follow the **neutrality pattern**.
3) **Working-class** people in **tiring** or **dangerous jobs** follow the **opposition pattern** to get away from the stresses of work.
4) This theory has been **criticised** for ignoring the impact of **age**, **gender** and **personal choice** on leisure. For example, **Deem (1986)** argues that women who **work in the home** don't have **boundaries** between **leisure** and **housework** — these women are always '**on call**' to tackle any emotional and domestic issues. Women who have **paid work** can **separate** their work and leisure time **more clearly**, but they still often spend **free time** doing **domestic work**.

***Postmodernists** Say That **Class**, **Gender** and **Ethnicity** Don't Mean So Much*

1) In recent years, sociologists have suggested that people do not feel constrained by **social class**, **gender**, or **ethnic** background, and are now much more likely to build their identities through **symbolic consumption** (see below).
2) An example of this is the 'new man', who is caring, sensitive and does the housework.
3) In these cases, individuals use **leisure time** and **products** from **culture industries** to build **identities** for themselves.

Symbolic Consumption and Consumer Culture

1) In our **industrial capitalist** society, we **buy goods** that have been made by the **cultural industries** (e.g. film, music, broadcasting). Buying goods has become part of modern, Western culture — it's known as **consumer culture**.
2) These industries create and sell things that fit into people's **cultural lives** — the stuff they **think about**, and **talk about**, and often the stuff that helps them to **define who they are**. This is called '**symbolic consumption**'.
3) When you choose a pair of trainers, you look for the **right brand** and the **right style**. You are buying what the shoes **stand for** — their '**symbolic value**'. What you're actually buying is part of your **identity**.
4) **Most industries** in the modern world have become **cultural industries**. Any industry that makes things with a **brand image** that **means something** to people, or **stands** for something, is involved in **cultural production**.

Lury (2011) argues that shopping is becoming a more common way to spend leisure time — this is partly because there are more products to choose from and more ways to pay for things.

Production, Consumption and Globalisation

Pluralists say we have *Power* through *Choice*

In a **consumer culture**, people have **consumer power** (they can choose the products they buy). **Pluralists** argue that **cultural industries** make products based on what society **actively decides** to consume. It's the **consumers** who **shape popular culture** — not the other way round.

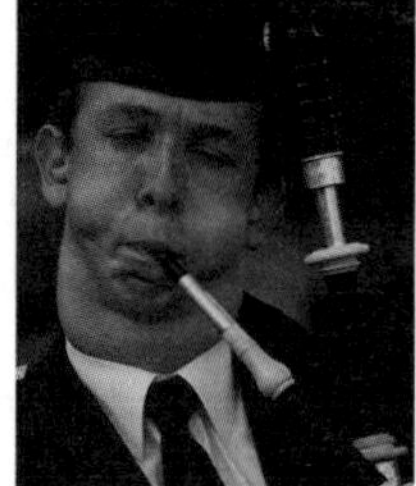

The chin-flator 5000. Surely a must-have?

1) Not everyone agrees with the pluralists. For example, **Ien Ang (1991)** suggests that the **opinions** of consumers are largely **ignored** by the cultural industry.
2) **Bauman** argues that **postmodern society** expects us all to play the **role of a consumer**, but that some people **can't** do this. Some people **want** to consume lots of cultural products, but their **freedom to choose** is limited by **lack of money**. They **can't use consumption** to create an **impression** of **who they are**. Bauman calls these people '**repressed consumers**'. (He refers to people who **can afford** to consume as much as they like as '**seduced consumers**'.)
3) Bauman also believes that consumer society gives you the **illusion** that your **identity** is flexible because you can change your way of living **at any time** by **changing what you consume**. However, consumer society still **forces you to make a choice** between the options that are on offer — this **limits** your power.

Clarke and Critcher (1985) argue that **capitalist society controls** the **choices** we make about **leisure consumption**:

- Leisure is **controlled by companies** who want to make **profit** — it's **cheaper** for them to give you a **limited number of popular choices** than to provide lots of different options. This means it's **harder** to create a **unique identity**.
- They argue that society encourages people to do **sports** so that there are enough **healthy people** to do the **work** that capitalist society is built on. This is a form of **manipulation** of leisure time.

Globalisation Has Influenced *National* and *Individual Identities*

Sociologists **disagree** over whether **globalisation** is having a **positive** or **negative influence** on national and ethnic identity.

Some think that globalisation is **bad news** for **ethnic identities** because everyone will experience the same, global culture — ethnic and national identities will **merge** and become **less distinct** and **less varied**. **Lemert and Elliott (2006)** and **Bauman** disagree with this — they say globalisation makes your identity **more unstable**, which creates **more** variety. You can try out lots of cultures and you **don't have to commit** to any part of your identity.

Some argue that globalisation **imposes Western culture** on other societies and **damages** traditional cultural identity. **Hall** disagrees and suggests that globalisation actually **strengthens national identity**:

1) **Hall (1992)** argues that both **ethnic minorities** and people in the **ethnic majority** group of a nation react to **globalisation of identity** by **emphasising** their own cultural roots.
2) Some people react by **breaking away** from the cultural identity **imposed** on them by their **nationality** or **ethnicity** — they create a **new identity** using lots of cultural influences.

Hall (1992) argues that **globalisation** means people don't have to construct their identity based on where they **live** — the growth of the **internet** means you can communicate with people across the world and **experience** different cultures. It's also getting easier to **travel** to other countries **cheaply**. Hall names this the '**cultural supermarket effect**'.

Practice Questions

Q1 Explain how identity and work were linked in industrial society.

Q2 What is 'symbolic consumption'?

Q3 Give two ways that globalisation has influenced identity.

Exam Question

Q1 Evaluate the idea that people can use consumer power to construct their own identity. [20 marks]

It says it's about shopping but it looks like work to me...

Phew... It's the end of the section. There's been a lot of heavy theory in this section. The usual suspects — postmodernists, Marxists, functionalists, feminists and interactionists — have an opinion about everything (you might have noticed). If you can get your head around what they say about culture and identity, then you'll find it a lot easier to pick up marks in the exam.

The Nature and Role of Family in Society

The family is one of the most important social groups in sociology — almost all people live in a family for some of their life.

Families and *Households* are *Not* Necessarily the *Same Thing*

A **household** is a group of people who **live together** who may or may not have family or kinship ties. In 2010, there were **25.3 million households** recorded in the Great Britain. **Families** make up the **majority** of households, but there are other types, e.g. **students** or **friends** sharing a house or flat, or people living alone.

A **family** is a type of household where the people living together are **related**. Most commonly, a family is also a **kinship** group. Kinship means being related by **birth** or **blood** — parents, children, grandparents, cousins. Families also include **non-kinship relationships** — foster children, guardians, step-parents and stepchildren, mother-in-law etc.

Here are the main types of family:

1) **Nuclear family**: Two generations living together (parents and dependent children).
2) **Traditional extended family**: Three or more generations of the same family living together or close by, with frequent contact between grandparents, grandchildren, aunts, cousins etc.
3) **Attenuated extended family**: Nuclear families that live apart from their extended family, but keep in regular contact, e.g. via phone or email.
4) **Lone-parent families**: A single parent and their dependent children.
5) **Reconstituted families**: New stepfamilies created when parts of two previous families are brought together. For example, two new partners who bring children from former partners together to create a new family group.

My architect didn't quite understand when I asked him to extend my house.

Functionalists Emphasise the *Positive Role* of the Family

Functionalists see **every institution** in society as **essential** to the **smooth running** of society. A **key functionalist study** by **Murdock (1949)** concluded that the family is **so useful** to society that it is **inevitable** and **universal** — in other words, you **can't avoid** having family units in a society, and societies **everywhere** have family units.

Murdock (1949) looked at 250 societies in different cultures

Murdock argued that some form of the **nuclear family** existed in **all** of the 250 different societies he looked at. He argued the family performed **four basic functions** – sexual, reproductive, economic and educational (social):

Sexual	Provides a **stable sexual relationship** for **adults**, and **controls** the sexual relationships of its members.
Reproductive	Provides new babies — **new members of society**.
Economic	The family **pools resources** and **provides** for all its members, adults and children.
Educational	The family **teaches children** the **norms** and **values** of society, which keeps the values of society going.

In the 1950s, American sociologist **Talcott Parsons** argued that the family always has **two basic and irreducible** (vital) **functions**. These are the **primary socialisation of children** and the **stabilisation of adult personalities**.

1) **Primary socialisation** is the process by which children **learn** and **accept** the **values** and **norms** of society. Parsons described families as '**factories**' where the next citizens are produced.

Remember: functionalists see the positive nature of the family as two-way — it's equally useful and beneficial to individuals and society.

2) For adults, the family **stabilises personalities** through the **emotional** relationship between the parents. The emotional relationship gives the **support** and **security** needed to cope in the wider society. It's a **sanctuary** from the **stress** of everyday life.

Some Say *Functionalists Ignore* the *Negative Aspects* of Family Life

1) The functionalist perspective has been **criticised** for **idealising** the family — focusing on the good bits and blanking out the bad bits. **Morgan (1975)** points out that Murdock makes no reference to **alternative households** to the family, or to **disharmony** and **problems** in **family relationships**.
2) The **functionalist** view of the family was **dominant** in sociology into the 1960s. Since then there's been **widespread criticism** that neither Murdock nor Parsons look at issues of **conflict**, **class** or **violence** in relation to the family. Some feminists argue that they also ignored the issue of **exploitation of women**.
3) The fact that functionalists **overlook negative aspects** of family life **makes their position look weak**.

The Nature and Role of Family in Society

Marxists See the **Family** as Meeting the **Needs** of the **Capitalist System**

Like functionalists, Marxists view the family as performing **essential functions** for modern industrial society. The key difference is that **Marxists** argue that the family **benefits** the minority **in power** (the **bourgeoisie**) and the economy, but **disadvantages** the **working class** majority (the **proletariat**).

1) **Engels (1884)** said the family had an **economic function** of keeping wealth within the **bourgeoisie** by passing it on to the next generation as **inheritance**. In other words, when a **rich person dies**, their **kids get their money**.
2) **Zaretsky (1976)** focused on how the family helped the capitalist economy. He argued that the family is one place in society where the **proletariat** can have **power** and **control**. When the **working man** gets home, he's **king of his own castle**. This relieves some of the **frustration** workers feel about their low status, which helps them to **accept** their **oppression** and exploitation as workers.
3) In capitalist society, a woman's role as '**housewife**' of the family means workers are **cared for** and **healthy**. This makes them **more productive** — a great benefit that the capitalist class (the employers) get for **free**.
4) The **family household** is a unit with the **desire** to **buy** the **goods** produced by capitalist industry, e.g. washing machines, cars, fridges. The family is a **unit of consumption**. The family buys the goods for more than they cost to produce and the **bourgeoisie get the profit**.

When the time came for home improvements, Steve decided to interpret Zaretsky literally.

All in all, Marxists argue the family is a **very useful tool of capitalism**.

The **Marxist** View is **Criticised** for being too **Negative**

The Marxist view of the family is all about it being a **tool of capitalist oppression**, and **never mentions nice things**, like bedtime stories for the kids, or trips to the zoo.

Criticisms of the Marxist view of the family

Marxist sociology is entirely focused on **benefits to the economy**, and benefits to the working man's **boss**. It **ignores other benefits** to individuals and society.

Traditional Marxist sociology **assumes** that the worker is **male**, and that women are **housewives**.

There is **no Marxist explanation** for why the family flourishes as an institution in **non-capitalist** or **communist** societies and there is little Marxist research on **alternatives** to the family.

Functionalists and Marxists both see the family as having a **key role** in society in **reproducing social structure** and **order**. The **key sociological debate** between them is whether this is **positive** or **negative** and **who benefits**.

Practice Questions

Q1 What do sociologists define as a household?

Q2 What are the key functions of the family, according to Parsons?

Q3 Explain the ways in which functionalist and Marxist perspectives on the role of the family are similar.

Q4 Explain the ways in which functionalist and Marxist perspectives on the role of the family are different.

Exam Questions

Q1 Give a definition of the term 'nuclear family'. [2 marks]

Q2 What functions might nuclear families perform? Outline three examples. [6 marks]

Cog in society's machine or tool of capitalist oppression — you decide...

If you're comparing functionalist and Marxist perspectives about the role of the family, make sure you cover the pros and cons of each view — and most importantly, make sure you answer the question. Remember, functionalists believe that the family is there to keep society chugging along smoothly, and Marxists believe it's there to help exploit the common worker.

The Nature and Role of Family in Society

There are lots of different feminist theories about the family — these theories are mostly left-wing and anti-traditional. It's worth looking at right-wing pro-traditional ideas too. And at the postmodernists, who say everyone can do what they like. Hooray.

Most ***Feminists*** *Believe the* ***Family Exploits*** *and* ***Oppresses Women***

1) From a **feminist perspective**, the **family** helps to **maintain the existing social order**. (If that sounds familiar, it's because functionalists and Marxists also talk about keeping up the existing social order.)
2) Feminists call the existing social order **patriarchy**. Patriarchy is the **combination** of **systems**, **ideologies** and **cultural practices** which make sure that **men** have power.
3) Feminist theory argues that the family **supports** and reproduces **inequalities** between men and women.
4) The idea is that women are **oppressed** because they're **socialised** to be **dependent** on men — and to put themselves in second place to men. The **family** has a central role in this socialisation — **male and female roles** and **expectations** are **formed in the family** and then **carried on into wider society**.
5) Feminist sociologists say that there's an **ideology** about men's **roles** and women's **roles** in the family.

An ideology is a set of ideas about the way things are and the way things ought to be.

There are ***Three Main Strands*** *of* ***Feminist Thought*** *on the* ***Family***

The three main strands of feminist thought are **Marxist feminism**, **radical feminism** and **liberal feminism**.

The distinction between the three theories comes from what they see as the **root cause of patriarchy**. For Marxist feminists it's the **capitalist system**, for radical feminists it's the **power dominance of men** and for liberal feminists it's **cultural attitudes** and laws that allow **discrimination**.

All three of these theories generalise quite a bit.

Marxist feminism — key points

Marxist feminism sees the **exploitation of women** as essential to the success of **capitalism**. The family **produces** and **cares** for the next generation of workers for society at almost **no cost** to the capitalist system. It's cost-free because society accepts that **housework** should be **unpaid**. **Men are paid** for work outside the home, but **women aren't paid** for work **inside** the home. If this sounds outdated, remember evidence shows that even when women work outside the home they still do **most** of the domestic labour (see p.66). **Benston (1969)** points out that if housework were paid even at **minimum wage** levels it would **damage capitalist profits** hugely.

Radical feminism — key points

Radical feminist theory also highlights **housework** as an area of **exploitation of women**, but... and it's a big but... radical feminists don't see this as the fault of the capitalist system. Radical feminists see the exploitation of women as being down to the **domination of men in society**. Radical feminism believes that **men will always oppress women**. **Delphy and Leonard (1992)** are radical feminists who see the family as a patriarchal institution in which **women do most of the work** and **men get most of the benefit**.

Liberal feminism — key points

Liberal feminists emphasise the **cultural norms** and **values** which are reinforced by the family and by other institutions in society. The family is only sexist because it **supports mainstream culture** which is sexist. Liberal feminists believe **social change is possible**. They try to put pressure on institutions such as the **legal system** and **government** to change laws and social policies which **discriminate** against women.

Feminist Theory has been ***Criticised***

1) All strands of feminist theory have been **criticised** for portraying women as **too passive**. It plays down the ability of individual women to **make changes** and **improve** their situation.
2) Feminist sociology **doesn't acknowledge** that **power might be shared** within a family.
3) Some feminist theory has been criticised for **not considering** the households in society which **don't** feature a **man and woman partnership**, e.g. **lesbian** and **gay** relationships and **lone-parent** households. The power structures in those families **don't get looked at**.
4) Some **black feminists** have pointed out that a lot of feminist theory doesn't address the fact that women from different **ethnic backgrounds** have different **life experiences**.

The Nature and Role of Family in Society

The **New Right** Believe the **Nuclear Family** is the **Bedrock of Society**

1) **New Right theory** gained influence in sociology in the **1980s**. It's based on the idea that the **traditional nuclear family** and its **values** (mum, dad and kids, parents married, dad in paid employment) are best for society.
2) New Right theorists reckon that **social policies** on family, children, divorce and welfare have **undermined** the **family**.
3) **Charles Murray** is a New Right sociologist who says the traditional family is under threat. **Murray (1989)** says that **welfare benefits** are **too high** and create a **'culture of dependency'** where an individual finds it easy and acceptable to take benefits rather than work.
4) New Right theorists are particularly concerned about giving lots of **welfare benefits** to **single mothers**. They also think that it's a very **bad idea** to have children brought up in families where adults aren't working.
5) New Right sociologists believe that the increase in **lone-parent** and **reconstituted** (step) families and easier access to **divorce** have led to a **breakdown in traditional values**. They say that this causes social problems such as **crime** to increase.
6) Some politicians have made use of New Right theory. It's had an influence on **social policy** — making it **harder** for people to **get benefits**.

There's more about the New Right on p.64.

Pine cladding — that's the real bedrock of society.

New Right theory has been **criticised** for **'blaming the victim'** for their problems.

Postmodernists Say **Diversity** in Family Structures is a **Good Thing**

1) The **central idea** of **postmodern views of the family** is that there's a much **wider range** of **living options** available these days — because of **social** and **cultural changes**. There are **traditional** nuclear families, stepfamilies, cohabiting unmarried couples, **single people** flat-sharing, more **divorced** people etc.
2) Postmodern sociologist **Judith Stacey (1990)** reckons there's **such a diversity** of family types, relationships and lifestyles that there'll **never** be **one dominant type** of family in Western culture again. She says that family structures in Western society are **varied** and **flexible**. This means a person can **move** from one family structure into another, and not get stuck with one **fixed** family structure.
3) Postmodernists say the **key thing** is the idea that contemporary living is so **flexible** that one individual can experience lots of different types of family in their lifetime. Postmodernists see this **diversity** and **flexibility** as **positive** — because it means individuals can always **choose** from several options depending on what suits their **personal needs** and lifestyle. People aren't hemmed in by **tradition**.
4) Sociological **criticism** of postmodern theory **questions** whether this movement through different family types is really all that typical. **O'Brien and Jones (1996)** concluded from their UK research that there was **less variety** in family types than Stacey reported, and that **most** individuals actually experienced **only one or two** different types of family in their lifetime.

Practice Questions

Q1 Identify three different strands of feminist thought about the family.

Q2 Give two characteristics of patriarchy.

Q3 Name two things that New Right theorists blame for family breakdown.

Q4 Why do postmodernists think there will never be one dominant type of family in Western culture again?

Exam Questions

Q1 How does postmodern society promote family diversity? Outline three ways. [6 marks]

Q2 Evaluate the idea that the nuclear family oppresses women. [20 marks]

If this is too difficult to learn, blame your family. Or blame society...

Another couple of pages all about different views of the family. Feminist theory is complicated because there are different varieties of feminism. Which one you go for depends on exactly how unfair you think family life is on women, and exactly whose fault you think it is. Don't forget to learn the reasons why sociologists say each theory might be wrong, or flawed.

Changes in Family Structure

The average family today doesn't have the same structure as the average family 250 years ago. Sociologists suggest various reasons for this, mostly to do with people moving to cities to work in factories.

Parsons said that **Industrialisation** Changed **Family Structure**

1) There are **two basic types of family structure** you need to know: **extended** and **nuclear** (see p.58).
2) There are **two basic types of society** you need to know:

Pre-industrial society — society before industrialisation. It is largely **agricultural** and work centres on **home**, **farm**, **village** and **market**.

Industrial society — society during and after **industrialisation**. Work centres on **factories** and production of goods in **cities**.

Industrialisation is the process by which production becomes more mechanical and based outside the home in factories. People travel outside the home to work and urban centres (cities) are formed. Industrialisation in the UK started in the 18th century.

Talcott Parsons (1951) said that nuclear families became dominant in industrial society

In **pre-industrial** society, the **extended** family is most common. Families **live and work together**, producing goods and crops to live from, taking the surplus to market. This is where the term **cottage industry** comes from.

In **industrial** society, the **nuclear family** becomes dominant. There is a huge increase in individuals **leaving the home** to work for a wage. The key social change is that industrialisation **separates home and work**.

Functionalists Say **Industrialisation** Changed the **Function** of the Family

Parsons was a functionalist — he thought that the **dominant family structure** changed from **extended** to **nuclear** because it was **more useful** for industrial society — i.e. the **nuclear family** is the **best fit** for **industrial society**.

1) Lots of **functions** of the family in **pre-industrial** society are **taken over by the state** in **industrial** society — e.g. policing, healthcare, education.
2) The nuclear **family** can focus on its function of **socialisation**. The family socialises **children** into the **roles**, **values** and **norms** of industrialised society.
3) Parsons said the industrial nuclear family is **'isolated'** — meaning it has **few ties** with local **kinship** and economic systems. This means the family can **easily move** to where the work is (this is called '**geographical mobility**').

In short, **family structure adapts** to the **needs of society**.

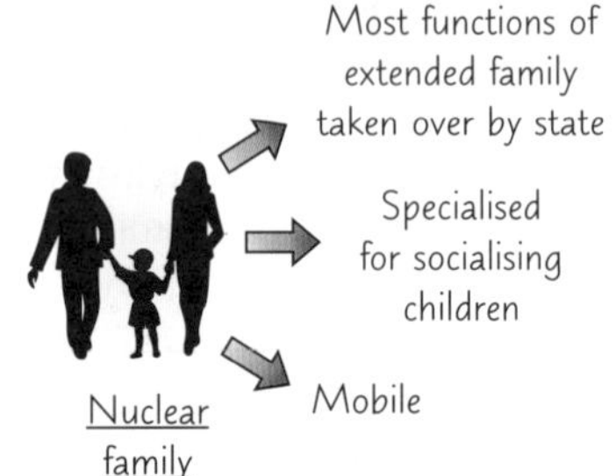

Functionalists Say **Industrialisation** Changed **Roles** and **Status** in the Family

1) Status for an individual in **pre-industrial society** was **ascribed** — decided at birth by the family they were born into. Parsons reckoned that in industrial society an individual's status is **achieved** by their success **outside the family**.
2) The idea here is that the **nuclear family** is the **best** for allowing individuals to **achieve status** and position without **conflict**. It's OK for an individual to achieve higher or lower status than previous generations. This allows for greater **social mobility** in society. People can **better themselves**.
3) Parsons says that **specialised roles** for men and women develop within the family. He thought that men are **instrumental** (practical / planning) leaders and women are **expressive** (emotional) leaders in a family. As a **functionalist**, Parsons said these roles come about because they're **most effective** for society. **Feminists** and **conflict theorists** disagree — they say these roles come from **ideology** and **power**.

Other Sociologists say it's all **More Complicated**

Functionalists are **criticised** for seeing the modern nuclear family as **superior** — something that societies have to evolve into. They're also criticised for putting forward an **idealised** picture of history. **Historical evidence** suggests there was actually a **variety** of family forms in the past.

Sociologist **Peter Laslett (1972)** reckons that the **nuclear family** was the **most common** structure in Britain even before industrialisation. His evidence comes from **parish records**. Also, **Laslett and Anderson (1971)** say that the **extended family** actually was **significant** in industrial society. Anderson used the **1851 census** for evidence. He said that when people moved to the cities for **industrial** jobs, they lived with relatives from their **extended family**.

Changes in Family Structure

Willmott and Young Said Families Have Developed Through Three Stages

British sociologists **Willmott and Young (1960, 1973)** did two important studies looking at family structures in British society from the 1950s to the 1970s. They mainly studied families in different parts of **London** and **Essex**. Their work tested the theory that the **nuclear family** is the **dominant form** in modern industrial society.

You need to remember their conclusion, which was that **British families have developed through three stages**. (Initially, they set out four stages, but there wasn't a lot of evidence for the last stage, so they dropped it.)

Stage One: Pre-Industrial	Family works together as an **economic production unit**. Work and home are combined.
Stage Two: Early Industrial	Extended family is broken up as individuals (mostly men) leave home to work. Women at home have strong **extended kinship** networks.
Stage Three: Privatised Nuclear	Family based on **consumption**, not **production** — buying things, not making things. Nuclear family is focused on its **personal relationships and lifestyle**. Called '**the symmetrical family**' — husband and wife have joint roles.
Stage Four: Asymmetrical	Husband and wife roles become **asymmetrical** as men spend more leisure time **away from the home** — in the pub for example. This stage got dropped.

A key part of the definition of a **symmetrical family** is the idea that both partners **work** either part-time or full-time. The economic contribution of men and women is **equally important**.

1) **Helen Wilkinson (1994)** argued that increasing numbers of women are working because the economy has moved away from the historically male-dominated **industrial sector** towards the traditionally female-dominated **service sector**.
2) Women's **attitudes** towards work and family have undergone a '**genderquake**' — Wilkinson notes that, in the **early 1990s**, women between the ages of **16 and 35** saw **work** and **education** as more important than **having children**.
3) Women have gained **economic influence** in the family through **employment** — this changes the **structure** of the family because **traditional gender roles** within the family are **broken down**.
4) In **2012**, a survey of social attitudes found that 41% of women and 36% of men believed that the **ideal** way to structure a family with dependent children was for **men to work full-time** and **women to work part-time**. This structure was seen as **more desirable** than only having a male breadwinner.

Other Sociologists have Criticised Willmott and Young

1) Willmott and Young (and other functionalists) have been criticised for **assuming** that family life has got **better and better** as structure adapts to modern society. They're described as '**march of progress**' theorists.
2) Wilmott and Young **ignore** the **negative** aspects of the modern nuclear family. **Domestic violence**, **child abuse** and **lack of care** for **older** and **vulnerable** people are all problems in society today.
3) **Feminist** research (see p.60) suggests **equal roles** in the 'symmetrical family' don't really exist.

Practice Questions

Q1 Give an example of social change caused by industrialisation.

Q2 What roles did Parsons believe men and women had within the nuclear family?

Q3 What is meant by the term 'symmetrical family'?

Q4 Outline one criticism of Willmott and Young's 'march of progress' theory.

Exam Questions

Q1 Give a definition of the term 'symmetrical family'. [2 marks]

Q2 Outline two ways that industrialisation has changed family structure. Explain each one. [10 marks]

My mum works at Sellafield — we're a real nuclear family...

OK — it helps to have a vague idea about history for this bit of sociology. You need to know what this 'industrialisation' business was. The idea is that when people went to live in cities to work in factories, society changed. Of course, it'd be far too much to expect sociologists to agree on all of this. Oh no. So you have another couple of pages of sociological debate...

Changes in Family Structure

Politicians sometimes try to promote certain family structures through their policies.

Governments *try to Influence Family Structure through* ***Social Policy***

1) The UK government often makes **laws** that are designed to influence **family life** or **family structure**. These laws are part of **social policy**.
2) Social policy laws cover areas such as **divorce**, changes to the **benefit system** which affect family income, reforms to the **education** system, **adoption/fostering** and **employment**.
3) **Donzelot (1977)** argued that **social policy** can be used by the state to **control** families. He argues that **professionals** such as health care visitors can use their knowledge to **control** family behaviour.

Social Policy *has Changed* ***Over Time***

1) The way that governments tackle social policy has **changed** since the Second World War.
2) In the 1945-1979 period, the state's social policy was quite **interventionist**.
3) **The Welfare State** (see p.87), which was set up by a **Labour government** in 1948, **supported families** through benefits, public housing, family allowances and free health care.
4) People paid into a **national insurance** scheme to pay for the welfare state. It was **universal** — everyone had the same benefits and services.

The NHS even covered floating baby syndrome...

The ***1979*** *Conservative Government Believed in* ***Reduced State Intervention***

The **Conservative Party** was elected in 1979 with **Margaret Thatcher** as their leader. Reacting to several years of political instability, they set about **reforming** the relationship between society and the state.

1) The Conservatives were influenced by **New Right** ideology. They believed that nuclear families were the **cornerstone of society**, but also thought that society as a whole should be **freed from interference** by the state as much as possible. They thought the UK had become a '**nanny state**' with too much government control over individual lives.

2) They set out to make individuals more **responsible** for their own lives and decisions — the state would **intervene much less** in private matters. So benefits were cut and **taxes lowered**. **Means testing** was introduced for some benefits with the aim of helping only those in **genuine need**. (Means testing is when you only get a benefit if your household income is below a set level.)

3) Mothers were encouraged to **stay at home** through preferential tax allowances. Families were pushed to take on more responsibility for **older people** through benefit cuts.

Mrs Thatcher's Conservatives echoed the concerns of Charles Murray, who first coined the phrase 'culture of dependency' (see p.61).

The Conservatives ***Legislated*** *to Protect People in a* ***Traditional Family***

The Conservatives valued **traditional**, **nuclear families**. In 1988, **Thatcher** described the **family** as "the **building block** of society. It's a nursery, a school, a hospital, a leisure place, a place of refuge and a place of rest."

The Conservatives created several laws that enforced the **rights** and **responsibilities** of individuals in families.

1) The **Child Support Agency** was established in **1993** to force absent fathers and mothers to **pay** a fair amount towards the upkeep of their children.

2) The **Children Act 1989** outlined for the first time the rights of the child.

3) The Conservatives also considered a law to make **divorce more difficult** — a compulsory **cooling off** period of one year was proposed before a couple could divorce. In the end they **abandoned** this idea because they couldn't find a way to make it work in practice.

Changes in Family Structure

New Labour *Promised a* **Compromise** *between the Old Ideologies*

New Labour came to power in **1997** led by Tony Blair.

1) They based their ideology on '**The Third Way**' — a middle ground between **left-wing** and **right-wing** politics. Their policies were designed to be **more pragmatic** and **less ideological** than either the 1979 Conservative government or previous Labour governments.
2) In their 1998 consultation paper '**Supporting Families**', they made it clear that **marriage** was their preferred basis for family life.
3) However they showed an awareness of, and concern for, **diversity** of family life.
4) In 2005 they introduced **civil partnerships**, a union a lot like marriage that is available to gay couples.
5) They also introduced laws allowing any type of cohabiting couple to **adopt children**.
6) They adopted some **New Right ideas** about **family policy** — e.g. they **cut** lone-parent family benefits, **supported** means-tested benefits and were **opposed** to universal benefits.

The **Coalition Government** *Promoted Family* **Stability**

After the **General Election in 2010**, no single party won a majority — a **coalition government** of **Conservatives** and **Liberal Democrats** formed under Conservative leader David Cameron.

1) The Coalition promoted **marriage** as a **stabilising** force in family life. For example, they pledged to remove the '**couples penalty**' that made those on benefits better off if they lived **apart**.
2) In 2014, they legalised **same-sex marriage**. However, not all **Conservative** politicians agreed — they thought that **civil partnerships** and **same-sex marriage** would damage family stability.
3) After the **financial crisis of 2008**, the Coalition introduced a policy of economic **austerity**, which aimed to **reduce** the amount of money the government was spending. This had an impact on **family life** in the UK.
4) In an attempt to **reduce** the welfare bill, the Coalition capped **housing benefit** in 2013 at £500 a week for couples and single parents with children — married couples were **not prioritised** in this policy.

In **2015**, a **Conservative** government was elected. This government **continued** the Coalition policy of **austerity** and thought families should take more **economic responsibility** for their children.

1) In 2015, the **Conservative** government announced a **cap** on **child benefit** — they decided that families with three or more children would not receive an increase in **child tax credits** or **housing benefit** after their second child.
2) The Secretary for Work and Pensions, **Iain Duncan Smith**, suggested that limiting **child benefit** to the first **two** children would promote '**behavioural change**' and discourage families from having too many children.

Practice Questions

Q1 What is social policy?

Q2 Give two examples of Conservative policies in the 1980s and 1990s that affected family life.

Q3 What was New Labour's attitude towards family diversity?

Q4 Give two criticisms of the New Right's attitude towards social policy.

Q5 Describe the attitude of the Coalition government towards marriage.

Exam Questions

Q1 How can social policy be used to control families? Use one example to briefly explain your answer. [2 marks]

Q2 Outline two ways that the government has tried to promote family stability since 2010. Explain each one. [10 marks]

My social policy — Thursday is the new Friday...

Politicians usually want to support the traditional nuclear family, but since 1979 they've generally also wanted to reduce state intervention in people's private lives. The financial crisis in 2008 led to economic policies that have had an impact on family finances in the UK — this is a more indirect kind of intervention in family life. Think of a way to remember that if you can.

Roles and Relationships Within the Family

As well as studying the place of the family unit in wider society, sociologists also research what happens within the family. The key focus is on the different roles and expectations of men, women and children within the family.

The **Rise** of the **Nuclear Family** led to **Joint Conjugal Roles**

Conjugal roles are the roles of **husband and wife** (or partner and partner) within the home. **Elizabeth Bott (1957)** studied how **jobs and roles within the family** were **allocated** to **men and women** in modern industrial Britain.

Bott's study is old, but it's a good foundation for the debate, so don't dismiss it — learn it.

Bott (1957) identified two ways household jobs can be shared

Segregated roles	Husbands and wives lead separate lives with clear and **distinct responsibilities** within the family. The man goes out to work and does DIY. The woman stays home, looks after the kids and provides emotional support.
Joint roles	Husband and wife roles are **more flexible** and shared, with less defined tasks for each. Usually **leisure time** is shared. Responsibility for **making decisions** is also shared.

1) **Willmott and Young (1973)** studied the changing structure of the British family from extended to nuclear (see p.63). They reckoned that the increase in the nuclear family meant that **joint conjugal roles** would develop. They predicted that **equal** and **shared responsibilities** would be the **future norm** in British families.
2) Willmott and Young's picture of **widespread equality** in marriage was **criticised** as soon as it was published.
3) **Oakley (1974)** pointed out that their study only required men to do a **few things round the house** to qualify as having joint roles. Their **methodology** overlooked the **amount of time** spent on housework — making 10 minutes washing-up equivalent to all the rest of the housework. Oakley's research found it was **pretty rare** for men to do a lot of housework.

Conjugal Roles are **Still Unequal**, although Most **Women** have **Paid Jobs**

Since the early studies by Bott, Willmott and Young, **new family structures** have developed. There are now lots **more families** where **both partners work outside the home**. Sociological evidence shows that an **equal share** of **paid employment** hasn't led to an **equal share** of **domestic labour**.

1) **Edgell (1980)** tested Willmott and Young's theory and found **none** of his sample families had **joint conjugal roles** in relation to housework. However, he did find **increased sharing of childcare**.
2) **Oakley (1974)** found that women took on a **dual burden** — taking on **paid jobs** and still **keeping** the **traditional responsibilities** for **home** and **children**.
3) **Gillian Dunne (1999)** studied **lesbian households**. She found that the **distribution** of **responsibilities** such as childcare and housework tended to be **equal** between the partners.

These are all **small-scale studies** — it's important to look at research using a much **larger sample**. The **British Social Attitudes Survey 2012** was a **large-scale study** that questioned about **3000 people** about **gender roles**. **Less than 15%** of those surveyed agreed that women should look after the home and family while men went out to work. There was also an **increase** in the number of people who thought that women with **school-age children** should **work full-time**.

Women Often Take Responsibility for the **Emotional Work** of a Household

Doing **emotional work** in a family means **reacting** and **responding** to other family members' emotions, **alleviating** pain and distress, and **responding** to and **managing** anger and frustration.

1) **Diane Bell (1990)** suggested that there is an '**economy of emotion**' within all families and that running this economy is the responsibility of women.
2) She says managing family emotions is a bit like **book-keeping** — women balance the family's **emotional budget**.
3) **Duncombe and Marsden (1995)** found that women in families are often required to do **housework and childcare, paid employment** and **emotional work** — amounting to a '**triple shift**' of work.
4) They found that married women were **happier** when their husbands **shared** some of the burden of emotional work, but women have the **main responsibility** for managing the whole family's emotions.

Roles and Relationships Within the Family

Industrialisation led to the *Creation* of the *'Housewife'*

1) **Oakley (1974)** thinks that the role of the **housewife** was **socially constructed** by the **social changes** of the **Industrial Revolution**, when people started **going to work in factories** instead of working at home.
2) **Married women** were often **not allowed** to work in factories. A new role of **housewife** was created for them.
3) Middle-class households had female **servants** to do domestic work. Working-class women did it themselves.
4) The **cultural values** that said women should be in charge of housework were **so dominant** that domestic work came to be seen as '**naturally**' (biologically) the role of women.

Decision-Making and *Sharing of Resources* can be *Unequal*

As well as looking at the **division of labour** and tasks in the home, sociologists have researched how **power is shared** in the home. The traditional role of the **man** holding **power to make decisions** was **so widespread** that the phrase '**who wears the trousers**' is often used to mean who's in charge.

Edgell (1980) interviewed middle-class couples

He found that **men** had **decision-making control** over things both husband and wife saw as important, whilst **women** had control over **minor decisions**. This is linked to the fact that men often brought **higher earnings** into a household.

Alas, no one knows who was wearing these trousers. It's a mystery.

Pahl (1989, 1993) researched money management by 100 dual-income couples

She concluded that the most common form of financial management was '**husband-controlled pooling**', which she defined as money being **shared**, but the husband has the **dominant role** in how it's spent.

Other studies look at the **meanings** that couples and families attach to control over money. They discovered that control over money in a relationship is often more about **convenience** than **power**. This approach is called the **personal life perspective** — these studies do not use **traditional family norms** and **ideals** as a background to **judge** participants.

1) **Weeks et al (2001)** found that couples tend to **pool** money in a joint account while keeping some money back in a personal account — they have **sole control** over their **personal** spending money.
2) **Carol Smart (2007)** discovered that **same-sex** couples don't link control over money with **inequality** in the relationship — they organise their money based on what is best for them **as a couple**. She argued that same-sex couples don't have the same **ideas** about **gender** and **money** that heterosexual couples have **traditionally** held.

Practice Questions

Q1 What are 'conjugal roles'?

Q2 Describe the differences between joint and segregated conjugal roles.

Q3 What is meant by the 'dual burden' of women in modern society?

Q4 How was the role of 'housewife' socially constructed, according to Oakley?

Q5 Identify two areas of inequality in conjugal relationships other than household chores.

Exam Questions

Q1 Give a definition of the term 'conjugal roles'. [2 marks]

Q2 Evaluate the idea that conjugal roles are still unequal. [20 marks]

My husband just threw our money in the pond — he says he wants to pool it...

These pages are mainly about inequality in the family. You know, who does the housework and looks after the kids — that sort of thing. Some sociologists look on the bright side and say that things are getting more equal now that more women have paid jobs. Others say they still aren't equal enough. Remember to look at the possible causes and social construction of inequality.

Roles and Relationships Within the Family

These pages examine inequality within families and the dark side of family life — domestic violence and child abuse.

Explanations** for **Inequality** are based on **Theories About Power in Society

Guess what? There are **functionalist**, **Marxist** and **feminist** theories on power in society.

1) For **functionalists**, men and women still largely perform **different tasks** and **roles** within the family because it's the **most effective way** of keeping society **running smoothly**.

2) **Marxist** sociologists interpret the fact that men and women have different roles as evidence of the **power of capitalism** to **control** family life. They say women and men have unequal roles because **capitalism works best that way**. Even with more women working outside the home for equal hours to men, the capitalist class needs to **promote women** as 'naturally' **caring** and **nurturing** to ensure workers are kept fit, healthy and happy. This role for women is maintained **ideologically** through the **media**, e.g. in adverts.

Alice and Sam were awarded first place in the couples balancing competition.

3) From a **feminist** perspective, inequality in household roles demonstrates **inequality in power** between men and women. A **patriarchal** society will produce **unequal conjugal relationships** because society's **systems** and **values** will **inevitably** benefit men at the expense of women.

So, all explanations of conjugal **roles** lead back to **different theories** about **power in society**.

These explanations all agree that different roles for men and women in the family help to **maintain the status quo** (keep things the way they are at the moment) in society — the disagreement between them is over **who benefits**.

*Some Sociologists See **Child Abuse** in Terms of **Power***

Sociologists study the issue of **child abuse** by parents and carers in terms of **power relationships**.
You need to be able to **explain abuse** as a **form of power** rather than explore **details** of abuse itself.

- A parent or carer is able to abuse a child by **manipulating** the **responsibilities and trust** which go along with the role of parent or carer.
- Families are **private** and **separate** from the rest of society. This makes it **less likely** for children to **report** abuse.

The year 2013-14 just means April 2013 to March 2014. This is because it's a financial year — these start in April in the UK, instead of in January.

1) **Social policies** have been **adapted** to give some **protection** to children. The **Children Act 1989** was set up so the state can **intervene** in families if social workers are **concerned** about children's safety.
2) In the year **2013-14**, almost **658 000** children were referred to **social services** in England. In **just under half** of these cases, the **main reason** for referral was because the child was thought to be at **risk** of **abuse** or **neglect**.
3) In the same year, social workers put **59 800** children in England under a **child protection plan** — this allows social workers to **monitor families** to **protect** children from **neglect** and **abuse**.

***Domestic Violence** Affects Many Families in the UK*

Research by Professor **Elizabeth Stanko (2000)** found that:

- A woman is **killed** by her current or former partner **every three days** in England and Wales.
- There are 570 000 cases of **domestic violence** reported in the UK every year.
- An incident of domestic violence occurs in the UK every **6-20 seconds**.

A lot of abuse goes unreported. Even though these figures are from a self-report survey (which is a more confidential method than interviews, for example), they still won't give the full picture.

1) The Home Office estimates that **16% of all violent crime** in the **UK** is domestic violence.
2) In the year **2011-12**, **7.3% of women** and **5% of men** in **England and Wales** had suffered from **domestic abuse**.
3) A **2012-13** survey found that **non-physical abuse** (**emotional** abuse or use of **financial** power to control a partner) was **more common** than **physical abuse**. This was true for both **male** and **female** victims.

Roles and Relationships Within the Family

Radical Feminists See **Domestic Violence** as a Form of **Patriarchal Control**

Radical feminist theory says **violence against women** is treated **differently** to **other violent crime**.

1) **Dobash and Dobash (1979)** found the **police usually didn't record** violent crime by husbands against their wives.
2) Since 1979, the police have set up **specialist domestic violence units**, but still the **conviction rate is low** compared to other forms of assault.
3) **Before 1991**, British law said a husband was **entitled** to have **sex** with his wife **against her will**. In 1991 **rape law changed** to say that a husband could be charged with raping his wife.
4) Evidence like that above is used by **radical feminists** to support their argument that **laws** and **social policies** in society have traditionally worked to **control women** and keep men's power in society going.

Radical feminists believe that **violence against women** within the **family** is a form of **power and control**.

1) The **social climate** helps to **maintain this situation** by making women feel **ashamed** and **stigmatised** if they talk about the violence. The shame and stigma are part of the **ideology of patriarchy** — the school of thought that says women should **know their place**.
2) Shame also comes from the idea that women **should know better** — they shouldn't get involved with violent men in the first place. There's a tendency to **blame the victim**.
3) Dobash and Dobash found that most women who left violent partners **returned** in the end. This was because of **fear of being stigmatised** — and because they were **financially dependent** on their partner.
4) **Abusive partners** often **condition** their victim into thinking that nobody cares and there's nowhere to go. The pressure not to leave an abusive partner comes from the **relationship** as well as from society.

Remember, not all feminists agree with the radical feminist view.

Radical Feminism is **Criticised** for **Overemphasising** the **Power** of **Men**

There are **two main criticisms** of **radical feminist** theory of the family:

1) It **overemphasises** the **place** of **domestic violence** in family life. **Functionalists** argue that most families operate **harmoniously**, while **postmodern theory** argues that individuals have much more **choice** and **control** to avoid, leave or reshape their family relationships.
2) It presents men as **all-powerful** and women as **powerless** when in reality women often hold some power over men. The journalist **Melanie Phillips (2003)** highlights the fact that **women abuse men too** and **male victims** are often **ignored** by society and the police. The pressure group **Families Need Fathers** campaigns for men to have **equal rights** in **family** and **child law**.

Practice Questions

Q1 What did the Children Act 1989 do?

Q2 What proportion of violent crime in the UK is estimated to be domestic violence?

Q3 What do radical feminists think is the cause of domestic violence?

Q4 Give two criticisms of the radical feminist view of domestic violence.

Exam Question

Q1 Apply your own knowledge and material from Item A to evaluate the idea that radical feminists overemphasise the power of men in society. [20 marks]

Item A

Some feminist sociologists argue that inequality of power between men and women is responsible for unequal roles between men and women in the household. They say this is because patriarchy dictates the values of society, and these are then transferred to the home. Radical feminists have argued that domestic violence is a form of patriarchal control, but they have been criticised for crediting men with too much power.

The roles in my family are always wholemeal...

When one person in a relationship has more power than another, there can be pretty serious consequences for the family. Make sure you can explain what Marxist, functionalist and feminist sociologists say about abuse of power in relationships.

Family Diversity — Changing Family Patterns

These pages are about which family types are getting more common, and which are getting less common.

Social Trends Indicate *More Variety* of *Families* and *Households*

Official government statistics clearly show that the **variety** of family types has **increased** in Britain since the **mid 20th century**. There's now no such thing as 'the British family' — there are several kinds of family structure out there.

Look at the evidence:

1) Two of the biggest **increases** in household type have been in **single-person** households and **lone-parent family** households. The vast majority of **lone-parent** households are **matrifocal** (families where **women** are the head).
2) **Single-person households** increased by 500 000 from 2003 to 2013 — this rise could be related to the increasing number of **divorced** people and a rise in people **over 65** living alone.
3) The **fastest growing** household type is **multi-family households** — these households **increased** by **56%** between 2004 and 2014 to 313 000. This trend is partly linked to the growing number of **beanpole families** — **grandparents** might live with one of their **grown-up children** and some of their **grandchildren** in a multi-family household.
4) **Cohabitation** (living with a partner) **doubled** from 1996 to 2012 to 2.9 million couples — this number is still growing.

Increasing life expectancy means that children can become close to their grandparents, and even their great-grandparents in some cases. This creates a more 'vertical' family structure, with links between generations at different stages in their life-course (see below). Sociologists describe this as a 'beanpole family'.

There are two **overall patterns**:

1) There's been an **increase** in the **diversity** of families in the UK. There are more **different kinds** of family.
2) **The nuclear family** is still the most **common** type of family, though the **proportion** of nuclear families is going down.

Rapoport and Rapoport (1982) Identified *Five* Types of Family Diversity

Organisational diversity	**Differences** in the way families are **structured**, e.g. whether they're nuclear, extended, reconstituted or any other form.
Cultural diversity	Differences that arise from the different **norms** and **values** of **different cultures**.
Class diversity	Different **views** are often held by **different parts of society** concerning families. For example, more **affluent families** are more likely to send their children to **boarding** school than **poorer families**, leading to a different **relationship** between the parents and children.
Life-course diversity	**Diversity** caused by the **different stages** people have reached in their lives. E.g. **family relationships** tend to be different for newly-weds with children, childless couples, and people with grown-up children.
Cohort diversity	Differences created by the **historical periods** the family have lived through. For example, children who reached maturity in the **1980s** may have remained **dependent** on their parents for longer due to **high unemployment**.

People can reach each stage of the life-course at different ages.

Increasing *Individualism* and *Personal Choice* is Linked to *Family Diversity*

Giddens (1992) argues that **individual choice** dictates family relationships — he calls this the '**individualisation thesis**'.

1) **Rigid class, gender and family roles** used to stop people from choosing their own **life-course** — he argues that these fixed roles **no longer exist** and people are free to make their own decisions.
2) People do not have to stay in relationships because of **fixed social expectations** — they are free to separate and go on to form **different types of families**, e.g. lone-parent families and multi-family households.

Postmodernists claim that there is no longer a **single dominant family structure** — postmodern society is **highly diverse** and its diversity is **increasing**. They see this diversity and fragmentation as the **new norm**.

- Improvements in **women's rights** and the availability of **contraception** have resulted in people having far more **choice** in their type of relationship.
- People now tend to create their relationships to **suit their own needs** rather than following the **traditional values** of **religion** or the **government**.
- Their relationships only last as long as their needs are **met** — creating even greater **diversity** and **instability**.

Postmodernists emphasise the rise of individualism as a crucial feature of postmodern society.

Family Diversity — Changing Family Patterns

Fewer People Marry and More People **Live Together Instead**

Marriage rates have **fallen** since the **early 20th century**. In 2009, the **lowest** number of **marriages** took place in the England and Wales since records began. However, the marriage rate began to **increase** again in 2010.

This does NOT mean a decline in family life, though:

1) While **marriage rates** have **fallen**, there has been an **increase** in the number of adults **cohabiting** in the last few decades. There were **nearly 1 million more** cohabiting couples in the UK **2014** than there were in **2001**.
2) **Duncan and Phillips (2013)** have discovered that the number of people who are in a **serious relationship** but who are **not** cohabiting or married may be as many as **half** of the single population of Great Britain. They are classed as **'living apart together'**.
3) **Social trends statistics** show that living with a partner doesn't mean you **won't** get married — it often just means a **delay** in tying the knot.
4) People are getting married **later** in life — between 1971 and 2011, the **average age** of men and women getting married in England and Wales **increased** by 8 years.
5) **Men** tend to **die** before women. **Widowed pensioners** make up a lot of **single-person households**. The **population** of the UK is **ageing** (see p.73), so this helps explain why there are so many single-person households.

The proportion of births outside marriage in England and Wales has increased rapidly since 1980 to 47% in 2013 — this change is largely due to the increase in cohabiting couples who are in serious relationships.

Divorce and **Separation** are Common in England and Wales

1) There's been a **steady rise** in the **divorce rate** in most **modern industrial societies**.
2) More than **40%** of all marriages in England and Wales end in divorce.
3) **Since 2000**, the percentage of marriages ending in divorce has **fallen** — this is related to people **marrying later** in their **life-course** and the increasing number of couples who **cohabit** before getting married.
4) **Serial monogamy** (having **several serious sexual relationships** one after another) is increasingly **common** in the UK — a significant number of divorces are granted to people who have been **married** and **divorced before**.
5) **Separation** often precedes divorce — in 2011, **32%** of divorces secured by **men** and **22%** by **women** followed **2 years** of separation. In the same year, **16%** of divorces for **men** and **9%** for **women** were granted after **5 years** of separation.

There are several **social**, **cultural** and **political** factors that explain why divorce is increasing in the UK:

- Divorce has become easier to obtain — it's now more **available**.
- Divorce is more **socially acceptable**.
- Women may have **higher expectations** of marriage, and **better employment opportunities** may make them less financially dependent on their husbands.
- Marriages are increasingly focused on **individual emotional fulfilment**.

Availability and acceptability are the buzz words in the debate on divorce.

The **link** between divorce and marriage breakdown isn't completely straightforward. You **can't assume** that **fewer divorces** in the past meant **happier marriages** — a marriage can break down but the couple still **stay married** and live together. This is called an **empty-shell marriage**.

Practice Questions

Q1 Which household types have increased in the UK in recent years?

Q2 Give five types of family diversity.

Q3 Why have single-person households become more common in the UK in recent years?

Exam Question

Q1 Give a definition of the term 'life-course diversity'. [2 marks]

86% of people get bored of reading about divorce statistics...

Sometimes I wonder what sociologists would do without all of those handy official government statistics floating around out there. Anyway, jot down your own list of trends in the size of the family, the number of single-person households, the number of divorces and the number of people who are cohabiting. You have to know which are going up and which are going down.

Demography and the Family

These pages will explore changes in the demography of the UK since 1900 and the impact of these changes on UK society.

*Population Size is Affected by **Births, Deaths** and **Migration***

Demography is the study of the statistics that measure the **size** and **growth** of a **population** (e.g. birth and death rates).

1) A population generally **increases** when **birth** rates are higher than **death** (**mortality**) rates. **Low fertility** or **high mortality** rates lead to a **decline** in population, as too few children are born to **replace** those dying.
2) **Immigration** into a country causes the population to **increase**, while **emigration** away from a country **decreases** the population.

Birth** and **Fertility** Rates Have **Decreased

The **birth rate** has **fallen** since the **early 20th century**. In **2014** there were nearly **700 000** births in England and Wales — there were **1 million** in **1901**. Fertility was **unusually high** after the **First** and **Second World Wars** and in the **1960s** — those born in these periods are called **baby-boomers**. The birth rate has **fluctuated** since the mid-1970s and is now **falling**.

- The **total fertility rate** (**TFR**) is the **average number** of children a woman would have if she followed the current fertility rates throughout her life. The TFR has generally **decreased** in England and Wales since the early 20th century — in **2014**, it was **1.83 children per woman**. There were unusual **peaks** in **fertility** during the **baby booms** of the 20th century.
- **Completed family size** (**CFS**) is the average number of children for a woman born in a specific year. In **England and Wales**, for example, a woman born in **1968** has a CFS of **1.92 children** compared to **2.34** for a woman born in **1941**.

*People are Having **Fewer Children** and Having them **Later in Life***

Government statistics for **England and Wales** show that **childbearing trends** have changed in recent decades.

- People are having **fewer children**. The average number of dependent children per family was **2.0** in **1971**, compared to **1.7** in **2011**.
- Women are having children **later**. The average age of a woman at the birth of her first child was **24** in **1971**, compared to **28** in **2013**.
- More people are **not having children at all** — **9%** of women born in **1945** were childless at age **45**, compared to **20%** of women born in **1966**.

1) Social changes have influenced these trends. **Contraception** is more readily available and **women's roles are changing**. The emphasis on the **individual in post-industrial society** is a key factor.
2) Children are **expensive** and **time-consuming**, and couples may choose to spend their **time** and **money** in other ways. The **conflict** between wanting a **successful working life** and being a **mum** has made many women **put off having kids until later**.

Mortality** and **Death** Rates Have Also **Fallen** Dramatically **Since 1900

- **Infant Mortality Rates**, or **IMR** (the number of deaths of children **aged 0 to 1** per 1000 live births), and **childhood mortality** dramatically **improved** in the first half of the **20th century**. In 1901, **16.6%** of boys and **13.6%** of girls in England and Wales died before their first birthday — infant mortality is now **less than 0.5%**.
- **Adult mortality** has also fallen — the **number of deaths** per year has stayed roughly the same since 1901, but the **increase** in **population** in the 20th century means that the **proportion** of deaths has actually **fallen**.

1) **Medical advancements** in the second half of the **20th century** reduced mortality — the introduction of **vaccines**, **blood transfusions**, **antibiotics**, and better care for **pregnant women** meant that more people **survived serious illness** and **childbirth**. The creation of the **NHS** in **1948** made health care **free** and **accessible** to all.
2) The government **improved public health** by **regulating** food and drinking-water quality and enforcing **laws** to **improve cleanliness**. Improved public **awareness** of how infections are **transmitted** also led to a decline in disease.
3) **McKeown (1972)** thought that **better nutrition** was a major factor in improving mortality rates in the UK because people were more able to **fight off infection**. Critics of McKeown point out that cases of **some diseases** (like measles) **rose** as nutrition improved.

Demography and the Family

The Overall **Population** of the UK is **Ageing**

Life expectancy is the average length of time a person is expected to live. **Falling mortality** rates have led to **increased life expectancy** — 1 in 3 babies born in **2013** will have a life expectancy of **100**. **Falling infant mortality** is largely responsible for this improvement, but other factors linked to **public health** have also contributed to the trend.

The UK has an ageing population

A population **ages** when the **number** and **proportion** of older people increases. This causes the **median age** of the population (the age when **half** of the population is **younger** and **half** is **older**) to increase.
A population needs a **TFR** of **2.1** to replace the **existing** population — this is called the **replacement level**.

1) The proportion of **over 65s** in the UK is **increasing** — almost a **quarter** of the UK population is expected to be **over 65** by **2035**. The proportion of **over 85s** in the UK has **doubled** since 1985.
2) Improvement in **mortality** rates and **increasing life expectancy** mean that more people now live **past the age of 65**.
3) When the **TFR** falls below replacement level, an **ageing population** develops. The **decline** in **fertility** rates since the **late 1970s** to below **replacement level** means that fewer children are being born.
4) As a result, the **proportion** of young people in the UK is **decreasing** compared to older age groups. The **proportion** of older people in the UK is also set to **increase** as the **baby boomers** born after the **Second World War** reach their **late 80s** and the **1960s baby boomers** move into their **60s** and **70s**.

These trends have created beanpole families (p.70), which include several generations. Older generations of the family are living longer and there are fewer family members in each generation.

An **Ageing Population** Changes the **Burden of Care** in Society

1) Society has a **responsibility** to care for the **vulnerable** (e.g. children and older people) — this responsibility is called the **burden of care**, and it puts pressure on resources.
2) The burden of care shifts towards **older** people in an ageing population — at the same time, there is a decline in the proportion of **working-age** people. This **increases** the **dependency ratio** and the young **struggle** to **meet** the needs of older people.

The dependency ratio is the number of people who are not of working age, compared to the number of working-age people who can support them (e.g. by paying taxes).

Hirsch (2005) suggests that people will either have to **work into their 60s and 70s** or **pay more taxes** during their working life to contribute towards the cost of **health** and **social care** in later life. He argues that **single pensioners** compete for housing with **single young people**. This makes house prices **rise**. Hirsch points out that older people often own their own homes, but young people have **fewer assets** (possessions and property), so they **lose out**.

In the **late 1980s**, the government commissioned **the Griffiths Report** on **care in the community**. The report looked at the **long-term care** of mentally ill, disabled and older members of society with the aim of making it **more efficient**.

1) Care of older people leaving hospital used to be carried out by various **NHS services** — this responsibility was shifted to **local council social services**. This was part of a movement away from **institutionalisation** (placing people in group homes, hospitals etc.) towards **care in the home**.
2) Delivering more minor **health** and **social** care in the **home** has improved the **independence** and **comfort** of older people who do not want to move into **retirement homes** or do not need **24-hour care**. However, since the **financial crisis** in **2008**, the government has given **less money** to local councils — this has resulted in **cuts** to **services**.

Poverty in Old Age is Linked to **Social Class, Gender** and **Ageism**

Ageism (discrimination against older people because of their age) tends to **increase** in ageing populations — the needs of older people are often seen as a problem. Ageism also involves underestimating the **value** of older people to society.

1) **Peter Townsend (1979)** studied **poverty** in the UK — he discovered that there was a **higher proportion** of older people in poverty compared to younger people. He argued that an **underclass** of pensioners developed because older people could no longer rely on **income from employment** (see p.83 for more on age and poverty).
2) People with **higher status** during their working lives were **less likely** to be in poverty in old age than people who were in a **low-status job** (who are **more likely** to have suffered **unemployment** and **illness** during their working life).
3) He linked this idea to **social class** — people who were in **poverty** throughout their working life were **less** likely to have **savings** and **private pensions** to support themselves in old age.
4) **Pilcher (1995)** argues that both **class** and **gender** affect income in retirement. Women often have **smaller** pensions because they might take time **away** from work while still of working age to care for children.

Demography and the Family

Net Migration Has Significantly *Increased* Since the *Second World War*

In the UK, **net migration** (the number of people **moving into** a country **minus** the number **moving away**) reached a high of **330 000** in the year 2014-15. The **foreign-born** population of England and Wales **nearly doubled** between **1991** and **2011**.

1) Before the Second World War, the **foreign-born population** of the UK was very **low**. After the war, a **labour shortage** prompted the government to encourage Polish soldiers to move to the UK.
2) The **British Nationality Act of 1948** made it easier for citizens of the **British Commonwealth** (countries that used to be part of the British Empire) to settle in the UK. This led to a wave of **mass immigration**.
3) Until the **1980s, emigration** from the UK to countries like **Australia** and **the USA** largely **matched** immigration into Britain. However, **mass immigration** in the 1990s **outstripped emigration** and **net migration** rose rapidly.
4) In the late **1990s, war** and **political conflicts** in South Africa, Afghanistan, Iraq, Somalia, Sri Lanka and Kosovo led to an **increase** in applications for **asylum** (protection) in the UK — applications **peaked in 2002** at just over **84 000**.
5) Between **2004** and **2007**, **new countries** joined the EU and **free movement** (allowing Europeans to move freely within the EU) was introduced. **New EU migrants** arrived in the UK and contributed to **rising net migration**.

Increasing ***Net Migration*** *Has Affected the* ***Structure*** *of* ***Society*** *and* ***Families***

1) The impact of **low fertility rates** on population size in the UK is **outweighed** by the impact of net migration.
2) Migrants **decrease** the **average age** of a country, as they tend to be **young** and of **working age**. Immigration **decreases** the dependency ratio (p.73) by **increasing** the number of people able to **support** children and older people.
3) The fertility rate for mothers **not born in the UK** is **higher** than that of mothers **born in the UK**. While this **increases** the dependency ratio by increasing the number of **children** in the population, the impact is **temporary** because children of migrants will reach working age and go on to **decrease** the dependency ratio.
4) Increasing net migration has also led to an increase in **multi-family households** (see p.70 for more on this).

Globalisation Has Increased *International* Migration

Globalisation happens when nations become more **connected** and **barriers** separating societies are **broken down** — this leads to more **international migration** and more **diverse reasons** for migration.

1) Since the **1990s**, British society has become far more **ethnically diverse** — migrants have brought different **cultures** and **religions** to the UK, which has created a **multicultural society**.
2) Globalisation results in different reasons for migration — over half of the **visas** granted by the UK government between **June 2014** and **June 2015** were for **educational** purposes, while more than a **quarter** were granted to **economic migrants** (people moving for work).

Eriksen (2007) argues that migrants in a globalised world tend to form **transnational identities** — they do not belong to a **single** country but a **network** of countries across the world. They are less likely to **assimilate** (learn the **language** of a country or adapt to its **culture**) because they do not see it as a **permanent** home. Immigration becomes a **political** issue — governments have to decide whether to promote **assimilation** or accept **multiculturalism**.

Practice Questions

Q1 How have birth and death rates in England and Wales changed since 1901?

Q2 Name three things that have caused mortality rates to fall in England and Wales.

Q3 Give two main reasons why the UK population is ageing.

Q4 What is meant by 'dependency ratio'?

Q5 What is globalisation and how has it affected UK society?

Exam Question

Q1 Outline two ways that an ageing population can affect society. Explain each one. [10 marks]

Net revision = total time revising minus time spent watching cat videos...

You need to know how demographic trends have affected families and wider society. Net migration and the UK's ageing population have had a big impact. Make sure you know what sociologists have said about why these changes are happening.

Family Diversity and Social Change

Sociologists have different theories about family diversity — some argue that the nuclear family is still the most common family structure. Others think that your social identity (see p.1) influences the type of household you live in.

Functionalists Think that the Growth in Diversity has been *Exaggerated*

1) The functionalist **Robert Chester (1985)** admits that there has been **some growth** in family diversity, but believes that the **nuclear family** remains the dominant family structure.
2) He argues that statistics show a **greater increase** in diversity than is actually happening. This is because **UK society** has an **ageing population** (see p.73) — the proportion of older people is **increasing**. This increases the number of people who are at a stage in their life when they're **not in a nuclear family**.
3) Chester has also suggested that nuclear families are becoming **less traditional** and **more symmetrical** (see p.63) to better fit modern living.

Death rates have fallen for several reasons, e.g. improving standards of living, advances in health care and a decrease in manual, heavy labour jobs (Social Trends 38, 2008).

The *New Right* think Family Diversity is *Caused* by Falling Moral Standards

1) **New Right** theorists believe that family diversity is the result of a **decline** in traditional values. They see it as a **threat** to the traditional nuclear family and blame it for **antisocial behaviour** and **crime**.
2) **Murray (1989)** suggests that **single-mother** families are a principle cause of crime and social decay, because of the **lack** of a **male role model** and authority figure in the home.
3) The New Right believe that **state benefits** should be **cut** and social policy targeted to **discourage** family diversity and **promote** marriage and the nuclear family.

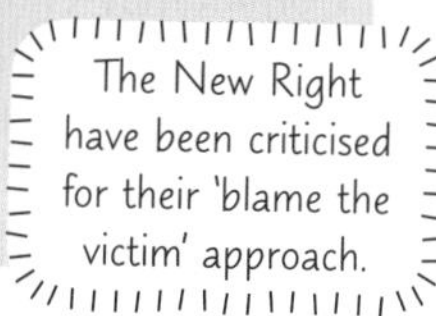
The New Right have been criticised for their 'blame the victim' approach.

The *Sociology of Personal Life* Focuses on *Individual Families*

The **sociology of personal life** looks at families from a different angle — it focuses on what the families themselves see as important in their lives rather than what sociologists **believe** is important.

1) The **individualisation thesis** states that people don't have to conform to **strict family roles** (see p.70). **Vanessa May (2013)** argues that it is based on an **idealised view** of freedom of choice. It **ignores** the differing levels of **choice** available to those who are not **white**, **middle-class males** — **social identity** affects ability to choose.
2) **Carol Smart (2007)** says that the term '**family**' is often linked to **traditional** ideas about family. She thinks the term '**personal life**' is better for studying family relationships, because it includes the **newer** kinds of relationships that exist in **postmodern** society.
3) Smart offers an **alternative** to the individualisation thesis — the **connectedness thesis** argues that individual choices are influenced by **relationships** and **past experiences**. **Class** and **gender** also influence our options where **structural inequalities** exist.
4) Smart and May both accept that **family diversity** has increased, but they believe that the importance of **individual choice** is more **limited** than postmodernists suggest.

Alex couldn't escape his family's obsession with doing the conga.

Ethnicity Can Influence *Family Type* and *Household Structure*

Immigration has had an impact on **family diversity** in England and Wales — the **2011** census found that a **higher proportion** of people who were **born abroad** lived in **multi-family households**, compared to people **born in the UK**. Also, in England and Wales, those born in **Bangladesh** or **Pakistan** were **most likely** to live in **extended families** with dependent children.

A study of **ethnic minorities in the UK** by **Modood et al (1997)** found that:

1) Whites and African-Caribbeans were most likely to be **divorced**. Indians, Pakistanis, Bangladeshis and African Asians were most likely to be **married**.
2) African-Caribbean households were the most likely to be **lone-parent families** — there is thought to be a higher proportion of **matrifocal families** (where women are the head) in African-Caribbean households in the UK.
3) **South Asian** families are traditionally **extended** families, but there are more **nuclear family** households than in the past. **Extended kinship links** stay strong and often reach back to India, Pakistan or Bangladesh.
4) However, there's **diversity** within each ethnic group.

Family Diversity and Social Change

Class and Sexuality Also Affect Which Types of Family You Experience

1) **Eversley and Bonnerjea (1982)** found that **middle-class** areas in the UK have a **higher** than average proportion of **nuclear families**. Inner-city **working-class areas** are more likely to have a higher proportion of **lone-parent households**.
2) **Weeks, Donovan et al (1999)** found that there had been an increase in the number of **gay** or **lesbian** households since the 1980s. This is due to changes in **attitudes** and **legislation**.
3) **Fertility treatments** have allowed **gay and lesbian** couples (and **single** and **older women**) to have children when they wouldn't have been able to before. This means that **family structures** exist that were **impossible** in the past.

Some Sociologists Say You Can Choose Who to Include in Your Family

The postmodernist **Beck** (1992) believes many people now live in '**negotiated families**' — family units that vary according to needs of the people in them. Negotiated families are **more equal** than nuclear families, but **less stable**.

Some sociologists argue that groups who do not fit the **traditional structure of a nuclear family** can often **decide** who they consider as family — **same-sex couples** and **lone-parent families** can choose **supportive people** to be part of their family.

Stacey (1998) has highlighted the existence of the '**divorce-extended family**' where mostly female members of an extended family stay connected by **choice** after divorce. A woman may **choose** to stay connected with her former **mother-in-law** or form a new relationship with her **ex-husband's new partner**. This is a result of **greater individualism** among women — they are able to form a **new family structure** based on their own **needs**.

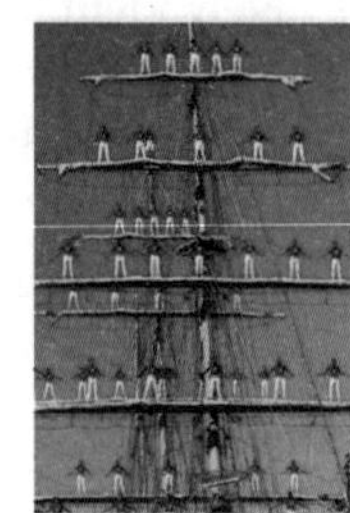
Once you start building a negotiated family, it can be pretty hard to stop.

Weeks, Donovan et al (1999) suggested that family commitment is now viewed as a matter of **ongoing negotiation** rather than something that lasts forever once entered into. **Weeks (2000)** believes that personal **morality** has become an **individual choice**, rather than a set of values influenced by **religion** or dictated by **society**. He sees modern **liberal attitudes** towards marriage, divorce, cohabitation and homosexuality as a major cause of **irreversible** diversity.

Weston (1992) has observed that **same-sex couples** often form a 'family of choice' by surrounding themselves with **supportive** members of their friends and family.

Practice Questions

Q1 Why do functionalists think that the growth in family diversity has been exaggerated?

Q2 On what grounds do New Right theorists oppose family diversity?

Q3 How has immigration contributed to changing family structure in the UK?

Q4 Give two examples of 'negotiated families'.

Exam Questions

Q1 Give a definition of the term 'negotiated family'. [2 marks]

Q2 Apply your own knowledge and material from Item A to evaluate the functionalist idea that growth in family diversity has been exaggerated. [20 marks]

Item A

Sociologists have many theories about the extent of family diversity. Some sociologists argue that people are abandoning traditional morals, with increasing acceptance of divorce and cohabitation. Immigration has also been highlighted as a contributing factor to family diversity, since family types vary by ethnic group. Alternatively, some sociologists argue that family diversity has been exaggerated because the nuclear family is still the most common family type in the UK.

Have you met the nuclear family? They make you feel right at-om...

The New Right think family diversity is the result of falling standards, Carol Smart reckons class and gender are more important than personal choice when it comes to family type, and Jeffrey Weeks thinks everyone just makes their own mind up. At least everyone agrees that diversity is increasing. Well, except functionalists. They say that families are just more symmetrical. Weird.

Childhood

These pages examine the social construction of childhood, the position of children in today's society, and the future of childhood.

Childhood is Partly a Social Construct

1) Sociologists say **childhood** is not only a **biological stage of development** but a **social construct** as well. The idea of how children are **different** from adults in their **values**, **behaviour** and **attitudes** isn't the same **everywhere** in the world, and it hasn't been the same for all **times**. In other words, it's **not universal** — different societies, with different **cultures** and **values**, can view childhood in different ways.
2) An example of this is how the age that you can **leave education** in Britain has moved from 12 to 18 in the last century. It would now be not only **socially unacceptable**, but also **illegal**, to leave school and **work full-time** at the age of 12.
3) The minimum legal age for **marriage** in Britain rose to **16** in **1929** — before that, girls could be married at **12** and boys at **14** (although in England and Wales they needed **parental permission**). Effectively, the age at which **childhood ends** and **adulthood begins** has moved in line with social attitudes.
4) **Jane Pilcher (1995)** highlighted the **separateness** of childhood from other **life phases**. Children have different **rights** and **duties** from adults, and are **regulated** and **protected** by special **laws**.

Ariès says a Cult of Childhood Developed After Industrialisation

Sociologist Philippe Ariès' work on the **construction of childhood** is a classic study.

Ariès (1962) looked at paintings

Ariès said that the concept of **childhood** in Western European society has only existed in the **last 300 years**. Before this, in **medieval** society, a child took on the role of an adult as soon as it was **physically able**. Children in medieval paintings look like **mini-adults**.

With **industrialisation**, social attitudes changed and people began to **value** children as needing **specialised care and nurturing**. The importance of the child reinforced the importance of the role of the **housewife** — it was the housewife's job to look after children.

This **'cult of the child'**, as Ariès referred to it, first developed in the **middle classes** and over time has become a part of **working-class values**.

Although Ariès' work is very important, he has been criticised — e.g. **Pollack (1983)** says that Ariès' work looks **weak** because it uses paintings for its **main evidence**.

Functionalists See the Position of Children in Society as a Sign of Progress

Some functionalist sociologists, including **Shorter (1975)**, make the '**march of progress**' argument:

1) Society has a functional need for **better-educated** citizens and **lower infant mortality rates**.
2) So school leaving ages have **gone up** and child protection has **improved**.
3) That means that the current position of children is the result of **positive progression** from the past.

The Status of Children Has Changed — Society is More Child-Focused

1) **Donzelot (1977)** has observed that theories of **child development** changed in the **19th century** — they began to argue that children needed to be **protected** and **supervised**. He linked this to **growing medical interest** in childhood development.
2) **Infant mortality** has dramatically **decreased** since the **early 20th century**. In **1901** just over **150** children aged under one died per 1000 children, but in **2012**, this rate had fallen to **3.9** deaths per 1000 children.
3) Families are also getting **smaller**. Fewer children die in infancy and families are **having fewer children** on average. **More attention is devoted** to each child and **more money is being spent** on their development, both within the family and wider society.
4) This is linked to the '**march of progress**' argument, which suggests that families are increasingly **child-focused** — parents want a **better life** for their children than they have experienced themselves.

Harry's family found an alternative to surrounding him in cotton wool.

Childhood

Children are Protected by **Special Laws**

1) Children are subject to laws that restrict their **sexual behaviour**, their **access to alcohol and tobacco**, and the amount of **paid work** they can perform. These laws act **in addition** to the laws that affect adults.
2) Children are offered **additional protection** by the **Children Act 1989**, which allows them to be **taken away from their parents** by the state if it judges the parents to be **incapable** or **unsuitable**.
3) But organisations such as the **National Society for the Prevention of Cruelty to Children** (the **NSPCC**) argue that they need greater protection. An NSPCC report by **Cawson et al (2000)** said that **16%** of children aged under 16 have experienced **sexual abuse** during childhood, and **25%** of children have experienced **physical violence**.

Child Liberationists Believe that Society **Oppresses** Children

Some see the increased **protection** of children and their **separation** from adult life as **oppressive**.

Diana Gittins (1985) argues that there is an 'age patriarchy' — adults **maintain authority** over children. They achieve this using **enforced dependency** through 'protection' from paid employment, legal controls over what children can and can't do, and in extreme cases abuse and neglect.

Hockey and James (1993) noted that childhood was a stage that most children wished to **escape from** and which many **resisted**.

Childhood **Varies** according to **Class, Gender** and **Ethnicity**

Some sociologists suggest that the **experience** of childhood varies depending on class, gender and ethnicity:

1) Children living in **poverty** tend to suffer **poorer health**, a lack of **basic necessities**, **lower achievement** in school, poorer life chances, and higher incidences of **neglect** and **abuse**. Children from low-income, **working-class families** are more likely to live in poverty — in **2013-14**, **17%** of children in the UK were living in **low-income households**.
2) **June Statham and Charlie Owens (2007)** found that **black** and **dual-heritage** children were **more likely** to end up in **care** than white or Asian children.
3) **Ethnicity** may **influence** where a child **lives**. For example, in England and Wales in **2011**, **22%** of **white British** people lived in rural areas, compared to **1%** of **Bangladeshis** and **Pakistanis**.
4) **Julia Brannen (1994)** said that **Asian** families were much **stricter** with their **daughters** than their **sons**.
5) **Hillman et al (1990)** studied children aged 7 to 15 and found that parents generally give **boys** more **freedom** than **girls** to travel around their local areas **unaccompanied**, **cross roads**, and go out **after dark**.
6) **Bonke (1999)** has discovered that **girls** perform more **household chores** than boys — this trend is particularly true in **lone-parent** households.

Households earning less than 60% of the median income.

Ideas of Childhood are **Different** in Different **Cultures**

Wagg (1992) argues that the construction of childhood **varies** across different **historical** and **cultural** societies. Because of these **cross-cultural differences**, children are not always seen as **vulnerable** and can have a **similar status** to adults.

Punch (2001) found that children growing up in the **countryside in Bolivia** were given **responsibilities** and **work** to perform at the age of 5. This **contrasts** with **Western attitudes** towards child labour that have developed since **industrialisation**.

Katz (2004) has found that **Sudanese** children have far **more freedom** to **explore** and **travel** around their local area than children in Western societies.

Children in less industrialised societies are often treated differently to children living in Western societies. Some argue that ideas of **Western childhood** are **projected** onto different cultures.

Judith Ennew (1986) argued that **humanitarian** and **welfare work** is often based on the belief that Western childhood is the '**correct childhood**'. The idea that childhood should be a **separate**, more **innocent** stage of life can be projected through this work onto cultures that may have **different views** on the needs of children.

Childhood

British Society Today is **More Child-Focused** than Ever

1) Children are now recognised as having unique **human rights**. The **United Nations Convention on the Rights of the Child** was ratified (agreed to) in 1990 by all the UN members (except the USA and Somalia).
2) In Britain, the **Child Support Act 1991** established the **Child Support Agency**. This gave children the legal right to be **financially supported** by their parents, whether the parents are **living with the child or not**. This Act also made courts have to ask for the **child's point of view** in custody cases and take the child's view into consideration.

Advertisers recognise the **financial power** of children — this is often referred to as '**pester power**'. They advertise a product to children because they know the children will **pester** their parents to buy the product.

Sociologists Have Looked at the Impact of **Postmodern Society** on Childhood

1) **Jenks (2005)** argues that the **20th century** was focused on the '**futurity**' of the child — children symbolised **future potential** and were the main concern of society. Adults **sacrificed** their needs to **protect** and **nurture** children.
2) Jenks believes that adult relationships are now **less dependable** due to **divorce** becoming more common — adults prioritise their relationships with children instead of **investing trust** in relationships with **friends** and **partners**.
3) Adults see children through a lens of **nostalgia** — children **represent** a lot of the things that **society has lost** over time (like **innocence**). This has led to increased **protection** and **surveillance** of children.
4) Critics of Jenks' theory say he makes too many **generalisations**.
5) **Palmer (2007)** believes children are now experiencing '**toxic childhood**' — children's lives are more **violent**, **stressful**, and **sexually active**, which leads to **teenage pregnancy**, **obesity**, **self-harm** and **addiction** to alcohol and drugs. She also argues that children's **development** has been **damaged** by the increasing speed of **technological advancement**.

Sociologists **Disagree** over the **Future** of Childhood

1) **Neil Postman (1994)** believes that childhood is **disappearing**.
2) Children grow up **very quickly** and experience things only available to adults in the past.
3) This is due to a **shift** from **print** and literary culture to **visual** culture. Lack of **literacy** is no longer a barrier to the adult world — children can access it through **watching TV**.
4) He argues that our definitions of 'childhood' and 'adulthood' will need to be **changed** soon.

1) **Nick Lee (2005)** disagrees with Postman.
2) He agrees that childhood has become an **ambiguous** area, but argues that parents have **financial control** and children can only spend as much as their parents allow.
3) So the **paradox of childhood** is one of **dependence** and **independence** at the same time.
4) **Opie (1993)** argues that **childhood culture** still exists **independently** of adult influence.

Practice Questions

Q1 Explain the view that childhood is partly a social construct.

Q2 Describe how functionalists see the role of children in society.

Q3 How do class, ethnicity and gender influence a person's experience of childhood? Give examples.

Q4 Give two ways in which 21st century British society could be said to be more child-focused than before.

Q5 What arguments have been put forward to support the view that childhood is disappearing?

Exam Questions

Q1 Give a definition of the term 'toxic childhood'. [2 marks]

Q2 How might children be oppressed by society? Use one example to briefly explain your answer. [2 marks]

Here's looking at you, kid...

It's all a bit dramatic really. Toxic childhoods. Disappearing innocence. Evil parent overlords ruling children. Ahem... sorry... got a bit carried away there. The main ideas on these pages are that childhood is partly socially constructed and that theories about it are not universally accepted. It's not enough to say that something is a 'social construct' — you need to say how and why.

Definitions of Poverty

Poverty is basically about not having enough money. However, sociologists don't all agree on exactly what constitutes poverty, and how badly off you must be to be 'in poverty'. There are quite a few definitions...

Absolute Poverty** is a Lack of the **Minimum Requirements** for **Survival

1) An individual is in absolute **poverty** if they can't afford the basic necessities — **food**, **warmth** and **shelter**.
2) **Rowntree (1871-1954)** set up the first major studies of poverty in the UK in **1899** and measured it in absolute terms. He made a **list of essentials** needed for life and recorded how many families could **afford** them. Those whose income was **too low** were classed as **in poverty**. People were shocked that a large proportion of **York** was in poverty.
3) There are criticisms of Rowntree's study. His definition of poverty didn't allow for any wasted food and it assumed the **cheapest** options were **always available**. The lists were compiled by **experts** and **didn't match the lifestyle** of the folk he surveyed. He did listen to his critics though, and for two further studies (published in 1941 and 1951), he **added more items** to the list of essentials. By this time, **more people** could afford the basics on the list. His conclusion was that **poverty was disappearing fast** in 20th century Britain.
4) Another **study of poverty in absolute terms** is **Drewnowski and Scott (1966)**. They devised a **"level of living index"** which worked out the income needed for **basic needs**, adding **cultural needs** to the list. However, it's debatable whether cultural needs like TV should be included in a study of **absolute** poverty.

Measuring absolute poverty means making assumptions about people's basic needs. It also assumes that everyone has the same basic needs. It disregards information about occupation, gender and age that might be relevant to deciding someone's basic needs.

***Bradshaw (1990)** Devised the **Budget Standard Measure** of Poverty*

1) **Bradshaw (1990)** used an approach similar to Rowntree's idea of **absolute poverty**. He studied the **spending patterns** of the least wealthy and used those patterns to calculate an **adequate budget**. Anyone earning less than the adequate budget was classed as **"poor"**.
2) The main difference between the approaches was that Bradshaw studied how people **actually spend their money** whereas Rowntree assumed people weren't poor if they earned more than the **usual total cost of essential items**.
3) Because Bradshaw's test isn't relative (see below), it gives clear and unambiguous statistics that are easy to **compare** between different studies. However, critics have argued that Bradshaw set a **very low 'adequate budget'**, so his conclusions are not a **true reflection of deprivation** in society.

Relative Poverty** is a **Comparison** with the **Average Standard of Living

1) Many sociologists favour the **relative** definition of poverty. This considers whether an individual is rich or poor in **relation** to **other people** in their society, rather than whether people have the basics like food and shelter.
2) The **downside** of relative poverty is that some people will always **appear to be "poor"**. Also, if the rich get richer **more quickly** than the poor get richer, then relative poverty will **increase** even though the lives of the poor **improve**.

Townsend (1979)** Introduced the Concept of **Relative Deprivation

1) **Townsend (1979)** devised a "**deprivation index**" — a list of 60 things **central to life** in the UK. The list included **social activities**, such as inviting other people over for meals, and **possessions**, such as owning a refrigerator.
2) From his list of 60 things, he selected **12** that he thought were **equally essential to the whole population**.
3) He then gave each household a **deprivation score** based on whether or not they had the items on his shortlist of 12 items.
4) Looking at his statistics, he found that the deprivation score **went up rapidly** after wealth dropped **below a certain threshold**. The threshold was about 150% of the 1979 basic supplementary benefit levels (now called income support).
5) So he said all households **earning below the threshold** were **"suffering from poverty"**.
6) Townsend calculated that **22.9%** of the population were suffering from relative poverty.

Barney was well stocked in all his essential life items.

- **Piachaud (1987)** has argued that Townsend's deprivation index is too **subjective** and **culturally biased**, citing shortlist items such as having **cooked breakfasts** and **Sunday joints**.
- **Wedderburn** also criticised Townsend's method for creating the deprivation index. She argued that he should have carried out **research** into the customary behaviour of people in society. It seemed to her as though he had just picked items based on his own **cultural opinions**.

Definitions of Poverty

Mack and Lansley (1985) Measured Poverty using a Consensual Approach

1) **Mack and Lansley (1985)** measured poverty in a similar way to Townsend, but acted on some of the criticisms his work had received. They defined poverty to be "an **enforced lack** of **socially perceived necessities**".
2) They used a **survey** to determine which items to include on their list of perceived necessities. They asked respondents what they considered to be the necessities. Any items that were classified as essential by **over 50%** of the respondents were added to their list. They ended up with a list of **22 items**.
3) They then surveyed households to find out what they lacked. Households could answer that they had the item, didn't want the item, or **wanted but couldn't afford the item**. Only those who said the latter were considered **deprived**. Mack and Lansley therefore argued that their figures would only reflect **involuntary** deprivation.
4) If a household involuntarily lacked **three or more items** from the list of necessities then they were classified as **poor**.
5) Mack and Lansley reported that **14%** of the British population were living in poverty in **1983**. When they repeated the study in **1990**, they found that this figure had risen to **21%**. In **2012**, a Poverty and Social Exclusion (PSE) report found that **33%** of the population were living in poverty according to this method.
6) The list of necessities **changes** over time — e.g. a **telephone** was considered a necessity in the 1990 study whereas it hadn't been in the 1983 survey. Critics have argued that because the surveys didn't produce **the same list of necessities**, the results are **not directly comparable**.

Subjective Poverty — whether people Think they're in Poverty

1) **Subjective poverty** is based on **how** poor people **feel**. It's their **own evaluation** of how much money they **need** to live a decent life. It all depends on their **expectations**.
2) Subjective poverty studies ask **questions** such as 'What **income** do you think is **necessary** to keep a household such as yours out of poverty?', and 'How far **above or below** that level is your household's income?'.
3) The Poverty and Social Exclusion Survey (2000) found that the proportion of people who consider **themselves** to be in poverty was **similar** to the 'scientific' consensual poverty figure. This means subjective poverty is a **good way** of assessing how **widespread** poverty is (although the **same people** aren't necessarily 'in poverty' according to **both** measures).

Social Exclusion — when people Can't Participate in Society

1) Social exclusion is about a much **wider range of deprivation** than just being short of money. It involves not being able to **participate** in **normal activities**, whether economic, social, cultural or political, as well as not being able to **access services**.
2) The **government** said social exclusion can occur when "people or areas suffer from a **combination** of **linked problems** such as unemployment, poor skills, low incomes, poor housing, high crime environments, bad health and family breakdown."
3) Factors such as **age** and **disability** contribute to social exclusion, but the Poverty and Social Exclusion Survey (2000) found that **poverty** has the **biggest effect**.
4) These problems trap people in a "**spiral of disadvantage**" (Department of Social Security, 1999) and **limit their opportunities**, as well as those of their children. For example, low income may mean having to live in an area with poor schools, reducing their children's later chances.

Practice Questions

Q1 What is absolute poverty?

Q2 Outline how Townsend measured relative poverty.

Q3 List three problems that can combine to cause social exclusion.

Exam Question

Q1 Give a definition of the term 'subjective poverty'. [2 marks]

Poverty is a bad thing, no matter how you measure it...

Many people think that absolute poverty isn't much of a problem in the UK. However, the dramatic rise in the number of people needing to use food banks over recent years may suggest otherwise. Learn the three definitions of poverty, and make sure you know that social exclusion is what happens when different problems all join forces to damage people's well-being.

The Distribution of Poverty, Wealth and Income

Wealth isn't equally distributed. In fact, the richest 10% of UK society own over half the country's wealth, whereas the poorest 50% have only 6% of the wealth. Also, people belonging to some social groups are much more likely to be poor than others...

Wealth and Income are Different

1) Wealth is defined in official statistics as the **value of all the possessions** of an individual **minus** any **debt**. It includes houses, land, money in the bank, shares and personal goods.
2) **Wealth** largely results from ownership of **business** and **property**. Most of this gets **passed down** to the **next generation**, so wealth **stays in the same families** for years. However, lots of the richest people in Britain have generated their own wealth.
3) The vast **majority** of the British population **doesn't have significant wealth**. For most individuals their money comes from an **income**. Income is defined as the **personal funds an individual receives** on a **monthly / yearly basis**. This is usually from a **job** but can be from **benefits**, or **interest** on a savings account.

£9.18 a month just doesn't go as far as it did in my day.

Recent Changes in Society Have Increased the Gap between Rich and Poor

1) Household **disposable income per head** has **grown steadily** in the UK since the early 1980s. This reflects **overall growth in the economy**, and could be said to show that **everyone is getting richer** to some extent.
2) On the other hand, the **gap** between **rich and poor** has **widened** in recent years (according to the Social Market Foundation, an independent public policy think tank). This means that the rich are getting richer whilst the poor are getting **relatively** poorer. Ahhh... the stuff sociology is made of...

- The gap between the income of the rich and the income of the poor **went down** in the **1970s**. Under the **Labour government (1974-1979)**, **benefits** given to the poor **went up** and taxes paid by the rich were **very high**.
- In the **1980s**, under the Conservative government, the **gap widened**. The top rate of tax went down so the **rich kept more of their earnings**. Taxes that everyone pays like **VAT** and **fuel tax** went up. The economy did well, so rich people earned more money on their **investments**. **Benefits** went **down**.
- **Adonis and Pollard (1997)** reported that the gap continued to widen into the 1990s. In addition to policies introduced during the 1980s, they identified the **increase in private education** as a factor affecting wealth distribution.
- An **Office of National Statistics** report by **Penny Babb (2004)** based on the 2001 census suggested that the gap between rich and poor continued to grow under New Labour. A **Centre for Welfare Reform** report by **Simon Duffy (2014)** suggests that the **Coalition's VAT increase** and **benefit cuts** hit the **poorest** section of society the **hardest**.
- There has been an **increase** in the number of **lone-parent households**, who tend to have less money (see the next page). This means the statistics show **more poorer households**.
- There are also more **dual-income households** — e.g. families where both parents work. Income is measured by household, so a **household with two people** in **good jobs** is relatively rich. This contributes to the statistics showing an **increase in rich households**.

Some Social Groups are More Likely to be Poor Than Others

The government measure of poverty in the UK is an income of **less than 60% of the median income**. (The **median** income is the **middle** income. **Half** the population **earn more** than the median, **half** of them **earn less**.)

It's a measure of **relative poverty** — it **changes** in line with the incomes of the rest of the population.

Social Class affects Wealth, Income and Poverty

1) This isn't surprising. The factors determining social class, such as type of **job**, are **closely linked** to **economic well-being**. People in unskilled, manual jobs tend to have **lower wages** and **less job security** than those higher up the socio-economic scale.
2) People in higher social classes are more likely to get **better qualifications**, leading to better-paid jobs. **Smith, Smith and Wright (1997)** suggest that a reason for this is that **market-driven educational reforms** (p.33) favour middle-class children.
3) Middle-class people can continue working for longer because they tend to have **better health**.

The Distribution of Poverty, Wealth and Income

Income *Also Seems to be Related to* ***Ethnicity***

1) Census data shows that **White British** and **Indian** people are **much more likely** to be in **paid work** than **Bangladeshi**, **Pakistani** and **Black African** people. The difference for **women** is **much greater** — probably due to **cultural** reasons, e.g. women in some cultures are traditionally expected to stay at **home** to look after the children.
2) Studies have also shown that Bangladeshis, Pakistanis and Black Africans are generally **less well paid**.
3) **Family structure** also has an impact — the ethnic minorities which tend to have **more children**, or a greater proportion of **lone-parent families** (see below), are likely to be less well off.
4) **Racism** and **discrimination** are also thought to **limit the opportunities** of people from some ethnic groups. Also, if **English** is not someone's **first language**, this might pose another barrier.

Lone-Parent Families *are More Likely to be Poor*

1) Raising children is **expensive**, so families **with children** are **more likely** to be in **poverty** than families without them.
2) **Lone-parent families** are **more likely** to be poor than **two-parent families**. In 2015, the **Department for Work and Pensions** (DWP) found that **41%** of children in **lone-parent families** live in **relative poverty** — about **double** the proportion of children in **two-parent families** that do. It's hard to get **good work** and **look after kids** at the same time.

Women *are* ***Slightly*** *More Likely to be* ***Poor*** *than Men*

1) This difference is partly because women are **more likely** to be **lone parents** than men, and **female** lone parents tend to be from **less affluent** backgrounds in the first place. **Working mums** are more likely to be in **part-time jobs** that fit in with childcare, but that pay less.
2) **Single female pensioners** are **more likely** to have **low incomes** than single male pensioners.

Age *is a Factor too*

1) **Children** in the UK are statistically **more likely** to live in low-income households than the population as a whole. DWP (2010) data has shown that unless an adult in their family **works full time**, there's a **high chance** that a child will be in **relative poverty**.
2) **Pensioners** are now **less likely** than non-pensioners to live in **poverty**, even though the opposite was true until about 15 years ago. This could be due to **more generous benefits** for pensioners.

These benefits include things like payments to help with winter fuel bills.

Disabled *people are More Likely to have* ***Low Incomes*** *too*

1) Disabled adults are **twice as likely** as non-disabled adults to live in low-income households. This is because disabled adults are **more likely** to be **low paid** or **not in work**.
2) They often either **can't work** or face **discrimination** in the job market. They may have also had poorer access to **education**, making them **less qualified** on average than other people.

Practice Questions

Q1 Give three reasons why the gap between rich and poor has widened since the 1980s.

Q2 Explain why a person's social class affects their chance of being in poverty.

Q3 Give two reasons why disabled people are more likely to be in poverty than others.

Exam Question

Q1 How is wealth different to income? Use one example to briefly explain your answer. [2 marks]

Disposable income — money you can throw away...

Remember that the gap between rich and poor went down, then up again. It's mainly related to tax and benefits — fun stuff. It's also important to remember that the information on these pages is all based on statistics. It doesn't mean that every single person in these groups is going to be living in poverty, just that they're a bit more likely to be — some over-65s are loaded...

Explanations of Poverty

Unsurprisingly, different schools of sociological thought have different explanations of why poverty exists.

Early Theories **Blamed the Poor** for Being Poor

1) The first theories of poverty **blamed the individual** for the poverty they were in.
2) The **19th century** sociologist **Herbert Spencer** said the **poor** were those in society who had **failed** to do the best for themselves. He suggested that they were **immoral**, **lazy** and more interested in **booze** than an **honest day's work**.
3) Spencer said the **state shouldn't intervene** to help the poor because the poor are a useful **example to others** not to follow that way of life.

Rich footballers are always impeccably moral and teetotal.

Oscar Lewis said **Culture** was the **Cause of Poverty**

Lewis (1959, 1961, 1966) studied the poor in Mexico and Puerto Rico

Lewis thought that the **values**, **norms** and **behaviour** of the **poor** were **different** to the rest of society and these values were passed on from generation to generation. He said individuals **learn** how to be poor and learn to **expect** to be poor through the subculture of poverty they're socialised into.

He reckoned that this **culture** of resignation, apathy and lack of participation in wider society initially starts as a response to poverty but then becomes a culture which keeps people in poverty. He called it a '**design for life**'.

1) Lewis's work was **controversial** and **criticised** from the start. Similar research done at the same time found **highly organised community facilities** and **political involvement**.
2) **Schwartz (1975)** concluded that the poor **weren't culturally different** from the well-off.

1) Situational Constraints theory says that the poor have the **same values and norms** as the **rest of society** and any difference in the **behaviour** of the poor is because they're **limited** by their **poverty**. For example, unemployment restricts lifestyle options.
2) **Coates and Silburn (1970)** studied poor areas of Nottingham. They found that **some people** in poor areas **did feel resigned to being poor**, and that it wasn't worth trying to get out of poverty. But... they said this was a **realistic assessment** of an individual's situation. It **wasn't proof** of some kind of **alternative value system**.
3) Coates and Silburn's research supported the idea that **poverty leads to other forms of deprivation** which can trap people into a **cycle of deprivation**. This means poverty is **practically hard to get out of**, not culturally hard to get out of.

Functionalists Say **Unequal Distribution** of **Wealth** is **Good** for Society

1) Functionalism says that some people are richer or poorer than others because **society functions that way**. It says that there needs to be a way of allocating people to **suitable roles and jobs**. The **top jobs** need to be **rewarded more highly** than others to motivate **intelligent people** to train for them.
2) American sociologist **Herbert J. Gans (1971)** identified many **functions of poverty**, for example:

- Poverty makes sure that there are people willing to do **dirty, dangerous or menial jobs** for low wages.
- Poverty **creates jobs** in occupations serving the poor, e.g. social workers.
- Poor people make the rest of the population feel **more fortunate**. It's also easy to **blame** this section of society for social problems. Alternatively, **helping** the poor (e.g. through donating to **charity** or **volunteering**) provides people with an opportunity for '**emotional satisfaction**'.

3) Functionalist arguments have been **criticised** — they assume the best jobs are allocated on the basis of **talent** when in reality **discrimination** by social class, age, ethnicity and gender often influences who gets the top jobs.

Explanations of Poverty

Marxists Blame Capitalism for Inequalities in Wealth and Income

1) According to Marx and his followers, **capitalism thrives** on **inequality of income** — if wealth was distributed equally there wouldn't be any profit for the capitalists. The capitalist class **needs profit** to maintain its **power in society**.
2) Marxism says **exploitation** is an **essential part of capitalism**, and inequalities in **wealth** and **income** are a central part of that exploitation.
3) **Kincaid's (1973)** explanation of **why poverty is needed** goes like this:

As you may have noticed, the Marxist explanations are quite similar for most things. Capitalism, exploitation, etc., etc...

- The low-paid provide a **cheap labour supply** for the **capitalist class**, which keeps **profits high**.
- The varying pay levels within the working class keep individuals **competing** against each other to get the best jobs. This **divides the working class**. Marxism says that if the working class all **united together** they'd be a **threat** to capitalism — so it's in the **interests of capitalism** to keep the **working class divided**.
- Kincaid believes poverty is **not an accident** — he thinks it's an **inbuilt part** of the capitalist system.

Marxist Explanations of Poverty Have Been Criticised

1) Marxist explanations of poverty **don't explain** why some groups are more likely to experience poverty than others. Marxists treat poverty as a **characteristic of capitalism**, and as something that the **working class as a whole** suffers. They don't look for much **detail** about the experience of poverty for **individuals** or **groups**.
2) Marxism **ignores** the effects of **gender** and **ethnicity** on poverty. It doesn't explain why **women** are more likely to be poor than **men**, or why **Bangladeshi** households are more likely to be poor than other households.
3) **Capitalism** creates **wealth** in the economy. Increase in wealth contributes to the **reduction of absolute poverty**.

Weberians Say Distribution of Wealth is Based on Market Situation

1) Weberian sociologists (followers of **Max Weber**) say that the distribution of wealth and income is based on what they call **market situation**.
2) An individual's market situation is how **valuable** their **skills** are for society and how **scarce** their skills are. It's about **supply and demand** of skills. High demand for your skills makes them worth more.
3) For example, currently **plumbers** can earn **higher wages** than other skilled manual workers, because there's a **shortage** of plumbers and people **need their skills**. So plumbers have a good market situation at the moment.
4) Weberians say **poor people** have a **poor market situation**.
5) There **isn't always the same demand** for the **same skills** — the same people don't always have the best market situation. This means there's always some **movement of wealth in society**.
6) **Dean and Taylor-Gooby (1992)** think that **changes in the UK labour market** have led to increased poverty. There are more casual and temporary jobs, but less job security and far fewer "jobs for life". Dean and Taylor-Gooby say this means more people are likely to experience poverty at some point.
7) Individuals **compete** to improve their market situation:

- **Powerful people** like judges, politicians and the directors of big companies can **do the most** to keep themselves in a good market situation.
- **Low-status** workers don't have much power to improve their labour market situation. **Townsend (1970, 1979)** believes that this is the key **explanation for poverty.**

The Feminist Perspective says that Things are Worse for Women

1) The official figures say that women in the UK are only **slightly more likely** to be in poverty than men, and that this is due to women being more likely to be **lone parents** or **single pensioners** (see p.83).
2) However, feminists say that the **real situation** is far more **unequal**. They claim that because lots of poverty research focuses on the **formal economy** and **work**, the experiences of women's **domestic lives** are often ignored.
3) For example, some studies have shown that:

- in **couples**, men tend to have **more money** to spend on **themselves** than women.
- women are more likely to make **sacrifices**, such as going **without food**, to provide for their children.

Explanations of Poverty

New Right Theorists Blame Dependency on Welfare for Poverty

1) **Charles Murray (1993)** said there's a sector of society who have a **culture of dependency** on the **state** and an **unwillingness to work**. He called this group the **underclass**.
2) Murray identified the **rising number** of **lone-parent families**, **rising crime** and **attitudes** of **resistance to work**. Murray accepts that **not all** poor people are work-shy but he thinks a **significant group** just don't want to work.
3) In Murray's opinion, **Welfare State benefits** are **too high**. He says this means there's not much encouragement to get off welfare and get a job.
4) Another right-wing sociologist, **Marsland (1989)**, thinks that the **level of poverty** is **exaggerated** by other writers. He says society should **keep a small level of poverty** to **motivate** others to work. Marsland agrees with Murray that the **Welfare State is too generous** and encourages a **culture of non-work** amongst some groups.

Tinkerbell and Lewis were unwilling to work.

Sociological **criticism** of Murray says his **evidence** for the existence of an underclass is **too weak**. **Walker (1990)** found very little evidence of **different values** and **behaviour** among the poor. His opinion was that **blaming** the poor **distracts** from the **real causes** of poverty such as the **failure** of **social policy**. It also ignores factors such as **unemployment** and **disability** that individuals can't control.

Social Democrats Blame Poverty on Structural Causes

1) Social democrats believe that the **capitalist system** and the way **society** is **structured** will always mean that some groups hold a **weak economic position** in the labour market (e.g. the disabled).
2) They believe **inequality** in **wealth and income** is the root cause of poverty, so they want government policy to **redistribute wealth** and **resources** from **rich** to **poor**.
3) The big idea is that the state **can** work to stamp out poverty — and that the state **should** work to stamp out poverty.

Social democratic theory believes that inequalities can be addressed by the state through increased welfare spending.

Practice Questions

Q1 Why did Spencer argue that the poor are good for society?

Q2 What did Lewis (1959, 1961, 1966) mean by the term 'design for life'?

Q3 Give an example of how poverty is helpful to the capitalist class, from a Marxist perspective.

Q4 How does an individual's market situation affect their wealth?

Q5 According to Murray (1993), what are the characteristics of the 'underclass'?

Exam Questions

Q1 How might an uneven distribution of wealth be good for society? Outline three ways. [6 marks]

Q2 Apply your own knowledge and material from Item A to evaluate the idea that capitalism is to blame for poverty. [20 marks]

Item A

Some sociologists argue that an inequality of income benefits a capitalist system, as it allows the poor to be exploited to the advantage of the rich. An inexpensive supply of labour allows the capitalist class to generate high profits, and maintain their power in society. In this way, poverty can be seen as an essential part of capitalism.

Blame the victim or blame the system...

It's not as easy as you might think to explain why people get stuck in poverty. Each of these theories makes some sense, but they don't account for all the factors. When you're answering questions about why poverty exists, remember the downsides of each theory, and that there are lots of different groups in society — the reasons why they experience poverty may differ.

Social Policy and Poverty

Welfare means all the institutions that look after people — whether they're state-provided or not.

Four Sectors provide Welfare — **Public**, **Private**, **Voluntary** and **Informal**

Public (or State) Welfare

The **British Welfare State** was set up in the 1940s and was designed to wipe out the **social problems** of society, such as **poor health**, **poor housing** and **poverty**. It provides **services** which are **funded**, **regulated** and **run by the state**, e.g. the **NHS**, the free **education system** and the **benefits system**. The idea was that people **in work** would pay into a **national insurance scheme** which would pay for the Welfare State, making it **free** at the point when you actually **need it**.

This system is **still in operation**, but there are also **three other sectors** providing welfare.

Private Sector

These services are **run by companies for profit**. They often offer **alternatives** to state services — e.g. **private hospitals** and **schools**. They're not state-funded but they have to **meet state regulations**. The individual **pays for these services directly**.

Voluntary Sector

These services are provided by **charity**. They often provide **extra** facilities and services beyond what the state provides, e.g. the **hospice** movement and **Age UK**. They have to **conform to state regulations**. Voluntary services **may get some state funding**. The individual receives these services **free** or at a **subsidised low cost**.

Informal Sector

This means services and help provided by **friends and family**. The informal sector often provides services **in addition to state services** or when there **isn't enough state provision**. Examples: **family carers**, **family childminders**. There's **little** or **no state funding** or **regulation**. It's usually **free** to the individual but **costs the provider money**.

Benefits can be **Universal** or **Means-Tested**

Universal benefits are paid to everyone regardless of wealth.
Means-tested benefits are targeted at those **most in need**, such as those on **lower incomes**.

	Universal benefits	Means-tested benefits
Advantages	• Simple and cheap to administer. • No stigma attached to them. • Promote idea of citizenship.	• Less money is paid out, reducing welfare spending.
Disadvantages	• Wastes money, as many recipients don't need them.	• Costly to administer. • People in need might not claim them due to social stigma or because they don't know about them. • People whose income is just above the threshold may be left in need.
Examples	Winter fuel payments for pensioners	Free school meals, child benefit

The **New Right** believes in the Reduction of the **Welfare State**

1) The **New Right** thinks that a **generous welfare state** actually **makes people poorer**.
2) British New Right thinker **Marsland (1989)** thinks all **universal benefits** should be abolished because they **encourage dependency**. He says that **means-tested benefits** should be used to support those in the most desperate need for the shortest possible time. He argues that this will encourage people to "stand on their own two feet".
3) **Right-wing policy** encourages **business** so that **wealth will be created**. Right-wing politicians would prefer everyone to make their own money and decide how to spend it, instead of paying lots of tax or getting benefits from the state.
4) American sociologist **Murray (1993)** recommended a "**moral**" benefits system to discourage people from forming **lone-parent families**. He thought that unmarried mums should get no benefit at all.

Some **criticisms** of the **New Right solutions**:

1) Means-testing benefits cause a '**trap**' — getting a low-paid job may mean you **lose the benefit** and are **no better off**.
2) Poor people may end up with **second-class services** if other people are expected to use **private providers**.

Social Policy and Poverty

State Welfare Provision has been *Declining*

1) The British system is based on **welfare pluralism** (the combination of all four types of welfare provision). Since the 1979 Conservative government, there has been a **steady growth** in **private**, **voluntary** and **informal sector welfare** and a **relative decline** in **public sector welfare**. For example, local authority care homes have been closed and replaced by private care homes, and housing associations (many of which are charities) have taken over many council houses.
2) The shift from **public sector** to **private sector welfare** is supported by New Right sociologists such as **Marsland** and **Bartholomew**. They reckon the **free market economy** is the **best way** to ensure services are provided at the **lowest prices** and the **best quality**. This is because **private welfare providers** have to compete, giving individuals **choice** and **value**. They suggest that if the tax burden was reduced, most people would be able to be **self-reliant** (e.g. by buying health insurance) and welfare could be focused on those in **dire need**.
3) The '**Big Society**' was a **key element** of the Coalition government's policy (2010-2015). It aimed to encourage **businesses** (private), **charities** (voluntary) and **informal providers** to take over a **greater share** of welfare provision from the state. Some people argue that the 'Big Society' gives communities and organisations the **freedom** to develop their **own responses** to problems at a **local level**.
4) It was also an **austerity measure** to reduce state spending. Although the government would provide **grants** and **loans** to the private organisations and charities, they believed it would still be **cheaper** than the state intervening directly.
5) Not everyone is convinced that this is a **good solution**:

- Some people argue that the private and voluntary sector won't be able to provide such **comprehensive welfare** as the state. State welfare has **greater funding** and can **guarantee** to provide assistance.
- *Whose Society? The Final Big Society Audit* (2015) by the think tank Civil Exchange found that the Big Society had **failed** to do what it set out to. It said that a '**big society gap**' had opened up in **deprived areas** which have **lower levels** of **charitable giving** and **volunteering**.
- **Informal carers** are saving the government a **huge amount** of money. However, despite many carers being eligible for **carer's benefits**, many people feel that the system **doesn't** meet their needs and carers may end up **workless**, **isolated** and in **poverty** themselves.

Social Democrats Believe *Social Policy Reforms* Could Solve Poverty

1) Social democratic theory says **increasing welfare provision** will help to **solve poverty**.
2) **Mack and Lansley (1985)** suggest a big increase in benefits. They conducted a public opinion poll in which British people said they were **prepared to pay higher taxes** to get rid of poverty.
3) **Townsend (1979)** sees the solution to poverty in the **labour market**. He says **social policy** must have the job of **reducing inequalities** in the labour market.
4) The poor are most often unemployed or low-paid. This means **policies** are needed to **improve wages** and conditions and to **protect workers' rights**. The **National Minimum Wage** and **Working Families' Tax Credit** brought in under the New Labour government are examples of this kind of intervention.
5) British sociologists **Walker and Walker (1994)** argue for an "active employment strategy" where the government would actually **create work** for the unemployed.

Social democratic theory has been **criticised** by people on the **right wing** and on the **left wing**.

1) **New Right** theorists say the social democratic policy of **strengthening the Welfare State** and increasing the power of social policy would be an **absolute disaster** in terms of solving poverty. The New Right say these things led to the increase in poverty in the first place.
2) Left-wing **Marxists** say the **state** will always **serve the interests** of those in **power**, which means that nothing the government does can make a big difference to poverty in capitalist society.

Edwin's attempt to parallel park had been an absolute disaster.

Social Policy and Poverty

There's also the *'Third Way'* Approach

Recent governments have used a philosophy which **combines** both the **New Right** and the **social democratic** approaches — it is called **'the third way'**.

New Labour (1997-2010)

1) When New Labour took power in Britain in 1997, they claimed their social policies would reduce poverty significantly. The theme was that the poor need **"a hand up not a handout"**. The "hand up" part means the state should have **social policies** which **help the poor** — rather like the social democratic theory. The "not a handout" part means people **shouldn't depend** on benefits — rather like **New Right theory**.
2) They said the state has a responsibility to **help people in real need**, but individuals have a **responsibility to help themselves**. The **"New Welfare Contract"** of 1998 said that the **government** had to **help people find work**, make **work pay**, help with **childcare**, help the **poorest** old people and help those who really **can't work**. In turn, **individuals** had to look for work, be as **independent as possible**, support their own family, save for retirement and not defraud the taxpayer by claiming benefit when they shouldn't.

<u>New Labour Reforms aimed at making sure working pays more than benefits:</u>

- **Working Families' Tax Credit** — tax reductions for the **low-paid who are working**.
- **National Minimum Wage** — to ensure every employer **pays more than benefit levels**.
- **Income Tax cuts** — they halved the **starter (lowest) rate**, meaning poorer families **keep more** of what they **earn**.

The Coalition Government (2010-2015)

1) The **Coalition government** continued the Third Way approach. The 'Big Society' (p.88) was part of this.
2) They introduced **changes** to the benefit system so that people moving into work didn't **suddenly** see all of their benefits stop — their aim was for people to be able to see that the **more they worked**, the **better off** they were.
3) They also introduced **'sanctions'** for people who repeatedly **refused work** (they lose their benefits for some time).

Marxists *say* ***Nothing*** *Will Work Except the* ***Overthrow of Capitalism***

1) Marxists believe that the root cause of poverty is the **inequality** central to the **capitalist system**. Therefore, the Marxist solution to poverty is the **removal** of the **capitalist system**.
2) Marxists say that while the capitalist system keeps on going, poverty will still be around — **no matter** what **social policy** you throw at it. **Westergaard and Resler (1976)** think no big **redistribution of wealth** can happen until capitalism is overthrown and replaced by a **socialist** society where **wealth is communally owned**.
3) The most **common criticism** of the Marxist approach is the **evidence** that **socialist** and **communist societies haven't eradicated poverty**. People were poor in Soviet Russia and there is poverty in Cuba.

Practice Questions

Q1 Give two reasons why non-state welfare providers may perform better than the state welfare sector.

Q2 What's the difference between universal and means-tested benefits?

Q3 Why do the New Right think that the Welfare State can be too generous?

Q4 How do Marxist theorists believe poverty could be eradicated in Britain?

Exam Question

Q1 Give a definition of the term 'welfare pluralism'. [2 marks]

<u>Sounds great on paper — but will it work in real life?</u>

Although the theories here are different, they all make some kind of sense on paper. It'd probably be great if everyone earned enough money to buy the best kind of private welfare. It'd probably be great if the state provided really good public welfare for everybody. In real life it's hard to make things work. At the moment, the jury's still out on the Third Way idea.

The Labour Process

These two pages are about labour, as in work — not the Labour Party (we want no confusion here).

Division of Labour — Breaking Down Work into Very Specialised Tasks

1) **Specialisation** is a common way to **organise** a work force. We've always needed people to **specialise**, because **no one person** can learn **all** the skills a society needs.
2) In **pre-industrial** agricultural societies, villages would **divide up** the work according to **individual strengths** — this led to the creation of **craft jobs** such as woodworker, cook, blacksmith and farmer. These craftsmen were **skilled** and carried out a **range of tasks** within their jobs, e.g. a blacksmith would make **all kinds** of metal objects and tools, carrying out **all the steps** in the process himself.
3) However, during the **industrial revolution**, the **division of labour** became more **extreme**. In factories, it was far **more efficient** for workers to learn how to do a **single task**. They'd do this **over and over again** and could do it very **quickly**.

For example, in 1776 the economist Adam Smith wrote about pin-making factories, in which some workers made the pinheads and others the points. Nobody made a whole pin, or even knew how to. This allowed many more pins per worker to be produced each day.

Marx and Durkheim saw the Division of Labour Differently

Karl Marx saw the organisation and control of labour as exploitation... but Emile Durkheim took a different view.

Marx argued that the whole capitalist system exploits the working class

1) Marx said that the rich **control the means of production and distribution** (e.g. factories and shops). This means that the working class have **no choice** but to work for the rich.
2) This means that the rich can pay the working class **whatever they like**, so workers aren't paid the **full value** of their labour.
3) Work becomes **meaningless** and **empty** for the working class, which leads to **alienation** (where the worker becomes **detached** from **society** and **themselves** due to a **lack of control** over their own future).
4) According to Marx, **division of labour** in a factory **increases alienation**. The work is broken into small, easy, repetitive tasks that don't have any **meaning** on their own. This process is called **deskilling**.

Durkheim was far more positive about the division of labour

1) He saw it as **constructive** because it exists in **all societies**. The **more progress** a society makes, the **more specialised** its members become.
2) Durkheim also claimed that the division of labour is a **natural law**. This argument is based on **biology**. Each part of a living creature has a **specialist purpose** — e.g. the heart pumps blood, the stomach digests, etc. Durkheim argued that **society** should be based on the **same idea**.
3) In **contrast** to Marx's idea of **alienation**, Durkheim thinks the division of labour creates **social solidarity**. His argument is that it makes people **depend on each other more**, so they **value** each other more **highly**.

These viewpoints make more sense if you remember that **Marxism** is a **conflict theory**, and **functionalism** (**Durkheim**) is a **consensus theory** (see p.3).

Taylor and Ford encouraged the Division of Labour...

1) In the early twentieth century, **F.W. Taylor** (an American engineer) promoted the idea of '**scientific management**'. He argued that it was **most efficient** to **remove** the need for **knowledge** and **decision-making** from workers' jobs and give each person a **very simple task**. All **planning** and **creative work** should be done by **managers**.
2) When the industrialist **Henry Ford** designed his first **car assembly lines**, he based them on Taylor's ideas. Every worker did **one small job** towards building each car, and nobody needed to be a **skilled mechanic**. This is known as the **Fordist model**.

...But Others have Criticised it

American Marxist **Harry Braverman**, criticised **scientific management**. In 1974 he wrote that the **deskilling** in the Fordist model made workers feel like they were **no more than machines**. It also **took power away** from workers, by making them **easier to replace** if they threatened to go on **strike**.

The Labour Process

Technology can *Deskill* Workers

1) **Modern technology** makes life **easier** for workers in many ways, but it also means **people** are **less vital** to production. Workers on **production lines** being replaced by **machines**, processes becoming more **automatic**, and the more widespread use of **ICT** mean more and more tasks can be done by **technology**, not **people**.
2) Some sociologists argue that technology has led to **upskilling** (where workers learn **additional skills**) or **reskilling** (where workers learn **new skills**) to cope with the new technology. However, others have argued that only workers who are **highly skilled** in the first place will be able to upskill or reskill, while the rest are **deskilled** or **replaced**.

> 1) **Braverman (1974)** looked at new technology from a **Marxist** perspective. He argued that technology **further deskilled** workers, who were already deskilled by the Fordist model. He also said it **reduced** workers' **bargaining power** even more — machines would never strike for more pay or better conditions.
> 2) **Andrew Friedman (1977)** criticised Braverman's analysis — he found that workers in British car factories **did** still **strike** for **better conditions**. However, Friedman also said **union power** had a lot to do with **economic factors**. The workers were **stronger** when general unemployment was **low**, but **weaker** when unemployment was **high**.
> 3) **Michael J. Piore (1986)** had a different view — he argued that technology actually makes a workforce more **flexible**. When machines can be programmed to do **different tasks** (e.g. 3D printers can print different prototypes), the workers need to be able to **adapt** as well. Their work is more **diverse**, so they **reskill**, and there is less of a **gap** between the **workers** and the **management** (as well as better communication between them).

High unemployment means it's difficult to get another job, so workers might not want to risk losing their current one.

Shoshana Zuboff said *Technology* increased *Managers' Control*

1) **Zuboff (1988)** studied **office work** in the 1980s. She found that **technology** was used to **increase** the bosses' **power and control** over workers.
2) Her study showed that computers were being used to **take jobs away** from **human beings** and to **increase surveillance** of **office staff** — for example by **keylogging** (recording what you type).

> Zuboff said that there are **three laws of information technology**:
> 1) **Everything** that **can** be **automated will** be **automated**.
> 2) **Everything** that **can** be **informated** (turned into information) **will** be **informated**.
> 3) **Every** digital application that **can** be used for **surveillance** and **control will** be used for **surveillance and control**.

Ruby had gone to great lengths to prevent keylogging.

Practice Questions

Q1 What is the division of labour?

Q2 Give an advantage and a disadvantage of the division of labour in industrialised society.

Q3 Describe the Fordist model.

Q4 What is reskilling?

Q5 What did Zuboff's (1988) study discover about the use of technology in offices?

Exam Questions

Q1 Outline two ways that the division of labour may have a positive impact on the workforce. Explain each one. [10 marks]

Q2 Evaluate the idea that technology gives workers less control over their lives. [20 marks]

Don't leave Windows® open — your computer will get cold...

Is division of labour a good thing? Well, it depends on your sociological viewpoint. It's probably no surprise what Karl Marx had to say about the matter, but make sure you know other sociologists' views too. And remember, technology has come a long way since most of these studies were done, bringing about even more changes in the way we live and work.

Work and Life Chances

The job you do (and whether you have a job at all) influences many other aspects of your life (so say the sociologists).

Your **Work** Affects Your **Life Chances**

In sociology, **life chances** are the **opportunities** an individual has to get all the things their **society values**, such as money, security, status and comfort.

Peter and Jamie's life chances were looking pretty sweet.

1) The **sort of work someone does**, or if they have a job **at all**, affects their **life chances**.
2) Here are some examples of how the **opportunities** of a **low-paid manual worker** may **differ** from those of a **high-paid skilled worker**.

High-paid skilled worker	Low-paid manual worker
• Can afford **good quality**, **comfortable** housing in a **safe area**. • Can afford to **eat better** and access **better health care**, so generally **healthier** and **lives longer**. • Treated with **respect** due to **high-status job**. • Passes **advantages** on to **children** by supporting their **education** financially.	• Lives in **poor quality** housing in an area with a **high crime rate**. • Eats **less well** and **can't** always access **health care** easily. Is **less healthy** and **dies younger**. • Gets **little respect** due to **low-status job**. • Likely to pass **disadvantage** on to **children**, e.g. can't support them through **higher education**.

3) The examples in this table are **generalisations**. There's a lot of **variation** — e.g. some **high-paid workers** are so **stressed** that they smoke or drink heavily and **die young**. On the other hand, some **low-paid workers** live happily within their means in an area of the country with a low cost of living.

Work Satisfaction is **Important**

1) In general, higher-paid jobs involve **control** and **variety** for **workers**, leading to **work satisfaction** and **job fulfilment**. **Lower-paid jobs** tend to be more **routine**, leading to **poor work satisfaction** and **alienated workers** (who are purely doing the job to **get paid**).
2) **Robert Blauner (1964)** argued that **how technology is used** is the **key factor** in **work satisfaction**:

There's more on technology in the workplace and worker alienation on p.90-91.

- Blauner studied **car assembly line workers** and also **machine operators** in a **chemical factory**. Both of these sets of workers had **similar pay and status.**
- He found that car assembly line workers were **bored, dissatisfied** and **alienated**, whereas the chemical factory machine operators had **high levels of work satisfaction.**
- **Both** jobs involved **machinery**, but on the car assembly line the workers used the machines to do the **same task over and over**. They **could not control** the **speed** of their work — it was determined by the speed of the assembly line. They were also **isolated** from other workers.
- In **contrast**, the machines used in the chemical factory relieved workers of the **monotonous, repetitive tasks**, leaving them with the more interesting **decision-making** to do, such as when **maintaining** the machines. They also worked **in teams**, each with a responsibility for a **whole process**.

3) Recently, employers have begun to see **boredom and demotivation** in the workforce as a **problem**. They try to **improve conditions** by **rotating jobs** and giving employees **different responsibilities**.
4) However, **Marxists** see **all** working-class labour as **alienating**, and a cause of **misery** — whether the worker realises it or not. So, from a Marxist perspective, these changes are just ways to **distract** the workers from noticing that they're being **exploited**.

Work is associated with **Social Identity**

1) **Giddens (2009)** wrote about the **importance of work** in people's lives. He pointed out that for most people work is **not** just drudgery. It takes up a **large proportion** of their **time**, and when people find themselves **unemployed**, it's usually very distressing.
2) This is not only because of the **loss of income**, but also because we see our **social identity** (p.1) as closely tied to the **job** we do. It gives us a **routine** to follow, a **set of people** to socialise with and a **sense of purpose**.

Work and Life Chances

Workelessness can be ***Very Bad*** for ***Individuals***

1) Unemployment is **stigmatised** by society — unemployed people are often considered **lazy** and **unskilled**.
2) Long-term unemployment can lead to **poverty**. Studies also show that the **social effects** of unemployment can be very **damaging**. For example, in areas where there is high unemployment, social problems like **crime**, **violence**, **vandalism** and **drug use** tend to be more common.
3) Many sociologists have investigated the **effects of unemployment**:

- **Fagin and Little (1984)** found high levels of **illness** among **unemployed men**. They concluded that the sickness was a **strategy** for coping **psychologically** with feeling **rejected** by society.
- In 1997 a study by the **Joseph Rowntree Foundation** showed that long-term unemployment caused feelings of **isolation** and **low self-esteem**.

4) People who are **unable to work**, e.g. those with **disabilities**, can also suffer from **poverty** and **isolation**.
5) **Underemployment** is also a problem. This is when people who want **full-time**, **permanent** work are only employed in **part-time** or **temporary jobs**. The pay they receive might not be **enough** to keep them out of **poverty**. Underemployment also includes **highly-skilled** workers in jobs which **don't** utilise their skills, e.g. someone with a **law degree** working as a **bartender**. This may lead to a **lack of job fulfilment** and **low self-esteem**.

Retirement can have ***Similar Effects*** to ***Unemployment***

1) **Cumming** and **Henry's** Disengagement Theory (1961) suggested that worklessness in old age led to **isolation**, **detachment** and **unhappiness**.
2) **Hockey and James (1993)** wrote that retired people are **not treated like adults** by carers and family members. This is because **without a job** they have the **status of children**. This can lead to **low self-esteem**.
3) Although some people **enjoy** the increased **leisure time** that retirement brings, others still **want to work**. This can be because they're **bored**, they're **lonely** or their **pension** isn't enough to live on — or sometimes because they miss the feeling of **job fulfilment**.

Globalisation is ***Changing Employment*** in the ***UK***

1) **George Ritzer (1993)** wrote about **McDonaldisation**. He argued that an increasing number of jobs are like working in a **fast-food restaurant**, where every aspect is **standardised**, **predictable** and **controlled**. It's like an **extreme** version of **scientific management** (see p.90). This has come about as a result of globalisation (see p.1).
2) **Naomi Klein (1999)** describes how the **transnational corporations** (TNCs) have all moved their factories to **developing countries**, where wages are **cheap** and there are **no unions**. Mostly these are '**McJobs**' — **low status**, **badly paid** and offering **poor job security**. Meanwhile, in **developed countries** like the UK, TNCs mainly employ people in jobs such as **sales** and **marketing**.

No unions means that companies can get away with poorer working conditions.

Practice Questions

Q1 What are 'life chances'?
Q2 How can technology affect work satisfaction?
Q3 What is underemployment?
Q4 Describe one way in which globalisation has affected employment in the UK.

Exam Questions

Q1 How might your job affect your life chances? Outline three ways. [6 marks]

Q2 Outline two ways that worklessness may cause problems for individuals. Explain each one. [10 marks]

Fagin (1837) says that picking pockets is a suitable form of employment...

In the future, even more jobs could become automated — e.g. driverless cars may make taxi drivers obsolete some day. However, as Blauner found, technology doesn't always mean doom and gloom for employees — it depends on how the workers are using it. I'm all for new technology, personally — my state-of-the-art typewriter has made my job much quicker.

Definitions of Health

Sociologists see health as more than just not feeling poorly. Well, they do like to complicate things.

The Biomedical Model** says Health and Illness are **Natural, Physical Things

The **biomedical model** (favoured by scientists and health professionals) says that health and illness are caused by factors **within** the body.

This model has **three** key characteristics:

Key characteristics of the biomedical model

1) Health is seen as the **absence of biological abnormality**.
2) The human body is likened to a **machine** in that it needs to be **repaired** by treatment when it breaks down.
3) The health of society is regarded as dependent on the **state of medical knowledge**.

Related to this is the **biomedical view of disability**:

The biomedical model **looks in** at the patient and tries to **fix** the disability through medical practice.

Medical practice is **interventionist** — it's something that's **done to** the patient.

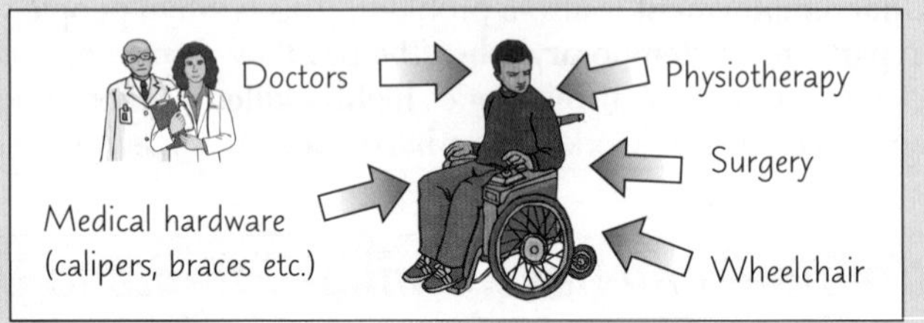

*The **Biomedical** Model has been **Criticised***

1) Some sociologists, e.g. **McKeown (1976)**, say that **improved nutrition and hygiene** have been more important in improving health than **developments in medicine** — starting with 19th and 20th century public health reforms.
2) **Marxist sociologists** in the 1970s accused biomedicine of distracting attention away from what they see as the real causes of illness — the **social causes**.
3) The biomedical approach can be viewed as **stigmatising** people who have an illness or disability — it views illness or disability as something **abnormal** that should be **fixed**.
4) **Tom Shakespeare (2000)** said that traditional approaches **individualise** and **medicalise** disability. They deal with the symptoms of each case and **ignore** social patterns.
5) **Ivan Illich (1975)** and others have argued that modern medicine actually **creates disease**.

Medicalisation is when human conditions start to be treated as medical problems and studied, diagnosed and treated medically.

Illich** Says the **Medical Elite** Actually **Cause Bad Health

1) **Illich (1975)** defines **health** as the **capacity** to cope with the **human reality** of **death**, **pain** and **sickness**. This is a very different definition to the mainstream biomedical definition.
2) Illich believes that medicine has **gone too far**, and that the **medical elite** (**doctors**) have started to '**play God**' — trying to **wipe out** death, pain and sickness. OK so far... he then says that **trying to control death and illness** is a bad move which **turns people into consumers** or even objects. In his opinion, this messes up people's natural capacity for health and **makes people ill**.
3) Illich uses the word **iatrogenesis** to refer to this kind of illness that's caused by modern medicine. He says there are **three types of iatrogenesis**:
    1) **Clinical iatrogenesis** — the **harm** done to patients by **ineffective** treatments, **unsafe** treatments or getting the **wrong diagnosis**.
    2) **Social iatrogenesis** — the idea that **doctors** have **taken over control** of people's lives, and individuals can't make decisions about their problems. More and more of people's problems are seen as **suitable** for **medical intervention**. This is called the **medicalisation of social life**.
    3) **Cultural iatrogenesis** — the **destruction** of **traditional ways** of **dealing** with and making sense of **death, pain and sickness**.
4) According to Illich, dying has become the ultimate form of **consumer resistance** (when you're dead, you can't buy any more Nike trainers, I'd imagine). **Death** isn't seen as something normal. It's become a **taboo**.

Definitions of Health

The *Social Model* says that Health and Illness are *Social Constructs*

1) The **social model** (favoured by **sociologists**) says that health and illness are caused by factors **outside** the body.
2) The **medical elite** haven't always **dominated** the definition and treatment of illness — it's a modern phenomenon, e.g. in the **1700s**, **mental illness** was often thought to be caused by **evil spirits** — a **religious** thing, not a **medical** thing.
3) In modern society illness is only recognised as serious if it has been **diagnosed** by the medical elite. The **social model** says **definitions of health and illness** are '**social constructs**' — not actually always related to **real physical symptoms**.

A '**social construct**' is an **idea that's created by a society** — as opposed to an idea that's based on objective and testable **facts**. It's specific to the **values and behaviour** of that society — it's not universal.

4) The **social model of health** looks to see which **environmental, social and behavioural factors** have contributed to make someone ill. **Social factors** (such as diet, housing or stress) make some people more likely to become ill than others.

A social view of disability:

- The social model looks **outwards** from the individual to the **environmental** and **social** factors which disable an individual, e.g. lack of access, rights and opportunities.
- A person using a **wheelchair** might feel more disabled by the **lack of a wheelchair ramp** than the fact that they can't use their legs to walk.

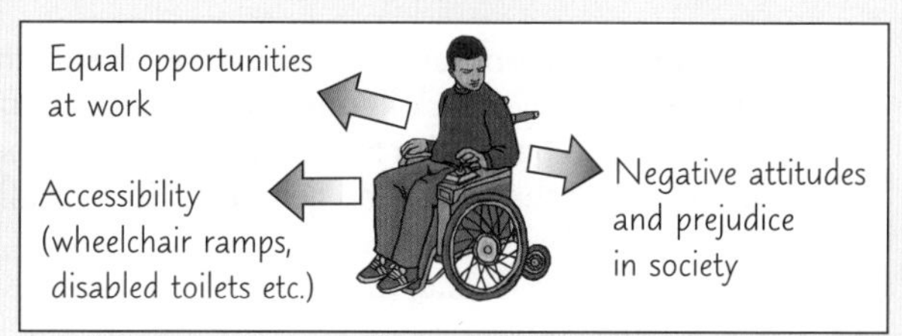

The *Social* Model has been *Criticised* too

1) Illness is often **not subjective**, and **isn't** affected by changes in the social environment.
2) The social model of disability **ignores impairments**, such as **pain**, which cause the disability.

E.g. Whether or not you have food poisoning is not subjective.

An **impairment** is a **physical feature** or **characteristic** (e.g. **blindness**), whereas a **disability** is an **inability** to do something because **society** hasn't made a **provision** for it (e.g. a blind person using a **cash machine**). Impairments **don't always** cause disability, but disability is **always** due to impairment.

The *Body* is a *Social Construction* Too

1) The **ideal** body **size and shape** is socially constructed, e.g. today's **media** often portray a very **slim ideal** for a woman and a **muscular ideal** for a man. However, in the **past**, being thin was associated with not having enough to eat and **indicated poverty**, so a more curvaceous figure was more desirable.
2) The **typical body shape** of a society is also a result of the **dominant cultural attitudes** to diet and lifestyle, e.g. the **fast food culture** of the US is linked to **increased obesity**.
3) However, the ideal body **isn't just** a social construction. A high body mass index (BMI) is **objectively linked** to increased risk of a range of diseases.

Practice Questions

Q1 What is the difference between the biomedical model and the social model of health?

Q2 What does 'iatrogenesis' mean?

Q3 Explain the difference between an impairment and a disability.

Exam Question

Q1 Why might the body be viewed as a social construct? Use one example to briefly explain your answer. [2 marks]

All I care about is why I feel ill...

Hmm... the social model of illness seems a bit odd at first — how can it be society's fault that I've got a sore throat... But when you look into it, you have to admit that things like clean water, proper sewers and a good diet are at least relevant to health. As always, you're expected to know the key points of each theory, as well as their faults and pitfalls.

Inequalities in Health

Your chances of staying healthy, and of recovering if you do get ill, depend on which social group you belong to and where you live. Sociologists have given various explanations for this.

Health Inequalities *are Strongly Linked to* ***Social Class***

1) Most sociologists **agree** that **economic deprivation** is probably the **major factor** causing health inequalities, even if they don't agree exactly **why**.

- The **working class** in England and Wales have a **higher infant mortality rate** than the UK national average. The **wealthiest social groups** have **lower infant mortality rates** than the national average.
- **Working-class** people are statistically **more likely** to suffer from **serious medical conditions** such as heart disease, strokes and cancer.
- **Working-class** people are more likely to **die before retirement** age than the national average.

Social Trends 33 (2003) report, Office of National Statistics.

2) A major government survey, '**Inequalities in Health Working Group Report (1980)**' (also known as the **Black Report**) confirmed that the poorer you are, the less healthy you're likely to be. It also found that those with the **most** need for health care get **least**, and those with the **least** need get **most**. This is called the **Inverse Care Law**.

Cultural Explanations *Blame Bad Health on* ***Variations*** *in Attitude*

Some sociologists attribute **differences in health** to the **values** held and choices made by **different social groups**. These are called cultural explanations. **Cultural deprivation theory** is a cultural explanation that looks at differences between social classes.

1) **Cultural deprivation theory** says that the **working class** lead **relatively unhealthy lifestyles** with relatively **poor diets**, more **smoking**, less **exercise** and more **drinking** — these are known as **behavioural factors**, as well as cultural ones.
2) It also says that the working class are less likely to take advantage of NHS **public health measures** such as **vaccinations**, **health screening** and **antenatal care**.
3) **Howlett and Ashley (1991)** found that **middle-class** people are better **informed** about health, with more **understanding** of health issues. Therefore, they tend to follow **healthier lifestyles**.

Cultural deprivation theory suggests that society needs better **health education** to make people more **aware** of health issues. It's resulted in lots of **government initiatives** through the **Health Education Authority** — trying to get people to give up smoking, eat less fatty food, etc.

Structural Approaches *link Health Inequalities to* ***Deprivation***

Many sociologists, such as **Shaw et al (2008)**, **disagree** with cultural explanations. Instead they believe that **differences** in health and illness are caused by the way **society is structured**. The **middle class** is healthier than the **working class** because society gives the poor **less chance** to keep healthy.

1) **Healthier diets** can **cost more**, and **gyms** are often **very expensive**.
2) **Smoking and drinking** may be related to **stressful lives**, not **cultural values**.
3) Working-class people are **less likely** to be able to afford **private health care**.
4) Living in **poor housing** can cause health problems, e.g. **damp housing** contributes to **child respiratory problems**.
5) Living in **high-crime areas** can contribute to **stress**, as can worrying about **bills** and making ends meet.
6) The fact that working-class people often **don't take advantage** of **public health facilities** has also been blamed on feeling **intimidated** by health care and **health care professionals**. Health care professionals are **mostly middle class** and health care in general can seem like it's set up to suit middle-class people.

The **Black Report (1980)** concluded that **material factors** were the **major cause** of health inequalities.

Inequalities in Health

There are **Gender Differences** in Health and Mortality

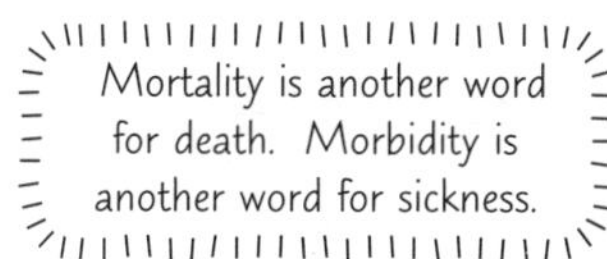

1) On average, **women** live **four years** longer than men in the UK. **Men** are more likely to **smoke** and **drink heavily** and are more likely to have **physical, dangerous jobs**. They also take more **risks**, leading to an increased risk of accidental death (e.g. in road accidents or through drowning) — this is a **behavioural** factor. All these factors may contribute to their **lower life expectancy**.
2) However, data shows that women have **more morbidity** throughout their lives. They also spend a greater proportion of their life with a **disability**, and **go to the doctor** more often.
3) The differences may be caused by **biology**, e.g. due to pregnancy and childbirth. Women also suffer more from **mental health issues**, such as depression and anxiety. However, **Hilary Graham (1984)** also suggested that women are more likely to go without **food** and **heating** to save money in times of **financial difficulties**, which could contribute to their increased health issues.

Brad and Tony were fairly sure they knew how to swim.

There's a **Relationship** Between **Ethnicity** and Health Too

1) The rate of **heart disease** is significantly higher in men and women of **Indian** origin.
2) **African-Caribbean** people have a higher incidence of **stroke, HIV/AIDS infection** and **schizophrenia.**
3) **Suicide** rates are **relatively high** amongst **Asian** women.
4) **Sickle-cell anaemia** is most common in people of **African** origin.

1) **Cultural factors** might have an impact too, e.g. research found that **British Chinese people** were **less likely** to seek help for **mental health problems** because of **social stigma**.
2) Some ethnic groups are more heavily concentrated in the **lowest social classes**. This is a **material factor**, and is likely to be the **most significant factor** in deciding the health of different ethnic groups.

Where you live in the UK is Also Important

1) **Morbidity** and **mortality** rates vary between different **regions** of Britain:
   - People in **Scotland** are more likely to die of lung cancer than people in **England**.
   - People in the **south of England** live more of their lives without a **disability** than people in the **north of England**.
2) There are also differences on a **smaller scale** — neighbouring areas of a city can have very **different** health statistics. There are thought to be **two factors** contributing to this:
   - **Social class** — there are **local variations** in income and deprivation.
   - **Social capital** — this refers to the existence of **social networks** and a sense of **community spirit**. Research has shown that where these things exist, people are **more likely** to have **better health and well-being.**

Practice Questions

Q1 What is the Inverse Care Law?

Q2 Describe the mortality and morbidity gender trends in the UK.

Q3 Why are people in some ethnic groups likely to have higher rates of morbidity than others?

Exam Questions

Q1 Outline two arguments that support the idea that social class can affect health. Explain each one. [10 marks]

Q2 Evaluate the idea that cultural variations by social class are the most important factors in determining health. [20 marks]

Apparently it's not all down to deep-fried chocolate bars then...

It's mostly down to the good old class system — and once again, it's the working class that suffers. They really do get the rough end of the deal. I reckon Marx would have something to say about that — it's a shame he doesn't pop up on these pages. Ah well, I'm sure we'll hear from him again at some point. What's a sociology section without a good bit of Marxism?

Access to Health Care

The National Health Service was set up to give free and equal health care for all. It was mostly a success. Mostly.

*There are **Inequalities** in the Health Care **Provided** by the **NHS***

The **NHS** was set up in 1948. It aimed to provide **free** and **equal** health care for **everyone** in the country. Unfortunately, although the NHS was **generally a success**, it **doesn't give 100% equal health care** to all.

*There are **Regional Inequalities**...*

1) The NHS in England is split up into **regional 'trusts'**, each with responsibility for their own **budget**. This means that money is **spent differently** in different areas of the country, so some regions have access to **different levels** of care.
2) **Specialist** hospitals, e.g. heart hospitals, **aren't spread out equally** across the country either.

*... as well as **Social Class Inequalities***

1) NHS hospitals are now carrying out an increasing number of **private treatments and operations** to raise funds. Some sociologists and politicians claim that this is creating a **two-tier system** in the NHS — people who can **pay** get seen **more quickly** and may get **better treatment**, whilst those who can't are left **waiting**.
2) **Working-class people** are **less likely** to attend screening programmes, e.g. for cervical cancer. A Cancer Research survey found that people from deprived backgrounds are less likely to be **aware** of the screening offered, as are people with **lower literacy levels**. Other reasons may be **practical**, such as **childcare problems**, or not having **paid time off work**.

*The **Inverse Care Law** can be Applied **Today** to **Inequalities** in **Health***

Remember the Inverse Care Law from p.96.

The **Inverse Care Law (Tudor-Hart, 1971)** states that people whose **need** for health care is **greatest** are actually **least likely** to get it.

Working-class areas tend to have the worst health facilities, the **fewest doctors** and the **fewest hospitals**.

Julian Le Grand's survey (2003)

- Le Grand's conclusion was that the middle class get far more benefit from the NHS than the working class. The benefit the middle classes got wasn't in proportion to their actual health needs.
- Le Grand found that the working class were 20% less likely than the middle class to get a hip replacement despite being 30% more likely to need one.
- Even with something as simple as consultation times in GPs' surgeries, Le Grand found that professionals were likely to get on average two minutes more of a doctor's time than working-class patients.

This evidence supports the idea that the health care system is biased towards middle-class people.

Research by **Cartwright and O'Brien (1976)** suggests that **middle-class patients** tend to have a **better relationship** with their **doctor** than working-class patients. Working-class patients said they **felt** like the **doctor doesn't listen**.

*Your **Age** can Affect Your **Access** to Health Care*

1) Research has shown that **older people** often **don't** get the **same treatment** as younger people suffering from the same problem. This is sometimes due to **health care rationing** — there isn't enough money to treat everyone so the people who'll get the **most benefit** get **priority**. There may also be a **greater risk of complications** for older people undergoing operations.
2) In a survey of older people, **over half** agreed that their symptoms were often **dismissed** as **'just old age'**. Older people may also put their own symptoms down to old age and **not bother** going to a doctor.

Access to Health Care

The *Inverse Care Law* Could Also Apply to *Ethnic Minority Groups*

1) **Ethnic minority** health needs were identified as **relatively high** in a report published by the **Department of Health in 1992**. Remember, "**relatively high**" doesn't mean "shockingly sky-high" or "loads higher than the white population". It means anything from a **tiny bit more** to a **lot more** than the **average population**.
2) Some sociologists think that **ethnic minorities** have **relatively poor health** because they're **less likely** to get the **full benefit** from NHS services. **Various possible reasons** have been suggested for this:

    1) The **cultural values** of the NHS might be **different** from those of some ethnic groups. Some advisers say the NHS **needs to adapt** to **fit** the **cultural values** of ethnic groups.
    2) Some people from ethnic minorities, especially older people, **might not speak enough English** to communicate well with health care staff.
    3) There's some evidence that **discrimination** and **racism** affect access to health care. For example, research in the 1980s found that **Asian women** in family planning clinics experienced racism.
    4) **Some ethnic minority groups** tend to see illness and disease as a part of life you can't do much about — and **don't bother** to go to the doctor.

E.g. an NHS Positive Practice Guide encourages employing mental health workers from the cultural backgrounds represented in the local population.

Women go to the Doctor *More* than Men

1) Women traditionally look after the **health of the family**, e.g. they take the children to the doctors. They also tend to use the NHS **earlier in life** than men, because of **contraception**, **pregnancy** and **childbirth**. This may make them **more comfortable** consulting a doctor than men.
2) Research suggests that to **achieve equality**, policies for different health issues should be **gender-sensitive**. They should take into account how conditions **affect** men and women differently, as well as differences in how men and women **seek treatment**. For example, a report found that locating **mental health services** in bars and clubs was more successful in **meeting the needs** of **young men**.

Rex had left it a little late to go to the doctor.

People with *Disabilities* face *Barriers* to Health Care

1) Research has found that **barriers exist** that prevent some people with disabilities from **accessing health care**. For example, **physical barriers** can make it difficult to use doctors' or dentists' surgeries, or they might have **communication difficulties** that make it hard to book appointments.
2) **MENCAP (2004)** found that people with **learning difficulties** often suffered from **discrimination** from health care professionals — they were sometimes **denied** treatments that would be offered to a non-disabled person. The study also found that **communication** was difficult, both in terms of the **patient** trying to describe their **symptoms** and the **doctor** trying to explain the **solution**.
3) Physical symptoms are sometimes **mistakenly** attributed to the person's disability, even when they are **completely unrelated**. This is called '**diagnostic overshadowing**' — it means people don't always get the treatment they need.

Practice Questions

Q1 Describe the 'two-tier' system in the NHS.

Q2 Why might older people not have the same access to health care as younger people?

Q3 Give three barriers that might prevent someone with disabilities from accessing health care.

Exam Question

Q1 Outline two arguments that support the idea that an individual's ethnicity might affect their access to health care. Explain each one. [10 marks]

Doctor, doctor — the NHS is biased against me...

Unfortunately, the NHS doesn't help everyone equally. People are at an advantage if they can read health literature, are able and willing to make an appointment, and are then able to talk to health professionals about their symptoms. Remember that social class, age, ethnicity, gender and disabilities can all affect a person's access to and understanding of health care.

Mental Illness

These pages cover different perspectives on mental health in the UK.

Mental Illness *in UK Society is* ***Unequally Distributed***

Sociologists and psychiatrists can't agree whether mental disorders have **physical causes** or **social causes**.

Sociologists have tended to favour the view that there is a **social basis** for mental illness. Given the **social inequality** in who has good or bad mental health, maybe the sociologists have a point. For example:

1) **Working-class** people are statistically **more likely** to be diagnosed with mental illness than **middle-class** people.
2) Women are statistically more likely to be diagnosed with **depression** or **stress** than men. They're also much more likely to be on **drug treatments** for **mental illness** — antidepressants etc.
3) **African-Caribbean individuals** are more likely to be **'sectioned'** under the Mental Health Act (**admitted against their will**). They are also more likely to suffer from **schizophrenia**. This is despite being **less likely** to suffer from **common** mental health problems than other people from minority groups.

Mental Health is Often ***Treated*** *using the* ***Biomedical Approach***

1) The biomedical approach to mental illness focuses on the **abnormal individual** rather than the **environment** that the individual lives in. It concentrates on the **physical symptoms** of mental illness. For example, a **biomedical approach to schizophrenia** might say it's caused by a **chemical imbalance in the brain**.
2) The biomedical approach is **cure-orientated**. It emphasises the importance of treatments involving **drugs or surgery** for depression.
3) The biomedical approach suggests that treatment is best carried out in the **medical environment** (e.g. a hospital rather than the community) and should always be carried out by the **medical elite** (doctors).

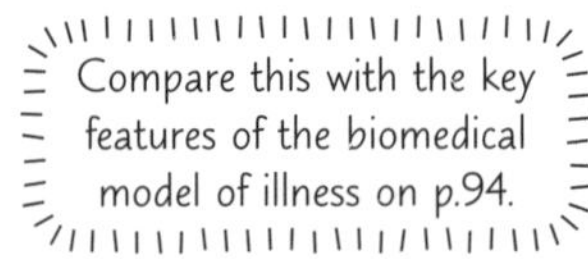

1) In the 1930s, mental disturbance was sometimes treated **surgically**. Doctors actually **severed** neural connections between certain parts of the **brain**. This is called a **lobotomy**. It often had unwanted side effects, such as adverse effects on the patient's **intellect**. Lobotomies aren't done any more, although more refined brain surgery is sometimes used in extremely severe cases.
2) In the 1940s, **electroconvulsive therapy (ECT)** was used to treat depression. It's still sometimes used to treat very severe depression. In ECT, an **electric current** is passed through the patient's **brain**, to create a **seizure** a bit like an epileptic fit.
3) **Drugs** are used to treat all sorts of mental illness. Some drugs have **severe side effects**.
4) Mental illness is also treated by **psychotherapy**, where the patient **talks** to a **therapist** who tries to get them thinking in a more healthy way.

Poverty *and* ***Low Social Class*** *have Links to Mental Illness*

1) There are **structural explanations** for the link between mental health problems and **low social class**. For example, **unemployment**, **social exclusion**, **poverty** and **stress** may make mental disorders more likely.
2) It's a **vicious cycle** too — people suffering from **poor mental health** are more likely to become **unemployed** and **socially excluded**, which may make their **mental health worse**.

Feminists *see* ***Women's Mental Illness*** *as a Result of* ***Patriarchy***

Joan Busfield (2001) thinks that women might be diagnosed with more than their fair share of mental health problems because of **sexism** in the **male-dominated medical elite**. She thinks that doctors **label** and **interpret** behaviour differently depending on whether it's a man or a woman doing it. For instance, an **angry, stressed, upset woman** might be labelled **mentally ill** but an **angry, stressed, upset man** might just be **'overworked'**.

1) **Marxist feminists** think that women's mental illness is caused by their **'dual oppression'** as **housewife** and **worker**.
2) **Radical feminists** suggest mental illness in women is a consequence of **patriarchal society** in which women have **low social status**, the **stress** of **housework** and **childcare** and the stress of **social isolation**.
3) However, **women** are also more likely to **seek medical help** than men (see the previous page), which may account for some of the difference in statistics.

Mental Illness

Inequalities in Ethnicity and Mental Health have Different Explanations

1) Some sociologists use **interactionist thinking** to explain inequalities in **ethnicity and mental health**. **Littlewood and Lipsedge (1982)** found that psychiatric doctors and nurses were more likely to use sedatives with **black** patients. They suggested that this was because the medical staff were **mostly white** and did not understand how to speak to patients who were **culturally different**. They looked to drugs as an **easy solution**.
2) Others have offered **structural** explanations. **James Nazroo (1997)** found that ill health in ethnic minorities in general was linked to **poor housing**, **stress**, **low status** and **poverty**. Mental health differences could be part of the **same pattern**.

The Interactionist Approach Sees Mental Health as a Social Construct

Thomas Szasz (1971) reckoned that **mental illness doesn't really exist**.

1) He thought that what we call 'mental illness' is really just another '**social construct**' — a **label** society uses to **control non-conformist behaviours**. He said that people who behave in a way that the rest of society sees as **unacceptable** or **dangerous** are defined as 'mentally ill'.
2) Szasz compared **sectioning** (see p.100) to the **persecution of witches** in the Middle Ages.
3) Szasz prefers a **system** where individuals are **free** to get psychotherapy **if they want to.** He says it's important that there's **no threat of force**, coercion or **loss of liberty**.

R.D. Laing was a psychiatrist who wrote in the late 1960s. He believed that 'mental illness' is really a natural response to being in an unbearable situation. He also thought that mental illness needn't always be a negative thing. He had an idea that **mental breakdowns** could turn into **mental breakthroughs**.

1) **Erving Goffman (1961, 1970)** saw mental illness as a **stigma** caused by **negative labelling**.
2) Goffman was particularly **harsh** on the **role of mental institutions** in **reinforcing these labels**.

Goffman (1961) studied patients and staff in psychiatric institutions

Goffman described three stages that patients tend to go through in response to being labelled 'mentally ill'.

Withdrawal	Patient doesn't communicate with other patients — doesn't believe he / she belongs with them.
Rebellion	Patient refuses to cooperate with staff.
Cooperation	Patient plays along with the staff idea of how a mental patient behaves. Patient starts to act crazy.

The staff respond to the patient's 'crazy' behaviour by **punishing** the patient — they take away the patient's liberty and privacy and they don't let the patient make choices. This is called '**mortification of the self**'. It ends up with the patient losing their personality.

The patient becomes **institutionalised**, which means they can't manage on their own outside the institution. After this, the staff can start from scratch, building up a 'sane' conformist personality.

If a patient said, "I don't belong here — I'm not mad", the staff might think, "that's just what a mad person would say — you must be mad".

Practice Questions

Q1 Which social groups are statistically most vulnerable to mental illness?

Q2 What is the biomedical approach to mental health?

Q3 According to Szasz, what is mental illness?

Exam Questions

Q1 Give a definition of the term 'mortification of the self'. [2 marks]

Q2 Evaluate the idea that mental illness is a social construct. [20 marks]

If you say you're sane, it's proof you're not...

There's a lot of stigma attached to mental illness. Some charities, such as Mind, are campaigning to end the stigma and discrimination that people suffering from mental illness face. Things are improving, but there's still a way to go. Anyway, learn about which groups are most likely to suffer from poor mental health — but remember, they're all generalisations.

The Role of Medicine and Health Care Professionals

Sociologists have differing views on the purposes that doctors and other health care professionals serve.

Functionalists See Illness as *Deviant* — Doctors *Control* this Deviance

1) According to **functionalists** like **Talcott Parsons (1951)**, doctors have an **important function in society** — they control the amount of time people take off **work** and **family duties**.
2) Illness is '**deviant behaviour**' which **disrupts** work and home life — you're not supposed to take time off sick.
3) Parsons said that sick people take on a "**sick role**". While a person is sick, they're allowed to stop functioning in their **normal role**. They don't have responsibility for making themselves better — but they are **expected** to **want to get better**, and to do whatever the doctor tells them.
4) Doctors have the **power** to **confirm** that the patient is **actually ill**. Doctors **allow** the sick person to take limited time off, and **make them better** by using their **expert medical knowledge**. Parsons thought that doctors always put the patient's needs before their own needs.

Critics of Parsons say the medical profession don't always put patients first — they say private medicine is proof that doctors are self-interested. However, it **can't be denied** that doctors really do give people **sick notes** so they can take sick leave.

Interactionists Look at *Doctor-Patient Interactions*

Interactionists (also called interpretivists) focus on the **social interactions between individuals** (see p.4). Research by **Szasz and Hollender (1956)** found there were **three types of interactions** between a patient and a doctor, which don't all match Parsons' 'sick role' concept.

Relationship	What happens	Example of condition
Activity/passivity	The doctor **does something to** the patient.	An operation such as a liver transplant
Guidance/co-operation	The doctor **tells** a **co-operative patient** what to do.	Acute conditions such as bronchitis
Mutual participation	The doctor **helps** the patient to administer **self-care**.	Chronic conditions such as diabetes

Marxists see *Medicine* as an *Institution* which *Supports Capitalism*

Marxists believe that the medical profession only do good for the **capitalist** class — they **keep class inequalities going**. Marxists say that medical professionals are in a position of **power** and have a **conservative** role in society.

1) Doctors keep the workforce **healthy** and **productive**. **Healthy** workers can **work harder** and won't have to take **time off sick**. This means **more profits** for the capitalist class.
2) Doctors **check** that **workers** aren't spending **too much time on sick leave**.
3) Marxists believe that doctors **hide the real social causes of illness** (poverty, class inequality etc.) by focusing on the individual and their physical symptoms.

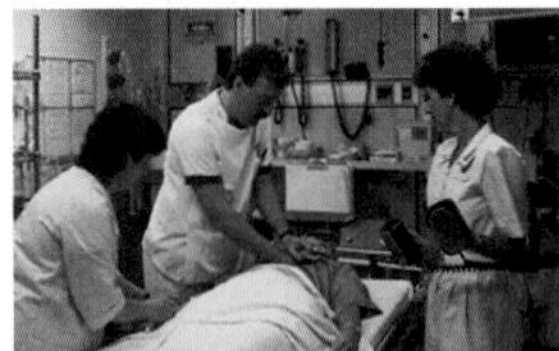
Donald had been deemed fit for work.

Some Marxists think that **doctors** are **agents** of **large drugs corporations** — they exist to produce **profits** for the pharmaceutical industry...

The *Global Pharmaceutical Industry* has been *Criticised*

1) The **global pharmaceutical industry**, sometimes nicknamed '**big pharma**', grew through researching and producing medicines that successfully cure and treat serious diseases. However, drug companies always want to make a **profit**...
2) Writers such as **Jacky Law (2006)** say that the industry has too much **power**, and accuse it of:
   - **Controlling** which 'illnesses' are **publicised** and **researched** — these being the ones that'll make them **most money**. They're even accused of identifying and promoting **new conditions** for the medicines they already have.
   - **Hiding drug trial results** that show the drugs **don't** work very well.
   - Providing **incentives to doctors** to endorse or prescribe their products.

   E.g. some people claim drug companies have caused the rise in ADHD, by persuading adults that if they're easily distracted then they have ADHD and need drugs.
3) The pharmaceutical industry has also been accused of making life-saving drugs too **expensive** for the people who need them. On the other hand, there are some companies that aim to provide **free** or **affordable** drugs to developing countries — for example, to cure **malaria** in **Africa**.

The Role of Medicine and Health Care Professionals

Feminists see the Medical Profession as serving Patriarchal Interests

1) Some feminists say that most **contraceptive methods** (e.g. the pill and IUDs) are designed for men rather than women. This doesn't mean men are supposed to use them — it means they have **significant health risks** for women that **men would never put up with**.
2) **Oakley (1984)** has said that the process of childbirth has been "**medicalised**". In other words, women giving birth are treated like there's **something wrong with them**. **Control** over giving birth is taken away from women and given to **men**. Male doctors are often in charge, not midwives or the women who are actually giving birth.
3) Women tend to have **subordinate** roles in medicine — **nurses** and **auxiliaries** tend to be **women**, while **consultants** tend to be **men**. Some feminists think that the role of being a nurse has been made to look like being a '**doctor's handmaid**' — a female servant **obeying** the male doctor.
4) **Cosmetic surgery** is criticised by some feminists as the 'medicalisation of beauty', and also as a **social control** over women.
5) Feminists see the diagnosis and treatment of **depression** in women as another kind of **social control**.

Weberians see the Medical Profession as Self-Serving

1) Weberians think that doctors **arrange** things so that they **keep** their **power** and **high status** in society.
2) They suggest that the medical profession is **self-serving**. They argue that the medical profession has managed to **shut out** other forms of healing such as homeopathy, aromatherapy, faith healing and other types of **alternative medicine**. This gives modern medicine a monopoly.

A Weberian is a follower of German sociologist, historian and economist Max Weber (1864-1920).

Postmodernists Believe the Power of the Medical Profession has Reduced

Postmodernists **don't** accept that the other sociological views explain the role of health care professionals **today**.

1) Traditionally, doctors held **all the knowledge** about medical conditions and treatments — this gave them **power**. Postmodernists say this has changed. The **internet** means people **empower themselves** by doing their **own research** and **diagnosing themselves**. However, some doctors complain that this often misinforms patients, causing **unnecessary worry** and leading them to **demand inappropriate treatments**.
2) Postmodernists believe that health care is now part of our **consumerist society**, e.g. patients can **choose** which NHS hospital to be treated at, based on mortality rates, etc. They can also **pick** from a range of **complementary and alternative treatments**, such as acupuncture or homeopathy (although not necessarily funded by the NHS).
3) Postmodernists also believe that society has become **medicalised** so that normal **life changes**, such as the **menopause** and **old age**, are treated as medical conditions. This transfers power from health professionals to both the **drug companies** (who advertise their products as **wonder cures**), and to the patient **consumers**.

Practice Questions

Q1 What is the 'sick role'?

Q2 According to Marxists, how does medicine support capitalism?

Q3 Give two reasons why the medical profession could be seen as patriarchal.

Q4 What is the postmodernist view on the power of the medical profession?

Exam Questions

Q1 How has the global pharmaceutical industry been criticised? Outline three ways. [6 marks]

Q2 Evaluate the idea that the medical profession has a lot of power in today's society. [20 marks]

'Big pharma' — making up diseases and convincing us we have them...

It all sounds like a conspiracy theory to me. But that doesn't mean it isn't true. Look back at the stuff on iatrogenesis on page 94, as that's relevant here — some people have accused the big pharmaceutical companies of this. Make sure you know all the different sociological viewpoints on these pages — some of them aren't that surprising. But who likes surprises?

Do Well in Your Exam

These pages will show you how to use all of your lovely sociology knowledge to get those all-important marks. The questions will test different skills, and require different lengths of answers, so always make sure that you read all of the instructions carefully.

Paper 1 is worth 50% of the AS-level

1) **Paper 1** is **1 hour 30 minutes** long. It's worth **60 marks** — **50%** of the AS-level.
2) It tests '**Education with Methods in Context**'. You have to answer **all** the questions.
3) The first **40 marks** are on '**Education**'. The final **20 marks** are on '**Methods in Context**' (the context is Education).
4) The **first three questions** are likely to be **short-answer questions** worth from 2 to 6 marks each. The **last three questions** are likely to be **longer essay questions** worth 10 or 20 marks each.
5) There are usually **items** (short texts about the topic) to read as part of the 20-mark questions. These highlight some of the **themes** or **theories** within the topic. You're told to '**apply the material**' in your answer, so you **have to read them**.

Alfred always brought lots of spare paper to his exams.

Paper 2 is also worth 50% of the AS-level

1) This exam is also **1 hour 30 minutes** long and worth **60 marks** — it's the other **50%** of the AS-level.
2) The exam has **two sections**:

- **Section A** is on '**Research Methods**'. You **must** to do this section. It's worth **20 marks**.
- In **Section B** you choose **one** topic and answer **all** the questions on it. It's worth **40 marks**. The topics are '**Culture and Identity**', '**Families and Households**', '**Work, Poverty and Welfare**' and '**Health**'.

Obviously, make sure you pick the topic that you've been taught.

3) Each section has a combination of **short-answer questions** and **longer essay questions**.
4) As in Paper 1, the **20-mark questions** usually start with an **item** to read. Again you're told to '**apply the material**' in your answer — so **read it** carefully.

You Get Marks for...

AO just means 'Assessment Objective'

AO1 — Showing what you know about sociology
You need to show that you **know** the sociological **theories**, **concepts** and **evidence** related to a topic. Make sure you **define** any sociological terms fully, and **spell** the names of any **sociologists** correctly.

AO2 — Applying what you know about sociology to a situation
To get these marks, you have to **relate** what you know to the topic **in the question**, e.g. you often have to give **reasons** for a pattern in society (such as **why** one social group is **more likely** to do something than another).

AO3 — Evaluating sociological ideas, and weighing up competing ideas to draw conclusions
This involves discussing **different perspectives** and **debating** which side is the **strongest**. At the end of **some** answers, you'll be expected to draw everything together to form a **conclusion**.

Short-answer questions don't require an essay. They're worth **2, 4 or 6 marks** and mainly test **AO1 and AO2 skills**.

Essay questions (worth between 10 and 20 marks) usually test **all three** Assessment Objectives.

For these questions you might **lose marks** if you don't:

- use **continuous prose** — so no bullet points.
- **organise information** clearly — it's worth **thinking through** your answer **before** you start writing.
- use **specialist vocabulary** where appropriate — so learn that **sociology jargon**.
- use appropriate **examples** to illustrate your points.

Don't forget about the basics:

- Write as **neatly** as you can.
- Use good **grammar** and **punctuation**.
- Check your **spelling** — especially of sociological terms.
- Make sure you **answer the question**.

Do Well in Your Exam

Here are some *Hints* for *Short-Answer Questions*

1) If you're asked for **two** things, give **two** things. **Not one**. Not three. Or four. Five is **right out**.
2) If you're asked for multiple things, spend **equal time and effort** on **each**. You **won't** get full marks for a **lopsided** answer.
3) Use the **number of marks** as a **guide** for **how long you should spend on each question**.
   The **more marks** a question is worth, the **longer** you should spend answering it.

Here are some *Example Exam Questions* and *Answers*

A Couple of *2-mark Questions* and *Answers* to Show You What to Do:

01 Give a definition of the term 'cultural capital'. [2 marks]

The language, skills and attitudes that children learn which help them to be successful in the education system.

Explain the term fully. Just saying 'language and skills', for example, would only get you 1 mark.

02 How might disability affect someone's likelihood of being in poverty? Use one example to briefly explain your answer. [2 marks]

Disabled adults are less likely to be in paid work [1 mark], so they tend to have lower incomes, making them more likely to be in poverty [1 mark].

You get one mark for the example, and one for the explanation.

4-mark Questions Usually Ask for *Two Things...*

There is a 4-mark question in the 'Research Methods' section of Paper 2.

03 Outline two disadvantages of a sociologist using focus groups. [4 marks]

If participants know they are being observed they might behave differently [1 mark], making the findings invalid [1 mark].

A focus group only consists of a small number of people [1 mark], so the findings may not be representative of the target population [1 mark].

Clearly outline each problem, e.g. don't just say, 'they might behave differently'.

Don't waste time writing about more than two problems.

...and *6-mark Questions* Usually Ask for *Three Things*

04 Why do girls outperform boys at most stages of education? Suggest three reasons. [6 marks]

Traditionally 'male' employment sectors such as heavy industry and factory work have declined [1 mark]. It can be argued that this has left boys with greater uncertainty over what they can aim for in life — some are disillusioned and feel no incentive to work hard at school [1 mark].

The number of female teachers has increased [1 mark]. This means that boys have fewer role models at school than before, which arguably means they are less likely to try to push themselves to achieve [1 mark].

The trend is also likely to be partly self-perpetuating. Boys are considered to be underachievers, so some teachers negatively label them [1 mark]. That negative labelling can become a self-fulfilling prophecy, causing boys to continue to underachieve [1 mark].

A new paragraph for each new point makes it clear that you've suggested three things.

05 How are children treated differently to adults in modern UK society? Outline three ways. [6 marks]

Children are banned from buying many harmful substances, such as alcohol and tobacco [1 mark]. This represents an extra protection for children in addition to the various laws that govern adults [1 mark].

Children are not expected to work and are financially supported [1 mark]. This is different from most adults, who are expected to earn enough money to support themselves [1 mark].

Children can be removed from abusive environments for their own protection [1 mark]. Children can't control this decision, whereas adults can decide for themselves whether to leave an abusive environment [1 mark].

Explain each point by stating the policy regarding children, and then saying how it's different for adults.

Do Well in Your Exam

Here are some *Hints* for *Longer Essay Questions*

1) This is where the **essays** start, so remember to write in **continuous prose**.
2) Come up with a **structure** before you start writing, and use **paragraphs** to show that you've **organised** your ideas. Start a **new paragraph** whenever you start a **new point**.
3) These questions will have marks for **AO1, AO2 and AO3**. So you have to show that you **know** all the theories and concepts AND that you can **apply** them to the issue AND that you can **evaluate** the arguments. In 16- and 20-mark questions, you also need to draw a **conclusion**.

Some people don't pay enough attention to structure.

10-Mark Questions — *Discuss* Ideas from *Different Angles*

In 10-mark questions, you're expected to **discuss different perspectives**. However, you **don't** need to draw a **conclusion**.

01 Outline two reasons why educational achievement may be shaped by social class. Explain each one. [10 marks]

Pupils from middle-class backgrounds are more likely to do well in GCSEs, take A-levels and go on to higher education than children from working-class backgrounds.

Briefly introduce the issue.

One reason for this is that negative labelling of children from working-class backgrounds can lead to self-fulfilling prophecies of failure. Teachers may not expect children from working-class backgrounds to achieve highly, so may place them in lower streams or sets where they do not have access to high levels of knowledge. This limits their opportunities to achieve in education. Pupils may also become frustrated with their low status and respond by forming anti-school subcultures where education is unimportant. This attitude will be a barrier to learning and doing well in exams. However, it could also be argued that this approach is too deterministic and that negatively labelled pupils are not always destined to fail. For example, Fuller (1980) found that African-Caribbean girls in London formed a subculture that worked hard to prove negative labelling wrong. Some working-class pupils are likely to do the same.

Use sociological terms correctly and explain them.

Evaluate the reason by looking at it from all angles.

A second reason is material deprivation outside of school. Working-class parents are less likely to be able to financially support their children through university, which may deter some working-class pupils from attending. Also, parents on low incomes might not be able to provide their children with educational books, which may put them at a disadvantage compared to middle-class children. In addition to this, Douglas (1964) found that children in unsatisfactory living conditions didn't do as well in ability tests as children from comfortable backgrounds. An example of such a condition is overcrowded housing, in which children may struggle to find a quiet place to study.

Apply your sociological knowledge to the issue.

Illustrate with examples.

There's a 16-Mark Research *Methods* Question on Paper 2

You'll probably be asked to write about the **problems** associated with a particular research method.

02 Evaluate the disadvantages of a sociologist using unstructured interviews. [16 marks]

Start by showing that you understand what the research method is.

Unstructured interviews are informal and don't have a rigid structure. They use open-ended questions and give mostly qualitative data. They're good for researching sensitive issues, but they do have several disadvantages.

One of the disadvantages of unstructured interviews is that they take time to do and a long time to write up, so they can only be done with a small sample. This makes them less representative than questionnaires, which can be done with a larger sample. Also, the people who agree to participate in unstructured interviews might have certain characteristics in common, making the sample unrepresentative of the target population. For example, they might have time on their hands, or feel strongly about the issue. However, it could also be argued that this problem is outweighed by the insights of the qualitative data generated by unstructured interviews, and this data could even be used to inform further research using a larger, more representative sample.

Discuss each problem in detail, using the strengths of the method to evaluate them.

Unstructured interviews also require a skilful interviewer, which makes them more challenging. The interviewer must gain the interviewee's trust and use questions to draw out more information on their views. This is particularly true for sensitive issues, such as domestic violence. Interviewer effects also mean that data from unstructured interviews is likely to be less valid than data from closed questionnaires. For example, the interviewee might give the answers they think the interviewer wants to hear, and they may have answered an anonymous questionnaire more honestly. However, Becker (1970) suggested that an aggressive interview style could produce more useful answers, so perhaps the interviewer's influence on the interviewee can actually be a strength of the method, if it's approached thoughtfully.

Illustrate with examples where appropriate.

Another disadvantage of unstructured interviews is that they generate mostly qualitative data, which is harder to analyse and draw conclusions from, meaning that the interpretations of the data may be less reliable results. Positivists, who prefer a more scientific approach to research, would criticise unstructured interviews for this. However, from an interpretivist perspective, collecting such explorative, individualised data would still be beneficial.

Use sociological terms correctly.

In conclusion, the characteristics of unstructured interviews would be seen as disadvantages if reliable, objective, quantitative data is required. However, if taking an interpretivist approach, perhaps the only problems are the time and skill investments needed.

Draw your points together in a conclusion.

Do Well in Your Exam

Here's an Example **20-mark Question** about **Methods**

1) Here's an example of a **longer exam question** based on an **item**. It's the kind of question you get in the '**Methods in Context**' part of **Paper 1** — you have to apply a **sociological method** to an **educational issue**.
2) In this example, you'll notice that the **sociological method** is the **same** as the one on p.106. This is to show how **different** your answer needs to be when **applied** to a topic.

03 Apply your own knowledge and material from Item A to evaluate the advantages and disadvantages of using unstructured interviews to investigate the link between social class and educational achievement. [20 marks]

Read the item carefully. It'll give you ideas for what to write about.

Item A
Investigating social class and educational achievement

Sociologists have studied the extent to which there is a link between social class and standards of achievement in education. Some sociologists believe that a negative attitude towards schooling (often reinforced by a peer group) can affect educational achievement. Some also note that such attitudes are more common amongst working-class students. This trend may be due to the approaches of teachers. Alternatively, it may be due to factors outside of school affecting attitudes to education.

Sociologists researching the link between social class and educational achievement may use unstructured interviews. Unstructured interviews have the advantage of allowing students to elaborate on their views, but they do take a considerable amount of time, so are usually only used for small-scale research.

Unstructured interviews take the form of an unrestricted, free-flowing conversation between the researcher and the subject, providing qualitative data through a range of open-ended questions.

Give a brief description of the research method you're discussing.

A key advantage of using unstructured interviews for researching social class and educational achievement is that they allow the researcher to build up a rapport with the interviewee. This can be important for encouraging a child to open up and be honest in their answers, resulting in more valid data. Furthermore, unstructured interviews allow the researcher to follow up any ambiguous or unusual responses, to gain greater clarity and detail. This could be very important if a child struggled to articulate themselves clearly. This is why unstructured interviews are most appropriate when taking an interpretivist approach to research, which is focused on empathising with individuals and discovering the motivations and emotions behind their behaviour.

Unstructured interviews are a good way to research individuals' attitudes, which may be key when researching educational achievement. For example, Willis (1977) used a range of methods, including unstructured interviews, to research the working-class anti-school subculture. The boys in this subculture had very negative attitudes towards education and were disruptive in school. The unstructured interviews allowed him to build a rapport with the boys and gain an insight into their motivations and beliefs. This opportunity for rapport wouldn't have been possible using methods such as official statistics or questionnaires.

Apply your sociological knowledge to the research method you're discussing.

Another advantage of using unstructured interviews to research this topic is that it is a sensitive and subtle approach for working with young people. For example, Labov used this method when investigating whether 'linguistic deprivation' might be a factor in working-class children underachieving in education. A different approach, such as formal, structured interviews, may have been intimidating to the children in the study.

Discuss both strengths and weaknesses.

On the other hand, there are some disadvantages of unstructured interviews as a research method. Firstly, the results are not always reliable. For example, if another sociologist repeated Willis's research with a different group of working-class boys, they may get different results. In addition, the research sample tends to be small because it's a time-consuming and therefore expensive method. For example, Willis used a sample of only twelve boys. It's difficult to generalise from the results, because answers tend to be specific to individual subjects. This also makes it difficult to make direct comparisons between one interviewee and another.

Show that you're applying the item at least once in your answer.

Furthermore, unstructured interviews may not be the best approach for studying how negative labelling by teachers can affect educational achievement. Teachers may be unwilling to admit to having lower expectations of working-class students, as they want to show themselves in the best possible light. In this situation, observation may be a better approach, as it would avoid this bias.

Positivist researchers would also find alternative methods more appropriate. For example, a self-completion questionnaire using a large sample would be more likely to provide reliable, quantitative data that could be used to make generalised conclusions. A possible correlation between factors outside of school, such as economic deprivation, and educational failure might be easier to research using a positivist approach, because quantitative data on household income and exam results could be compared.

In conclusion, unstructured interviews are, to some extent, a useful research method for the topic of social class and educational achievement. They are particularly appropriate for interpretivist sociologists researching individuals' views on this reasonably sensitive issue. However, they would be less useful for large-scale research, such as collecting data from a representative sample of many schools across the UK.

Sum up with a short conclusion.

Do Well in Your Exam

You'll get a ***20-mark Question*** *on* ***Education*** *and also on your* ***Chosen Topic***

1) These questions will ask you to evaluate a sociological viewpoint — make sure you **weigh up** both its strengths and its weaknesses before writing a **clear conclusion**.
2) Refer to the content of the **item** at least once, but **don't** just copy a bit of it — you need to **analyse** it by discussing an argument for or against it.

04 Apply your own knowledge and material from Item B to evaluate the idea that illness is a social construct. **[20 marks]**

Item B

Some sociologists disagree with the view that people whose bodies work differently to what is considered the biological norm have something wrong with them. In modern society, an increasing variety of problems are seen to require the intervention of doctors and drugs. As the numbers of drugs and treatments available change, so does society's view of what constitutes an illness.

A social construct is a concept that is created by society, rather than one that is based on objective, scientific facts. The social model says that illness is a social construct — it's the idea that illness is created by environmental and social factors.

Define the key sociological terms that you're discussing.

Environmental factors, such as stress, poor diet and poor housing, do mean that some people are more likely to be ill than others. For example, working-class people are more likely to suffer from heart disease and cancer, according to ONS data (2003). Indeed, McKeown (1976) supports the social model by arguing that improved nutrition and hygiene have been much more important in improving health over the previous centuries than advances in medical knowledge. On the other hand, the biomedical model sees illness as the effect of the body not working normally. Supporters of this model point out that some medicines, such as antibiotics and vaccines, have resulted in diseases such as diphtheria, which were a huge problem in the past, being rare in the UK today. This contradicts the social model of illness.

You can back up what you say using data sources and relevant sociological knowledge.

Some sociologists would argue that illness is a social construct because, in modern society, an illness is only recognised as serious if it is diagnosed by the medical elite. Doctors may be required to label someone as ill for social reasons, such as getting a sick note for time off work, and the patient may even persuade the doctor to label them as such. Despite this, illnesses can often be viewed objectively — scientific tests can often be done to show someone has something biologically wrong with them. Also, there can be very real symptoms, such as pain, that prevent the patient from carrying out their role in society and force them to fulfil the 'sick role' instead, as Parsons termed it.

Evaluate the argument using opposing points of view.

It is true that whether or not an individual interprets their symptoms as an illness in the first place can depend on social influences. Medicalisation means that an increasing number of problems are now seen as requiring medical treatment. For example, the menopause used to be thought of as a normal part of life, but it is now considered to be a medical condition. Furthermore, as more drugs become available, society's idea of whether a condition is an illness changes. The global pharmaceutical industry has the power to decide which conditions to develop new drugs for — often the ones with the greatest potential for profit. The industry is also accused of constructing new illnesses and convincing people that they have them in order to sell more drugs. For example, the existence of adult ADHD is debated by some medical experts. All these factors would point towards illness as a social construct.

You need to apply the item, but it's also great to link it with your own knowledge, like this.

Mental illness is a further example of a type of illness that may be socially constructed. If someone behaves in a way that society finds unacceptable, they can be sectioned. In this case, a doctor is effectively using the label of mental illness to control non-conformist behaviour (Szasz, 1971). Their treatment in a mental institution is likely to reinforce the label, so the individual eventually conforms to it, replacing their original personality with one better suited to institutional life. Goffman refers to this as the 'mortification of the self'. However, as with other illnesses the biomedical approach points to the physical causes of mental illness (for example, a chemical imbalance in the brain), which can be successfully treated with drugs.

Illustrate your points with examples.

In conclusion, when investigating illness it is certainly difficult to deny the real, physical symptoms of pain, or the fact that symptoms can often be scientifically linked to a biological cause. Despite this, the idea that illness is a social construct can still be valuable — if not as an alternative model that explains all illness, then as a useful approach for putting the biomedical model into perspective.

Sum up with a short conclusion. Make sure that it answers the original question.

Evaluate the view that revision will get you quite a lot of marks...

The more stuff you learn, the more you'll be able to write about. But you have to keep it all relevant. It's all too easy to start off answering the question, but end up waffling on about something else. If the topic is questionnaires, don't go on about interviews for ages. Remember to start a new paragraph for each point, and back things up with supporting evidence.

Glossary

absolute poverty Not having the essentials needed for life — food, warmth and shelter.

achieved status Status you get by working for it.

alienation Having no control over the products of your work and becoming detached from yourself and society as a result.

ascribed status Status you have from birth.

beanpole family A family structure where a small number of members from each generation all live together in one household, e.g. a retired couple living with their daughter, son-in-law and grandchildren.

biomedical model A model of health and illness that considers only factors within the body. It ignores social, psychological and environmental factors.

bourgeoisie Marxist term for the capitalist ruling class. They own the means of production (e.g. factories, equipment, raw materials).

capitalism An economic system based on private ownership of the means of production, distribution and exchange of commodities. In the capitalist system, labour becomes a commodity which employers buy for wages. Capitalism is associated with free trade and individual enterprise. It started in Europe and the US and has spread to become the dominant economic philosophy in most countries.

census A government survey of all people within a defined geographical area. The British census is an obligatory survey of the entire population that is carried out every 10 years.

class A way of stratifying society, on the basis of people's social and economic status. Class is hierarchical — some classes are more privileged than others. The 'class system' is criticised by Marxists.

collective consciousness The shared values and norms that hold society together.

commodity fetishism When capitalist society encourages people to become obsessed by products that are not essential to survival.

communism A system of government which is theoretically based on a classless society and where private ownership has been abolished. It is influenced by the ideas of Marx and Engels.

conformity Adherence to the norms and values of society. The opposite of deviance.

conjugal roles Husband and wife roles — who does the paid work, who does the washing-up etc.

consensus Fundamental agreement within a society, especially about that society's basic values. Functionalist theory suggests that, as a result of socialisation, the people in a society all share the same norms and values and this contributes to consensus.

cultural capital The skills and cultural know-how that children learn from their parents.

cultural deprivation theory This theory says working-class culture makes people disadvantaged.

culture The 'way of life' of a society or group. Culture is made up of things such as language, customs, knowledge, norms and values. It is passed on by socialisation.

culture of dependency The idea that generous welfare policies create a culture where people are happy to claim benefits instead of looking for work.

dependency ratio The number of people who are not of working age (e.g. children, pensioners) compared to the number of working-age people.

deviance Something that goes against society's norms and values. Deviant behaviour is behaviour that society doesn't approve of.

differentiation The division of society into different groups. These groups may be based on a person's abilities, on biological features like their age or sex, or on cultural differences like class or religion.

disability A limited ability to perform certain tasks because society hasn't made provision for an impairment.

emotional work Dealing with the emotions of a family.

ethnic group A group of people with a common culture — language, religion and way of life.

ethnocentric Centred around the values and interests of one particular ethnic group.

ethnography Research which studies the culture and way of life of a community by looking at social relationships, organisations, customs and practices. It is usually done by observation, and may also use interviews and case studies.

extended family A family which includes more than just parents and children, e.g. including grandparents, cousins, uncles and aunts.

Glossary

false consciousness Marxism says that workers are in a state of false consciousness about their place in society. They have learnt ruling-class values and beliefs through education, the media and religion, which prevent them from realising how unfair capitalist society is.

false needs Things people think they need but which don't really satisfy them. Marxists say these false needs have been created by a capitalist culture which encourages consumerism.

feminism A broad movement which believes that social organisations and culture have been dominated by men to the exclusion of women. Feminists claim that this has devalued and disadvantaged women into a marginalised status. Feminist sociologists think that mainstream sociology has ignored the lives of women. There are many varieties of feminism, e.g. liberal feminism, Marxist feminism and radical feminism.

Frankfurt School A neo-Marxist group that formed in Germany in the 1930s. They combined Marxist ideas with psychology.

free market An economic system that lets supply and demand control prices, wages etc., rather than the government.

functionalism An important sociological perspective about how society works, founded by Durkheim, which argues that everything in society exists for a reason. Functionalists believe that society is made up of a number of institutions, each of which has a useful function and helps society to run smoothly, e.g. the family, the education system, religion. These institutions work in harmony because of agreed norms and values, and this is essential for society to survive. Functionalists say that individuals internalise these norms and values (socialisation).

gender Sociologists say that gender (femininity and masculinity) is a social construction. Being male or female is the biological sex you're born with, while masculinity and femininity are identities you're socialised into.

globalisation The breaking down of traditional national boundaries as globally people become more interconnected. This happens due to factors such as the growth of multinational companies, improvements in communications and technology, increased migration of people between societies, and the global marketing of cultural products.

Hawthorne effect When participants are aware they are being observed and this affects their behaviour.

hegemony The domination of one group of people over others, or of one set of ideas and values over others.

hidden curriculum The social norms and values that are taught at school, but not as part of the regular curriculum. Includes conformity, respect for authority and other cultural values.

hierarchy A system which ranks people according to status. Any system where you have a boss in charge of people is a hierarchy.

household A group of people who live together. They needn't be related.

hypothesis A statement that makes a prediction which can be tested and proven to be true or false. Hypotheses are often used by scientists to predict how different factors are related. They are tested using experiments and research.

iatrogenesis Health problems caused by the modern medical system.

identity An individual's sense of self. This can be influenced by social factors such as class, gender, religion and ethnicity.

ideological state apparatus Institutions like the media, schools, Church and family which can spread the ideology of the state.

ideology A set of ideas and beliefs about the way things should be — often politically motivated.

impairment A physical characteristic or symptom (e.g. deafness) that a person has.

institutional racism When the policies, attitudes and actions of an institution discriminate against ethnic minorities — sometimes unintentionally.

institutions of society Structures that contribute to the running of society, e.g. the family, the Church, the education system and the health care system.

interactionism Also known as 'interpretivism'. A sociological approach which focuses on the actions and thoughts of individuals. Society is viewed as the product of interaction between individuals. Interactionists favour research methods that look at individual people's motives and feelings.

labelling theory This theory says that the labels given to someone affect their behaviour. Labels also affect how other people treat someone, e.g. teachers might treat a child labelled a 'troublemaker' more strictly.

life chances The opportunities people have to gain the things that society values and to improve their own quality of life.

longitudinal study A study done over a period of time.

marketisation of education Encouraging competition between schools in order to create a market within education, where parents have more choice.

Glossary

Marxism A theory and political ideology based on the views of Karl Marx (1818-1883). Marxists are opposed to capitalism, which they believe is based on the exploitation of the working class (proletariat), who do the work, by the ruling class (bourgeoisie), who own the 'means of production'. Most of the profit from the work that the working class do is kept by the bourgeoisie. The bourgeoisie arrange society to keep the workers down. Original Marxist ideas have been developed and adapted by neo-Marxists.

master status A label that dominates the way a person is seen, to the extent that all their other qualities are disregarded. For example, a person who is labelled as 'mentally ill' may find that their other qualities are ignored, because the label 'mentally ill' takes on master status.

means-tested benefit A benefit that people only get if they are below a certain level of wealth.

media Ways of communicating with large numbers of people, e.g. newspapers, TV, magazines, radio and the internet.

medicalisation Taking a previously non-medical human condition and treating it as a medical problem that needs to be studied, diagnosed and treated using medical means.

meritocracy A system where the best (most talented and hard-working) people rise to the top.

metanarrative An overarching, all-encompassing story which gives meaning to history and events.

multiculturalism The existence of lots of different cultures (e.g. ethnic, religious, national) in one society or community.

neo-Marxism A movement developed in the 20th century by some of Marx's followers who revised and adapted his ideas to make them more relevant to modern society. Neo-Marxists often stress the importance of culture in sustaining capitalism, e.g. through the hegemony of capitalist ideas.

New Right Movement which gained influence in sociology in the 1980s. New Right theory believes in the 'moral superiority' of the traditional nuclear family, and tends towards the view that sexual tolerance and single mothers are bad for society. Problems like poverty and unemployment are seen to be caused by an over-generous welfare state.

non-conformity Not going along with society's norms and values.

norm A social rule about what is correct and appropriate behaviour within a particular culture, e.g. queuing in a shop.

nuclear family Parents and their dependent children living together.

operationalisation Defining a concept and deciding how to measure it.

patriarchy A society where men are dominant. Feminists often describe male-dominated societies and institutions as 'patriarchal'.

peer groups People of the same or similar social status and age, e.g. a group of teenagers.

pluralism The belief that society is diverse and reflects the needs and views of everyone via democracy and the free market.

positivism A theoretical point of view which concentrates on social facts, scientific method and quantitative data (facts and figures). The positivist view is that human behaviour is determined by external social factors, and so is outside the control of the individuals in society.

postmodernism A theory which says there is no one objective truth or reality that everyone experiences.

postmodern society The world after the modern age — with flexible working, individual responsibility and people constructing their own identity.

primary data Completely new data that has been collected first-hand by the researcher.

privatisation When private organisations or companies are allowed to gain ownership of assets or companies that used to be owned by the government on behalf of the public.

proletariat The working class who, according to Marx, form the majority of society and are exploited by the bourgeoisie.

qualitative methods of research Methods like unstructured interviews and participant observation that give results which tell a story about individuals' lives.

quantitative methods of research Methods like surveys and structured interviews that give results you can easily put into a graph or table.

relative poverty A measure of poverty that decides whether a person is in poverty by comparing their situation (e.g. level of income) to the situations of others in society.

reliability Data is reliable if other sociologists using the same methods on the same group collect the same data. Quantitative data is usually the most reliable.

secondary data Data gathered using existing sources of information, such as official statistics, newspapers, emails, and diaries.

Glossary

self-fulfilling prophecy When people behave in the way that they know others expect them to behave.

social construct An idea or belief that's created in society, and doesn't come from a scientific fact.

social democrats People who think the state should redistribute wealth, and that there should be a strong welfare state paid for out of taxes. Social democrats believe in social equality.

social exclusion Where individuals can't participate fully in society, often because of related problems like poverty, unemployment, poor skills, bad health or family breakdown. These people often find it hard to access public services.

social model of health A model that regards health and illness as social constructs that are influenced by factors outside the body, e.g. damp housing and diet.

social policy Government decisions which affect society, e.g. raising taxes, changing the benefits system, privatisation.

socialisation Passing on cultural values and norms from one generation to the next, so that they become internalised, i.e. part of everyone's way of thinking.

sociology of personal life A sociological approach that values what individuals themselves think is important, instead of focusing on what sociologists think should be important to them.

stereotype A generalisation about a social group — often inaccurate and insulting.

stratification The way society is divided up into layers, which form a hierarchy.

stratified sample A sample with the same proportions of gender, class, age etc. as the population you're studying.

subculture A group who share values and norms which are different from the mainstream culture. A culture within a culture.

subjective poverty A measure of poverty based on how poor an individual person actually feels, rather than on more standard, official measures.

superstructure In Marxist theory, the superstructure is the institutions in a society which aren't economic (such as legal, political, cultural and religious institutions) and the beliefs and values which these institutions propagate. It has a role in maintaining and sustaining the economic infrastructure.

symbolic consumption Buying products for their symbolic value (e.g. what they stand for) to reflect aspects of your identity.

symmetrical family A family structure where conjugal (husband and wife) roles are equally shared.

target population A whole group of people (e.g. disabled women, black males) that a researcher wants to draw conclusions about using research carried out on a sample of that population.

third-way politics A political viewpoint that combines elements of right-wing self-sufficiency and left-wing social democracy.

triangulation Combining different research methods and data to get the best results.

underclass A social group at the bottom of the social hierarchy. New Right sociologists think they're lazy and dependent on welfare. Left-wing sociologists think they're disadvantaged by the welfare system.

underemployment When people who want to be in full-time, permanent work are employed in part-time or temporary jobs. Also, when a highly-skilled worker performs a job that requires less skill.

universal benefit Benefit that everyone gets, whether they're rich or poor.

validity Data is valid if it gives an accurate picture of what's being measured.

value-free research Research that isn't biased, and isn't influenced by the researcher's beliefs.

values General beliefs held by society and by individuals about what is important or what is right and wrong, e.g. freedom of speech is a value of Western society.

wealth The worth of everything a person owns (e.g. property, possessions, savings) minus any debts that they owe.

Welfare State The British Welfare State was set up in the 1940s with the aim of wiping out the social problems of society (poor health, housing and education, poverty and unemployment). The Welfare State was designed to be free at the point where people actually needed it (e.g. a visit to hospital) and was paid for by people in work contributing to a national insurance scheme.

Index

Index

Index

Index